"For the last half century, Methodist historians and theologians have focused their energies on the life and thought of John Wesley. Collectively, this work constitutes a golden age in Wesley studies. We must now build on this work by exploring the rich and complex history of the Methodist movement *after* Wesley. In North America and around the world, Methodism easily ranks among the most dynamic and influential forms of Christianity in the modern age. Jeffrey Barbeau's *The Spirit of Methodism* is a splendid introduction to its charismatic leaders, animating beliefs, and global impact. For those who want to think about Methodism as a living religious tradition, I can think of no better place to begin."

Jason E. Vickers, professor of theology, Asbury Theological Seminary

THE *Spirit* OF *Methodism*

From the Wesleys to a Global Communion

Jeffrey W. Barbeau

ivp
Academic

An imprint of InterVarsity Press
Downers Grove, Illinois

InterVarsity Press
P.O. Box 1400, Downers Grove, IL 60515-1426
ivpress.com
email@ivpress.com

InterVarsity Press® is the book-publishing division of InterVarsity Christian Fellowship/USA®, a movement of students and faculty active on campus at hundreds of universities, colleges, and schools of nursing in the United States of America, and a member movement of the International Fellowship of Evangelical Students. For information about local and regional activities, visit intervarsity.org.

Cover design: Cindy Kiple
Interior design: Daniel van Loon
Images: Canadian Methodist church: Toronto, Metropolitan (Methodist) Church, Canada, Nineteenth Century
       Engraving / Private Collection / © Liszt Collection / Bridgeman Images

ISBN 978-0-8308-5254-3 (print)
ISBN 978-0-8308-6665-6 (digital)

Printed in the United States of America ∞

InterVarsity Press is committed to ecological stewardship and to the conservation of natural resources in all our operations. This book was printed using sustainably sourced paper.

Library of Congress Cataloging-in-Publication Data

Names: Barbeau, Jeffrey W., author.
Title: The spirit of Methodism : from the Wesleys to a global communion / Jeffrey W. Barbeau. Description: Downers Grove : InterVarsity Press, 2019. | Includes bibliographical references and index. Identifiers: LCCN 2019019943 (print) | LCCN 2019022282 (ebook) | ISBN 9780830852543 (pbk. : alk. paper) Subjects: LCSH: Methodist Church--History. | Methodism--History. Classification: LCC BX8231 .B295 2019 (print) | LCC BX8231 (ebook) | DDC 287.09--dc23

LC record available at https://lccn.loc.gov/2019019943

LC ebook record available at https://lccn.loc.gov/2019022282

P	23	22	21	20	19	18	17	16	15	14	13	12	11	10	9	8	7	6	5	4	3	2	1
Y	38	37	36	35	34	33	32	31	30	29	28	27	26	25	24	23	22	21	20	19

In memory of

Carl W. Munson

1917–1999

and

Florence E. Munson

1918–2012

Contents

Acknowledgments

THANKS ARE DUE TO MANY COLLEAGUES, students, and friends who contributed to this work. David Congdon helped to cast a vision for the shape of this project. David McNutt and the staff at IVP Academic provided wisdom, support, and encouragement throughout the process; Lisa Renninger facilitated the addition of images. Two anonymous readers of the manuscript provided helpful feedback and critique. Several current and former students assisted with research on this project, including Susanne Calhoun, Alicia Mundhenk, Alyssa Evans, Rhett Austin, Loren Dowdy, Timothy Chen, and Samuel Boateng. I am grateful for my friends, especially Beth and Brian Jones, as well as members of Grace United Methodist Church in Naperville, who have helped me to understand our heritage better.

Above all, my work on Methodism belongs not only to a deep love for the church but also to my commitment to family. My wife, Aimee, is among the most remarkable means of grace in my life. I also write with deep gratitude for my parents and brother, Darren. I hope that my own children will one day understand how the history of the church of their childhood has formed them in faith—even in most unexpected ways. I dedicate this work to the memory of my grandparents, Carl and Florence Munson, who exemplified the Christian life in their prayers and their presence, their gifts and their service, and, in so many ways, their witness.

Abbreviations

AME	African Methodist Episcopal Church
AMEZ	African Methodist Episcopal Zion
EUB	Evangelical United Brethren Church
JLFA	*The Journals and Letters of Francis Asbury*
MC	The Methodist Church
MEC	The Methodist Episcopal Church
MECS	The Methodist Episcopal Church, South
MPC	The Methodist Protestant Church
SPG	Society for the Propagation of the Gospel in Foreign Parts
UMC	The United Methodist Church
WCC	World Council of Churches
WMC	World Methodist Council

PROLOGUE

Methodism in Crisis

ALMOST EVERYTHING I KNOW about Christianity, I learned as a child. At least that's what I sometimes think. Each week my grandparents brought my brother and me to a cluster of brown brick buildings that stand alongside the main road in my hometown of Hyde Park, New York. Since my parents didn't regularly attend church, the weekly ritual of gathering us for Sunday school was uncomplicated. My brother and I knew that a few minutes before the beginning of lessons, the phone would ring in our home. The two of us would push and shove each other to avoid being responsible for answering the call, standing dutifully close to the phone while simultaneously avoiding the obligation to pick it up. More than one ring of the phone meant trouble, and neither of us wanted to be responsible for waking our parents. Most weeks, my brother and I hatched a plan: we'd quickly explain that we simply weren't ready or had overslept and wouldn't be able to make it due to illness. If the task fell to me, I knew what had to be done. I swiftly lifted the receiver, but before I could get a word out, my grandfather would exclaim, "We're on our way!" and abruptly hang up the phone. No matter how groggy or sickly we made our voices, our plan almost always failed. Within minutes, our grandparents would arrive in our driveway and shuttle us off to church.

Once we arrived, we sang songs, played games, and worked on Bible lessons with newsprint and flannel board figures, just like other children at Methodist churches all over the world. I received my first Bible in that local church, and it was inscribed with our pastor's name. Somewhere along the way I heard the names of John and Charles Wesley. During the main church service following Sunday school, I went to the front of the sanctuary and listened to stories about the Wesley brothers and learned about how Methodism spread far and wide across the world. I may even have heard of Francis

Asbury or sung along to a hymn by Fanny Crosby. To be sure, years passed before I could name a single other Methodist from Great Britain, North America, or the rest of the world. Yet no matter how little I knew, my participation meant that I belonged to a vast, global communion.

What holds this worldwide communion (often called a "connection") together? The most common answer is *grace*. The heart of Methodism is not an abstract doctrine, however, but the active presence of the Spirit of Christ. For nearly three hundred years, preaching, teaching, and writing about the grace of the Holy Spirit has served as the glue holding Methodists together from different nations, cultures, classes, and experiences. We are brought to the love and knowledge of Jesus Christ by the Spirit, and Methodists love to talk about Jesus because we believe the Spirit is actively working all over the world to bring about renewal and change.

In this book, I offer a fresh look at Methodism by explaining the history of the movement, exploring the lives of laity and clergy, and providing a coherent vision of Methodism today. Methodists tend to oversimplify the movement. Some focus on evangelical beliefs attributed to John Wesley and neglect significant developments since the mid-1700s. Others ignore the origins of the movement in favor of progress, innovation, and new understandings of Christian faith in a pluralist world. The proliferation of competing narratives has resulted in confusion in both the pulpit and the pew alike. Methodism, many believe, is in a state of crisis.

This book provides a coherent account of Methodism through the global history of the movement, attention to influential Methodists through the centuries, and guidance for thinking about the challenges that threaten to further divide Methodist churches in this generation. Part history, part narrative, and part reflection, this book is my effort to help sort out why Methodism seems destined for division in a time of confusion. In short, I provide a historical and theological framework for understanding Methodism to help Methodists (and those who want to know them) think clearly about the meaning of one of the most influential and fruitful movements in Christian history.

Of course, even referring to "Methodists" creates a somewhat artificial boundary. I spent a lot of time thinking about the strengths and weaknesses of various labels as I prepared to write this book. For example, I could write broadly of the entire "Wesleyan" family that finds its origins in the teachings of the Wesley brothers. Such a capacious word captures a wide range of churches and believers through the last three centuries, including United Methodists, Nazarenes, Free Methodists, Salvation Army, and many other Holiness, Pentecostal, Methodist, and Wesleyan churches around the world. The use of "Methodist" or "Methodism," by contrast, is seemingly narrower. In fact, a closer look at the composition of the World Methodist Council (WMC) reveals a wide body of Methodist and Wesleyan churches including more than eighty different denominations and more than eighty million people worldwide! Since the largest single communion within that body is The United Methodist Church (UMC)—a church that celebrated fifty years of global ministry in 2018, while simultaneously engaged in a heated struggle over the identity and future of the movement—I will refer to "Methodism" throughout this book to orient the conversation with the hope that Wesleyans of all varieties discover common resources for reflection.[1]

If we take a step back from debates over terminology, a larger problem comes into view. Reading the latest headlines will lead even the most optimistic Christians to think the future looks bleak: "Mainline Protestants make up shrinking number of US adults."[2] News reports shout reminders of impending doom whenever Methodists gather together. What's worse, a closer look at the data doesn't give a very encouraging outlook either. While the US population expanded between 2007 and 2014, the number of mainline Protestants sharply declined. United Methodists, once the single largest religious group in the nation, have witnessed significant losses in membership for decades. In recent years, some United Methodist conferences reported that more than half of their churches failed to record even a single new profession of faith.[3] Members of churches in the majority world—especially the often-thriving churches in Africa and parts of Asia—obversely worry that the growth of churches will be stymied by confusion in the West as apparent departures from historic Christian teaching in matters of doctrine and practice threaten to sever longstanding ties. Members of local

> The terms **Methodist** and **Wesleyan** are often used interchangeably. More precisely, the terms *Methodist* or *Methodism* indicate various Christian denominations or forms of church polity. By contrast, the terms *Wesleyan* or *Wesleyanism* refer to particular theological traditions originating in the teachings of John and Charles Wesley. For both historical and theological reasons, not all Methodists are Wesleyans, and not all Wesleyans are Methodists.

churches everywhere may rightly ask, "What's so *united* about the United Methodists anyway?"

While Methodism has a presence throughout the world, some may find it difficult to believe that Methodism once constituted the single largest church denomination in the United States. The movement began in England with just a few individuals in the early 1700s. By the time of John Wesley's death in 1791, however, there were more than 57,000 Methodists in Britain and, shockingly, far more across the Atlantic. By 1900 Methodists in the United States rose to more than 4.5 million members, and at the time of the merger of The Methodist Church (MC) and the Evangelical United Brethren (EUB) in 1968, there were more than 10.5 million Methodists in the United States alone.[4] When one accounts for the close relationship between the Methodism and the emergence of American Pentecostalism in the early twentieth century, Wesleyans form a significant proportion of Christians in the United States today. In light of their diverse national, racial, and social history, Methodists should not be surprised that portraits of the movement vary widely. News reports of controversy may shock even lifelong members of the church. Confusion, anxiety, and anger abound.

For some, The United Methodist Church appears to drift in an ever more liberal direction. Questions surround the topic of human sexuality. Contrary to *The Book of Discipline*, ordained ministers have presided over same-sex marriages, and ministers in same-sex marriages have been ordained as clergy and elevated to the episcopacy. No controversy has rocked American Methodism so powerfully since the question of slavery. Some bishops have refused to enforce the disciplinary guidelines of the church, and jurisdictions of the denomination have rebuffed calls for action. More than a few parishes have taken a stand on social issues: they welcome interreligious dialogue, encourage solidarity with minorities against political injustice, and invite members of the LGBTQI community to openly worship and join the membership rosters of the church. These churches, in the eyes of some, have openly departed from historic Christian faith and practice.

For others, Methodism remains strangely trapped in the insular thinking of an earlier age. Pastors have denied membership to some who differ on disputed social and ethical stances of the church. Some churches seem to focus all their energies on winning converts while offering little to counter the status quo. While poverty and injustice plague the land, the laity refuse to stand up for the marginalized. The outlook of these churches, some say, looks more like a conservative political party than the body of Christ. Global Methodists from the majority world, for their part, are sometimes perceived as intractable and even antiquated in their beliefs. Yet these churches focus on evangelism, encourage a missional outlook that challenges cultural norms, and proclaim an ancient faith in a society increasingly skeptical of truth claims. Still, these churches, say critics, refuse to modernize in matters of doctrine and practice, setting roadblocks to institutional change for the West in the process.

One doesn't have to travel across the globe to recognize the diversity of Methodist churches. A decade ago, I took a new job and moved with my family to a different area of the country. Like others looking to settle in a new place, I found myself searching for a local congregation to join. The United Methodist churches I visited were all under the authority of the same bishop (and monitored by the same district superintendent), but each congregation was marked by differences that even the most uninitiated visitor could see. Some churches were large and bustling with activity. Visitors could come and go without ever being noticed. Others were small, intimate congregations where everyone seemed to know everyone else—and no newcomer could be missed. Beyond the size of these churches, each congregation varied widely in its personality, mood, and attitude. Some felt very formal with sanctuaries characterized by high, arched ceilings, elevated pulpits, and stained glass that bellowed institutional authority and the church's enduring connection to the establishment. To look around, one might imagine that the congregation had originally been Anglican or even Roman Catholic. Other churches, however, were marked by a rather different atmosphere that could be seen in the aesthetics of the sanctuary no less than the composition of the congregation. Some seemed quite content to break formalities by gathering in small groups facilitated by movable chairs. Still others allowed members of the congregation to share announcements and prayer requests audibly from the pews, revealing a distinctly democratic vibe. Some congregations included young families, while others maintained a predominantly elderly membership. Racial, cultural, and economic differences added layers of personality to each congregation I attended. In many cities, Methodist churches can be found within blocks of one another, tracing their heritage—not to mention subtle differences in belief and worship—to alternately

MC and EUB roots. These various practices are built into *The Book of Discipline* (the standard of church law and belief for the UMC) and can be complicated even further when one looks closer at differences between predominantly Native American, Hispanic, or African American congregations. All embrace the name of United Methodist (no less the wider Methodist or Wesleyan designations).

As members of local Methodist or Wesleyan congregations (of whatever sort), we may tend to forget or even ignore such differences, if we ever knew about them in the first place. Occasionally we are reminded of the diversity of the body on days associated with special offerings, when prayers are offered for far-flung congregations facing catastrophic circumstances, or during times of mission. However, as with members of other denominations, United Methodists hear reports of the imminent collapse of the church and wonder how things could have gotten so bad. Over time, though, we settle into routine and forget the experience of bewilderment that comes with moving to a new city, state, or country. We hear mention of Methodism and recognize the common bond—even if we are unaware of the strong affinities between members of United Methodist, African Methodist Episcopal (AME), and so many other churches today.

Consider two different scenarios. First, imagine you are elderly and have been a member of the same church your entire life. It's a United Methodist church today, but over the course of several decades, you've witnessed considerable change. When you were born, the church still identified as a Methodist Episcopal Church. Or perhaps you were too young to remember life in the church before the formation of The Methodist Church in 1939, but your parents often recalled the merger and you certainly remember the formation of the UMC in 1968. Or perhaps the UMC congregation you've attended all your life originally belonged to the EUB, so the union with The Methodist Church was met with some degree of skepticism. You find yourself repeating the constant refrain that the "United" in the UMC isn't simply a call to Christian harmony. In such a light, the hymns of faith, the decades of worship and preaching, and the many times of fellowship and sacrifice to raise funds for church camps and mission trips all belong to a common repository of "Methodist" (or "United Methodist") identity. You don't love the new contemporary service the pastor introduced, but you are happy if the service attracts younger members, particularly as signs of declining attendance and the possibility of schism hits closer and closer to home. After a lifetime of devotion to the church, the prospect of division is scary and frankly upsetting.

Now imagine you are a young person who is weighing the possibility of membership through confirmation, or perhaps you've recently joined a church that is United Methodist. Maybe the decision to find a church came as a compromise with a partner or spouse from another tradition or in the search for a place to educate children in a religious community where you've taken a job after high school or college. Soon you discover that the minister whose sermons you enjoy is moving, and a new pastor will be named by the bishop. You're confused by the prospect of change (and talk of "itineracy") and uncertain if this is the place for you. Perhaps you've been visiting a Sunday school class, and recently you've questioned the possibility of a denominational split. Maybe you heard that the beliefs of your local church are directly tied to the beliefs required of Methodists living halfway around the world. As a newcomer to the community, you think to yourself, *What have I gotten myself into?*

This book can't resolve divisions, answer every question, or promise resolution in times of uncertainty. No one is more aware of stories left out and events unmentioned than me. I haven't written this book to advocate for a church plan or model of administration either—though I do believe this story can inform how Methodists evaluate such decisions. Rather, I've written this book to provide a framework and coherent vision of the varieties of Methodism in the world today. Not only local "United Methodist" churches but many other congregations and even denominations belong to a broad heritage of Christians who maintain intrinsic and extrinsic connections to the earliest Methodists. It's strange to say, but even within a single denomination (such as the UMC), there is actually a wide range of *Methodisms* rather than a single Methodism. *Broad Church Methodism*, as I call this plural form, signifies the large family of churches in the Wesleyan tradition with its unique range of doctrine, forms of prayers and worship, and patterns of moral and social behavior. So, while it's not unreasonable to ask what difference the beliefs of John Wesley or any other Methodist should have for Christians today, recognizing the complexity of Broad Church Methodism can go a long way towards ending confusion and encouraging mutual understanding both within and between denominations.

I first began thinking about this book more than a decade ago. I was on staff at a new United Methodist church in the Bible belt of the United States that drew on early Wesleyan practices of small groups, weekly communion, and evangelistic preaching. My experience serving in that congregation contrasted with the United Methodist congregation of my childhood, where the appointment of the first female pastor occasioned confusion and threatened discord over the strong social emphasis she gave to the gospel. What had made these congregations so different? But also, what held them together? I'm doubtful that a mutual love for the hymns of Charles Wesley alone establishes the common bond (in fact, with the decline of hymns in many contemporary services, I doubt many Methodists could name more than one or two of Charles Wesley's more than eight thousand compositions today).

> The coinage **Broad Church Methodism** indicates the breadth of the movement from the earliest days of Methodist ministry in Britain to the worldwide expansion of Wesleyan churches today. Against the tendency to locate true Methodism in any one branch, movement, or perceived center, the term *Broad Church Methodism* underscores an inherent diversity within the movement that springs from the practical orientation of Wesleyan theology.

When I turned to histories of Methodism to find the basis of unity, I was surprised and disappointed. The wealth of scholarship on Methodism is immense, but there are few studies that both capture the development of Methodism from its early beginnings to the global movement *and* target interested laypeople or seminarians preparing for ministry in the local church. Scholars have plumbed the depths of controversies, doctrine, and fascinating movements in times and places around the world.[5] There are excellent surveys of the history of Methodism or of essential Wesleyan beliefs. Biographies of major Methodist clergy and laity continue to find audiences and break new ground. But the more I read, the more I discovered the need for a coherent account of how the parts form a whole. As I looked at the history of belief and practice—from the earliest days of the movement right up to present day congregations around the world—I found again and again that Methodists appeal to the work of God not only in their conversion or growth as believers but also in many other unexpected dimensions of life. Methodists belong to a long, rich, and diverse tradition of belief, but they weren't innovating or fashioning something entirely new either. Instead they developed ancient ideas in a new context that struck a chord with people of different backgrounds and ways of life.

Methodist commitment to the love of God, the gracious work of Jesus Christ, and the abiding presence of the Holy Spirit brought something fresh and vibrant and alive in each of the "waves" I trace in the three parts of this book, revealing the shifts in place, time, and thought that shaped Methodism over the course of nearly three hundred years of faith and ministry. In part one, I trace the emergence of the movement in Britain—its first wave, so to speak—through the tension between the establishment religion of the Church of England and the enthusiasm associated with the Wesleys, George Whitefield, and lay preachers who spread good news of God's work of assurance in the heart. I intentionally begin with one of the most well-worn stories in Wesleyan lore: the account of a young John Wesley, providentially plucked from the burning parsonage. While the persistence of this story has been criticized by some scholars, I hope to show how reports about the event indicate something at the heart of Methodist belief that contributed to the shape of the global communion today. Subsequent chapters reveal how others contributed to the movement, and eventually Methodism in Britain formed a network of churches that would spread faith throughout the world.

In part two, I turn to the second wave of Methodism in North America. This movement, which begins in the middle of the 1700s, was larger than the first, mirroring the rapid expansion of the United States. Early revival in the colonies under the leadership of Francis Asbury led to the foundation of a new church in the days of revolution. Just as the nation faced difficult questions over race and morality, so too did the Methodists. The church divided over slavery, and calls for moral reform further complicated the tenuous unity of the churches. While many Methodists managed to resolve their differences, old tensions between revival and respectability soon re-emerged and even continue to the present day as Methodists deliberate the future of the movement.

Finally, in part three, the largest and most expansive of the three waves, I show how early Methodist missionaries traveled the world and shaped the emergence of global Christianity. World Methodism brought revival to new lands and empowered local leaders to take charge of their social and political future. Methodism throughout the world developed in local contexts despite tensions with British and American authorities who sometimes hoped to shape new believers in their own image. Wherever conflict between church and culture festered, church growth remained stagnant. However, as churches empowered local, indigenous leaders, Methodism again and again expanded. Indeed, for almost every generation, the future of Methodism has looked uncertain. My hope is that this book—part history, part theology, part meditation—may help to illumine the way forward.

PART ONE

THE *Origins* OF BRITISH METHODISM

CHAPTER ONE

Warm Hearts

BRIGHT ORANGE AND YELLOW LIGHT streams from the top of a tall building. An inferno consumes the home, flames rushing from its fragmentary remains. White smoke rises to the sky. Against the flow of blazing heat, a crowd of desperate neighbors moves toward the fire. They hoist up one brave and desperate man. He grasps for a frantic child, who dangles from the upper window. Farther away, onlookers flee the conflagration. A cool darkness surrounds the rescued family. They shrink from the heat and the terrible sight of the child. One figure alone leans into the light. A father on his knee, hands clasped in prayer, reaching feverishly to the sky.

Figure 1.1. Rescue of John Wesley

Two haunting images in a single scene—a defenseless child and a fleeing family—resist closure in Henry Perlee Parker's portrait, "The Rescue of John Wesley from the Epworth Rectory Fire" (1840) (figure 1.1). The lack of a single focal point leaves viewers uncertain. Even the father's eager supplication on bended knee, whether pleading heavenward to God for providential deliverance or only in desperation that the child might save his life by risking the fall, is offset by a man leading a startled horse from the blaze in the distance. Antagonistic and contrary motions disrupt simple resolution, symbolizing tensions that have existed within Methodism from its earliest days.

The horror of the real event surpasses Parker's dramatic painting. The Epworth fire of 1709 nearly killed John Wesley (1703–1791), who was only five and half years old at the time. Wesley's father, Samuel, was a minister in the Church of England. Their family lived in the church rectory in Epworth, a small town in Lincolnshire near Sheffield. Sometime near midnight, flames consumed the family home. Sparks from the chimney fell on the roof and quickly spread. One of the girls felt a burning sensation on her foot and hurriedly ran to tell her parents. Samuel Wesley awakened the children in the adjacent room, a maid carried the youngest child from the nursery, and all but young "Jacky" followed along with the others. The family huddled in the downstairs hall, surrounded by the fire. The roof had weakened in only a matter of moments, and they feared that all was lost as the walls began to collapse around them. When the front door was finally opened (the key had been left upstairs in the commotion), flames rushed in from a strong northeast wind, threatening to consume them all. They finally escaped through windows the neighbors broke open to reach the family. Safely outside, they assessed the damage. They were scorched but unharmed, undressed and bitterly cold but together. Then, in the calm, Jacky's terrified cries reached them from the upper level of the burning home. The child, previously unnoticed, was unable to escape by descending on the severely weakened staircase. Samuel Wesley, hearing the terror-stricken screams of his son, frantically ran back inside. He couldn't ascend the stairs through the fire, no matter the effort. *My child is lost*, he thought. In unspeakable anguish, Samuel Wesley knelt down where he stood, commended his son to God, and "left him, as he thought, burning." John's mother later marveled, "The boy, seeing none came to his assistance and being frightened by the hanging of the chamber and his bed being on fire, climbed up to the casement, where he was presently spied by the men in the yard, who immediately got up and pulled him out just in that article of time that the roof fell and beat the chamber to the earth."[1]

John Wesley's mother recognized the infinite mercy of God in the event. Susanna Wesley was an independent woman by standards of the day. As with other mothers, she was primarily responsible for the education of her children and the development of their faith. Letters to her eldest son, Samuel Jr., provide a glimpse into her methods and temperament. She advised scrutiny of individual conscience, avoidance of temptations, and constancy in virtue. Although she never attended university, just as other women were barred from such studies at the time, she was far better educated than most of the Epworth townspeople and taught her children to carefully understand Scripture and the fundamentals of the faith.

Figure 1.2. Susanna Wesley

Samuel and Susanna both participated in the religious education of their children—ten of nineteen survived into adulthood, including three boys—but Susanna's piety deserves special notice. Each evening, she devoted time to one or two of her children for individual counsel in religious matters. Even when they lived away from home, she continued to guide them in letters she sent with extended discourses on Christian faith and practice. A few years after the Epworth rectory fire, Susanna's independent spirit resulted in public scandal. Her husband was away in London, so she began providing Sunday evening prayers and devotions for the family in his absence. In time, their neighbors began to attend the meetings as well—in fact, quite a few of them. Not surprisingly, Samuel Wesley was bound to find out after more than two hundred people had gathered for prayer and spiritual advice at his home. He wasn't pleased. But when he wrote to question his wife, she shrugged off any criticism of the propriety of a woman teaching and leading others with a reasoned defense of her responsibility to obey the Lord:

> I reply that as I am a woman, so I am also mistress of a large family. And though the superior charge of the souls contained in it lies upon you as head of the family and as their minister, yet in your absence I cannot but look upon every soul you leave under my care as a talent committed to me under a trust by the great Lord of all the families of heaven and earth. And if I am unfaithful to him or to you in neglecting to improve these talents, how shall I answer unto him, when he shall command me to render an account of my stewardship?[2]

Samuel Wesley (1662–1735) and **Susanna Annesley Wesley** (1669–1742), the parents of John and Charles Wesley, came from families with strong Protestant nonconformist backgrounds, though each elected to join the Church of England prior to their marriage in 1688. The couple lived briefly in London before Samuel received a living in Lincolnshire, where they eventually settled at Epworth and raised a large family. Susanna's regimented methods of religious education and self-discipline had a marked influence on the children and has often been heralded as a model of Christian piety. As members of the Church of England, which had separated from Rome and the authority of the pope during the sixteenth-century Reformation, the Wesleys affirmed the historic teachings of the creeds and the Thirty-Nine Articles of Religion (the Anglican confession of faith).[3] They regularly used the Book of Common Prayer, with Thomas Cranmer's timeless prayers and liturgy. Yet it is also worth noting that both Susanna and her husband, Samuel, were raised in dissenting families. While worshipers in the Church of England enjoyed the political and social privileges that came with membership in the national church, including the possibility of attending the universities at Oxford or Cambridge, dissenters assembled only under various restrictions or "disabilities." The Act of Uniformity (1662) had required that all ministers abide by the Book of Common Prayer, and dissenting or "nonconformist" ministers were barred from preaching within five miles of any town or city. Susanna attended her father's dissenting church until she joined the Church of England as a youth—an early sign of her independence. Samuel's father, John "Westley," was a dissenter who spent time in prison for refusing to use the Prayer Book after 1662. Samuel joined the Church of England shortly before moving to Oxford to attend Exeter College. The two married in 1688.

When her husband refused to change his mind on the matter, Susanna replied in a most unrelenting fashion: "Send me your positive command in such full and express terms as may absolve me from all guilt and punishment for neglecting this opportunity of doing good to souls, when you and I shall appear before the great and awful tribunal of our Lord Jesus Christ."[4]

Figure 1.3. John Wesley

Although his parents' influence and example continued to shape his decisions, John Wesley eventually left home to prepare for university life through education in languages and classics at Charterhouse School. He was devout and successful. By the end of the 1720s, John was a fellow at Lincoln College, Oxford, and a teacher of the Greek New Testament. When his younger brother Charles came up to Oxford for studies, John took special responsibility for a small group the two gathered together, leading the band of students into fervent acts of spirituality and Christian service. He was especially attracted to devotional writings that focused on right practice and the need for holiness in everyday life: Thomas à Kempis's *Imitation of Christ*, Jeremy Taylor's *Holy Living* and *Holy Dying*, and William Law's *Serious Call to a Devout and Holy Life*. These works inspired in John a deep piety and commitment to the church. The "Holy Club" dedicated themselves to fasting, regular participation in the Lord's Supper, and works of charity, such as visiting the sick and providing material goods for those in orphanages and prisons. In time, rumors spread about these Oxford students, their numbers increased, and the derisive label "Methodists" eventually stuck.[5]

John and Charles Wesley were lifelong members of the **Church of England**. As children, they learned from the Book of Common Prayer (BCP), which first appeared in 1549 and marked the reformation of the English church under the reign of Edward VI. The BCP contains prayers, litanies, and services for the Lord's Supper and other special occasions. The Wesleys also subscribed to the Thirty-Nine Articles of Religion, which provide the standard of doctrine and practice for the Church of England and the worldwide Anglican communion.

John Wesley's zeal brimmed over. Life at Oxford, though prestigious and comfortable, proved insufficient for a man of his temperament. In 1735, John convinced his brother Charles that they should risk the dangers of traveling across the ocean to serve as clergymen in the new colony of Georgia. Charles would have been quite happy to stay at Oxford, but he reluctantly agreed and quickly received ordination in the church for the task. The arduous journey challenged John Wesley's faith far more than any event before: as storms rocked the ship, John Wesley's trust foundered ("much ashamed of my unwillingness to die"). To his surprise, a group of German Pietists aboard the ship—Moravians, known for their belief in assurance of salvation and commitment to foreign missions—appeared entirely unmoved during the worst trials of the journey.[6]

Ministry in the new settlement at Savannah, too, proved far less glamorous than the young man had imagined. His methods of intense self-examination and devotion were not appreciated by the colonists, and an amorous relationship with a young woman, Sophy Hopkey, soured. He soon found himself a victim of his own impetuous decisions. John barred his paramour from the communion table, and her new husband and family brought an indictment against him. Wesley furtively left the colony, returning to England a broken man: "I went to America, to convert the Indians; but Oh! who shall convert me? Who, what is he that will deliver me from this evil heart of unbelief? I have a fair summer religion."[7]

The backdrop of the eager first rise of Methodism at Oxford and the abortive second rise of Methodism in Georgia makes the legendary third rise of Methodism in London even more powerful in Methodist family lore. Under the influence of Moravian Christians such as Peter Boehler, John Wesley gradually became convinced that he required a deeper experience of faith. Understanding John Wesley's earnest search for greater faith can be difficult to appreciate. After all, he was thirty-five years old, devoted himself to daily prayer and reception of the sacrament, taught the New Testament, led small groups of believers in daily devotions, and worked as a minister in the church and missionary in difficult circumstances abroad. Still, he believed that he needed more—more than the faith of his parents and more than an outward commitment to living in the way that follows Christ. Wesley believed he lacked the deeper, inward knowledge that he belonged to God. Then, as he sat reluctantly at a society meeting at Aldersgate Street on May

24, 1738, listening to a reading of Martin Luther's *Preface to the Epistle to the Romans*, John Wesley experienced divine assurance—an experience of faith he had never known before:

> About a quarter before nine, while he was describing the change which God works in the heart through faith in Christ, I felt my heart strangely warmed. I felt I did trust in Christ, Christ alone for salvation, and an assurance was given me that He had taken away *my* sins, even *mine*, and saved *me* from the law of sin and death.[8]

With these words, John Wesley gave witness to his trust in God. The event ranks among the seminal moments not only in Methodism but in the history of Christianity.

What actually happened at Aldersgate? A few observations may help to clarify the experience. First, John Wesley places Jesus Christ at the very center of the event. The work of Christ permeates the entire scene, so much so that one can hardly imagine the occurrence in any other way: "faith in Christ," "trust in Christ," and "Christ alone" saves him from sin and death. Second, Wesley links his experience of assurance to the Reformation. His explicit reference to Luther's *Preface to the Epistle to the Romans* reminds us of the central importance of justification and recalls Luther's fresh discovery of salvation by faith in the imputed righteousness of Christ. Third, the experience is highly individualistic. Wesley's repeated use of "I," "me," and "mine" demonstrates that the assurance of faith he experienced was intensely personal. To know God at Aldersgate is to experience the crucified Christ. How could it be any other way? To have faith in God is to do so by trust in the work of Christ, his sufficiency for salvation, and the knowledge that comes by Christ alone.

John Wesley may be best known for his presentation of **the way of salvation**. Wesley taught that grace abounds in every aspect of God's work in the Christian life, including a *prevenient grace* that prepares the way for a sinner to be reconciled to God, a *justifying grace* that brings pardon for sin, and a *sanctifying grace* that fills the heart with love.

Against the tendency to see religion as a matter of civil participation, social obligation, or family tradition, Wesley upended the Church of England with a reforming movement that appealed to those seeking a life-changing experience of faith in God. Few Methodists today surpass Wesley in his devotion to God at Oxford or Savannah, but Wesley came to believe that for all the good he was doing—his intense practices of prayer, regular participation in the Lord's Supper, and works of service to the community—he hadn't experienced the full transformation of Christian life promised in the Scriptures. Appeals to the inward witness of the Spirit abound in Wesley's sermons because his own experience of a deeper faith came through the gradual recognition that it wasn't enough to be the recipient of baptism, the child of a minister, or a scholar of biblical languages. Wesley knew that his heart had been transformed, and this transformation alone marks a true and living faith in Christ. The emphasis on interiority that Aldersgate memorializes does not eliminate the way that practices of small groups, sacramentality, self-discipline, mutual accountability, and holiness in social action all shaped Methodism in the subsequent decades, but ultimately these all spring from the work of Christ through the power of the Holy Spirit.

John Wesley and his circle of preachers proclaimed this message of inner faith so forcefully that many lost the right to speak in local churches. Wesley even returned to Oxford and delivered a scathing sermon distinguishing between the "almost" and the "altogether" Christian. The nominal Christian isn't one who lives in wanton disregard for faith, as we may be tempted to suspect. Rather, John Wesley thought the "almost" Christian lives a morally upright life and, in many respects, looks just like an "altogether" Christian in matters of religion and ethics. The "almost" Christian avoids gluttony and wickedness, labors for the good of others, and even uses the "means of grace" in practices of prayer, church attendance, and family devotions. The "almost" Christian is sincere, desires to follow God, abstains from evil, and lives as Christians are expected to live. When Wesley spoke to those gathered at Oxford, he made one thing particularly clear: he wasn't only casting aspersions on his listeners, he was also testifying to his own experience.

> I did go thus far for many years, as many of this place can testify: using diligence to eschew all evil, and to have a conscience void of offence; redeeming the time, buying up every opportunity of doing all good to all men ... endeavoring after a steady seriousness of behavior at all times and in all places. . . . Yet my own conscience beareth me witness in the Holy Ghost that all this time I was but "almost a Christian."[9]

Wesley's "almost" Christian doesn't pursue evil but pursues good. The "almost" Christian seeks God sincerely and wishes to please God in all things. Still more work remains.

What marks the "altogether" Christian? John Wesley's answer is difficult to quantify, for the mark of the "altogether" Christian is not found in a formulaic set of actions but the interior state of the heart. First, the "altogether" Christian has a heart filled with the love of God. The life is transformed from a wellspring of love that turns the mind, will, and emotions always toward the love of God. Second, the love of neighbor, as commanded in Scripture, drives the Christian to reject evil, avoid arrogance, and rejoice in love. Last, the "altogether" Christian lives a life in faith. Faith is a belief that springs from the experience of forgiveness. Faith brings about a life filled with ongoing repentance, love, and good works. Faith produces confidence that Christ reconciled us to God and saves us from eternal damnation.

Surprisingly, Wesley's experience of faith followed years of reading the Bible, devotional reading on faith and holiness, extensive service and witness to people in need, and ministry in Word and sacrament both in England and America. Even after all this, Wesley thought he needed transformation through faith in Christ. Against recommendations to be "still" before God, Wesley encouraged intentional activity. Don't wait passively before God, he advised, but faithfully seek him through the divinely appointed means of grace. Read the Bible, attend the Lord's Supper, and intentionally participate in opportunities for service. In time, perhaps even in an instant, the seeker may discover that Christ works in unexpected and life-giving ways.

> In his sermon, **"The Scripture Way of Salvation" (1765),** John Wesley rejects the tendency to think of salvation only as a future blessing or reward. Wesley explains, "It is not something at a distance: it is a present thing, a blessing which, through the free mercy of God, ye are now in possession of." In justification there is forgiveness of sins and peace with God, and in sanctification "we are inwardly renewed by the power of God."

Methodist history resembles a great work of art. Centuries-old paintings appear crisp and clear when viewed from a distance. Spectators may feel captivated by the moment, drawn into a scene, and caught up in the action.

Move closer to the painting, however, and fine lines may gradually become visible in such an artwork. Small blemishes, or *craquelure,* form over time as stretched canvases gradually loosen and changes in temperature and humidity produce tiny fissures on the surface. The portrait doesn't actually change upon closer inspection, but the slender lines serve as reminders of the distance between the original event and the spectator. These subtle blemishes, small signs of artificiality, may even disturb the belief that the artwork reproduces the original with precision.

Treasured stories from the earliest years of Methodism, viewed from the distance of three centuries, can be misleading. A boy pulled from a burning home. Young men at Oxford gathered for worship and service in devotion to God. A heart strangely warmed and a revival that spread to nations around the world. Look closer at early Methodism, however, and small fissures, previously invisible, appear in this stirring portrait. Tiny fractures remind us that these cherished stories provide order but resist complication. The stable familiarity of early Methodist history fosters the impression of unity and an uncomplicated vision of Christian piety, but a closer examination reveals subtle fractures and discontinuities that have shaped the identity of the movement even to the present day.

Take a closer look at Henry Perlee Parker's famous portrait, "The Rescue of John Wesley from the Epworth Rectory Fire" (1840) (figure 1.1). Created more than a century after the rectory fire that nearly killed John Wesley as a child, the painting differs in remarkable ways from the various eyewitness accounts of the blaze that have survived from the period. One notable detail reveals a surprisingly subversive

Figure 1.4. Close-up of second-generation Methodist James Everett (1784–1872) reaching from the ground for young John Wesley

undercurrent: the artist included a prominent nineteenth-century critic of British Methodism in his portrait of the rescuers. The man reaching for the child from the ground, just beyond the main group that surrounds the second-floor window, was none other than James Everett (1784–1872) (figure 1.4). Standing with outstretched arms, Everett appears ready to receive Jacky from those who have reached the boy first. Everett was a second-generation Wesleyan minister whose criticism of prominent Methodist leaders—such as the authoritarian Jabez Bunting (1779–1858)—resulted in Everett's expulsion from the Wesleyan conference and the formation of the United Methodist Free Churches in England.[10] Such inherent tensions within Methodism, however, did not begin in the second generation. Nor did the struggle over Wesleyan identity first commence at the *end* of John Wesley's life. Conflict presented itself from the outset.

What are Methodists today to make of this history? While some have touted stories of divine providence and stirring witness to Wesley's Aldersgate experience, others have diminished these events as simplistic and legendary tales. John Wesley faced this same problem as he looked back on the rise of Methodism. Not many years before his death, Wesley wrote about the movement to which he had devoted his life in "Thoughts upon Methodism" (1786). Against charges that Methodists were too focused on their personal experiences, Wesley affirmed the authority of the Bible above all. They were "Bible Christians," a people of the book, because the Scriptures were nothing short of "the whole and sole rule both of Christian faith and practice."[11] Yet, with this rule in mind, Wesley further explained that four enduring beliefs mark the life and character of the people called Methodists. First, Christianity is an "inward principle" known as the renewed mind or restoration of the soul to the proper likeness to God. Second, the basis of renewal is none other than the work of the Holy Spirit. Third, inward renewal is for the sake of Christ alone: holiness, righteousness, and any other blessing derive not from the work of the individual but Christ. And fourth, those who share the mind of Christ are true family—brothers and sisters together.

Wesley's description of the four marks of Methodist belief reorients the meaning and significance of early Methodist history. The rise of Methodism at Oxford, Savannah, and London began among a small group of earnest young Anglicans. In time, the movement spread as not only a renewal of the Church of England but part of a broader revival that quickly reached around the world. Perhaps for this reason, John Wesley shared his mother's belief that God alone had saved him from the flames: rescue from the fire came by the hand of God, an act of providential protection *for the sake of the church*. Notably, John Wesley did not return to his Aldersgate experience again and again in his later writings, as if Aldersgate signifies the singular measure of the Christian, but soon the story of a young man whose heart was "strangely warmed" became something of a commonplace among Methodists—a rallying cry for those who heard echoes of his story in their own experiences of faith.

"I felt my heart strangely warmed. I felt I did trust in Christ, Christ alone for salvation." In his explanation of the four enduring beliefs of the Methodists, Wesley provides a reminder of what he considered the seminal aspects of the movement. Far from mere happenstance, Wesley had experienced an interior renewal that profoundly changed his understanding of the Christian life. The heart strangely warmed came by a powerful work of the Spirit that gave new meaning and direction to his life. Spiritual renewal turned Wesley to Christ and "Christ alone" in faith and love for God and neighbor. These enduring beliefs, marks of Christian faith that others might discern in their own experiences, impelled the revival of Anglicanism that came to be known as the Methodist movement in Britain and around the world.

John Wesley's belief that God had saved him from the flames never amounted to a belief that Methodism was a permanent work. In fact, in his "Thoughts upon Methodism," Wesley begins with a startling admission: "I am not afraid that the people called Methodists should ever cease to exist either in Europe or America." He feared, rather, that Methodism would prosper without a corresponding commitment to the guiding principles that inspired the movement from its earliest days: "I am afraid lest they should only exist as a dead sect, having the form of religion without the power. And this undoubtedly will be the case, unless they hold fast both the doctrine, spirit, and discipline with which they first set out."[12] These striking words were not advice for some far-off, future generation, however, but a warning delivered amid the trials of the moment.

CHAPTER TWO

....

Divine Power

SOCIOLOGISTS HAVE DESCRIBED SOMETHING that many of us intuit but never quite manage to explain. Why is it that a single individual is often recognized for a great achievement, when so many others who participated in the accomplishment are forgotten? Few of even the savviest sports enthusiasts can name the losing team in decades-old championship matches, or the silver and bronze finishers in celebrated Olympic events. Though only set apart by the smallest margin, lesser figures who perhaps broke through similar barriers or smashed seemingly unbreakable records (but came in second place at the end) are overlooked. Or consider the success of political administrations—though policy may be set by a group of dedicated figures who worked together to accomplish a common goal, few people can name the supporting cast of vice presidents or members of a governmental cabinet. Across the arts and sciences, many examples could be given of individual figures who come to represent a larger group. The others remain in the shadows, recognized by a few but forgotten by many.

Sociologists such as Barry Schwartz, who writes of "the strange apotheosis of Rosa Parks" in the fight to desegregate American public transportation, have a name for this peculiar human tendency: *collective forgetting*, which refers to "the failure to transmit information about the past" such that "remembering and forgetting, knowledge and ignorance, are distributed unevenly among different communities, groups, and individuals."[1] Collective forgetting doesn't mean that entire communities all ignore the same people, but, more often, individuals of similar significance are "remembered differently *within*" groups and communities. The result is what Schwartz labels *oneness*: "a nonuniversal but powerful tendency for individuals and groups to simplify complex comparisons by choosing one prominent performer or entity."[2] In part, the phenomenon may be explained by the limits of human memory: most of us can only recall about four things at any time. We tend to organize information in easily managed groups. Put simply, it's easier to single out one individual than weigh the respective merits of many.

In Methodism, what might be called "the apotheosis of John Wesley" represents the tendency to think that the entirety of Methodism can be understood with reference to one man. There's little doubt that John Wesley should be remembered for his organizational leadership in the movement, not to mention his pastoral and theological acumen. Methodists have rightly codified John Wesley's writings, including his sermons and *Explanatory Notes* on the Bible, as the basis of Methodist doctrine and practice. Yet John Wesley's apotheosis also marks the condensation of a multifaceted historical and theological movement even in describing the earliest rise of Methodism in Britain.

More than any other leader, Charles Wesley has long been underestimated in the history of Methodism. A good case can be made that it was Charles who first gathered the small group at Oxford for prayer, study, and

service, and that it was Charles who first invited John to help guide the group and bring order to these young Anglicans seeking spiritual renewal. Charles traveled to America and served in Georgia, too, but he was no better equipped for the task than his brother. Before the trip, John convinced Charles to give up his plan to remain at Oxford, seek ordination, and take up the missionary journey to the colony. He also recognized his need for a deeper experience of God's grace and assurance of salvation while abroad.

Figure 2.1. Charles Wesley

Moravian Pietism appealed to Charles: he hungered for the certainty of forgiveness, the lifting of the burden of sin, and the freedom found in the fullness of divine love.

Days before John Wesley's famous Aldersgate experience, Charles Wesley had a similar discovery of Christian assurance. The event may well be one of the most profound examples of early Methodist piety. Charles's journal entries from May 1738 evocatively describe the days leading up to his own, lesser-known "Aldersgate" experience. Charles writes of a continual striving after deeper faith around this time. Nothing else, it seems, occupied his thoughts and prayers. One journal entry in this period gives us a sense of his longing for a total renewal of faith: "*Saturday, May 6.* God still kept up the little spark of desire, which he himself had enkindled in me, and I seemed determined to speak of, and wish for, nothing but faith in Christ."[3]

Notice the similarities between Charles and John: the sense of struggle, the explicit determination, and even the shared images of heat and fire in the sparks enkindled within. Charles continued in this state of openness and seeking, "hungry and thirsty after God," and desirous of the knowledge that "Christ loved me," throughout the month.[4] As with his brother, Charles found solace in the writings of Martin Luther. He read from Luther's *Commentary on the Epistle of St. Paul to the Galatians*, and his friend William Holland was so overwhelmed by their reading together that Holland breathed "out sighs and groans unutterable."[5] For his part, Charles wondered at the doctrine of justification by faith and "endeavored to ground as many of our friends as came in this fundamental truth . . . not an idle, dead faith, but a faith which works by love, and is necessarily productive of all good works and all holiness."[6]

German Pietism had a decisive influence on the early Methodists through an encounter between the Wesleys and several members of the **Moravian Brethren** on their voyage to Georgia. The Moravians originated in Bohemia and, under the auspices of Nikolaus von Zinzendorf, merged with Lutheran Pietists in Saxony in 1722. In 1738, John Wesley visited the village of Herrnhut on a pilgrimage, where he participated in the life of the community for several weeks.

Always a rather sickly individual, Charles was troubled in mind and body throughout the month. He describes a struggle with pleurisy, a condition of the lungs and abdomen, that left him weak and often bedridden. Though he tried leeches to bleed out the illness and called for the surgeon to bring him further relief, he found only temporary rest before his pains returned. He also sought divine remedy through the Eucharist. On May 19, Charles notes

In 1738, the German Moravian Peter Boehler established the Fetter Lane Society in London. Charles, John, and other London Methodists regularly attended meetings at Fetter Lane until the so-called **stillness controversy** led to their separation. The Moravian Philip Henry Molther taught a doctrine of quietism, in which the individual must wait in "stillness" for the assurance of true faith. John and Charles Wesley, by contrast, taught that Christians ought to use all the means of grace available while waiting for the inward witness of the Spirit.

pathetically that he "Received the Sacrament, but not Christ."[7] He even conferred with other believers where he was staying, such as Mrs. Turner, who claimed such assurance of her peace with God that she declared herself willing "to die this moment. For I know all my sins are blotted out."[8]

Finally, on May 21, 1738, Charles experienced the release from sin and assurance of salvation that he so desperately desired. The events of the day cast a new light on the rise of Methodism in London. After waking with great expectation, Charles met with John and a few other friends. They sang a hymn together—most likely "Hymn to the Holy Ghost":

> Come holy Spirit, send down those Beams
> Which gently flow in silent Streams
> From thy eternal Throne above:
> Come thou enricher of the Poor,
> Thou bounteous source of all our Store,
> Fill us with Faith and Hope and Love.
>
> Come thou, our Soul's delightful Guest,
> The wearied Pilgrim's sweetest rest,
> The fainting Sufferer's best relief:
> Come thou, our Passions cool allay:
> Thy Comfort wipes all Tears away,
> And turns to Peace all Joy and Grief.
>
> Lord, wash our sinful Stains away,
> Water from Heaven our barren Clay,
> Our Sickness cure, our Bruises heal:
> To thy sweet Yoke our stiff Necks bow,
> Warm with thy Fire our Hearts of Snow,
> And there enthron'd forever dwell.

All Glory to the sacred Three
One everlasting Deity,
    All Love and Power and Might and Praise;
As at the first, e'er time begun,
May the same Homage still be done
    When Earth and Heaven itself decays.[9]

Soon after, the assembled friends departed, and Charles devoted himself to prayer, recalling the promise that the Comforter would draw near and that, by the Spirit, the Father and Son would dwell with God's people.

Charles lay down to rest, when suddenly he heard the voice of a woman say, "In the name of Jesus of Nazareth, arise and believe, and thou shalt be healed of all thy infirmities!"[10] Struck to the heart, Charles arose and inquired of Mrs. Turner, who was in the household with him, if she heard the voice of the woman who spoke thus. She denied that any other was in the home. His heart sank, but he inquired again with "strange palpitation of heart" in hopes that the word was for him. Mrs. Turner finally confessed, "It was I, a weak sinful creature spoke, but the words were Christ's. He commanded me to say them and so constrained me that I could not forbear." Charles, distraught by these events, turned to both Scripture and a friend alike for comfort until his struggle finally ceased: "The Spirit of God strove with my own and the evil spirit, till by degrees he chased away the darkness of my unbelief. I found myself convinced—I knew not how, nor when—and immediately fell to intercession."[11]

In several respects, Charles's experience closely resembles some of the most famous conversions in Christian history. As Saul (later Paul) journeyed on the road to Damascus, he heard the voice of Jesus calling out to him and telling him to go to the city. Similarly, Charles Wesley's story is reminiscent of the conversion of Augustine in the

> John Wesley's falling out with the Moravians helped clarify the Methodist commitment to the use of what he called the "means of grace" in the Christian life. In his sermon "The Means of Grace" (1746), John clarifies this teaching: "The chief of these means are prayer, whether in secret or with the great congregation; searching the Scriptures (which implies reading, hearing, and meditating thereon) and receiving the Lord's Supper, eating the bread and drinking wine in remembrance of him." These, he explains, are "ordained of God as the ordinary channels of conveying his grace to the souls of men."

Garden of Milan.[12] Just as Augustine, who heard the words of a child playing a game calling out, *Tolle lege, tolle lege* ("Pick it up, read it; pick it up, read it"), so, too, Charles heard the voice of the woman as he lay resting. In fact, even as Augustine immediately turned to Scripture for signs of the divine promise, so also Charles took up the good book and read words that brought release from the torments of doubt and despair: "The words that first presented were 'And now, Lord, what is my hope? Truly my hope is even in thee.' . . . I now found myself at peace with God and rejoiced in the hope of loving Christ."[13]

Still, when Charles wrote in his journal of these profound events—events that preceded his older brother John's more famous Aldersgate experience by three days—he presented the whole under a single heading in large, neat letters:

THE DAY OF PENTECOST

In the mind of Charles Wesley, May 21, 1738, was not only a day of conversion or new birth. By an act of divine providence, the day of his conversion fell on Whitsunday (Pentecost Sunday). In what marks Charles Wesley's unique understanding of salvation, the day signified his belief that renewal in Christ is a necessarily pneumatological or Spirit-inspired event.[14] This illumines the fourth stanza of his noted "O for a Thousand Tongues to Sing" (also known as "For the Anniversary Day of One's Conversion"):

> Then with my heart I first believed,
> Believed with faith divine,
> Power with the Holy Ghost received
> to call the Savior mine.

The day of Charles's conversion was a day of profound spiritual renewal. In one unpublished hymn, he describes the promised outpouring of the Spirit as "Your day of Pentecost . . . You shall the Holy Ghost receive."[15] It was also a day of Pentecost-like miracles. Charles was awakened by what he always regarded as nothing less than a divinely inspired voice. Even after Mrs. Turner's confession, Charles continued to believe that the voice was identical to that of another woman.[16] Charles refused to think that Mrs. Turner's words were merely some sudden, impulsive act of deception. Rather, as Charles notes in the same extended journal entry, he affirmed her belief that Christ himself had commanded her to speak: "At night, and nearly the moment I was taken ill, she dreamed she heard one knock at the door. She went down and opened it; saw a person in white; caught hold of and asked him who he was; was answered, 'I am Jesus Christ' and cried out with great vehemence, 'Come in, come in!'"[17] The powerful dream left her "wavering and uneasy" for days but also filled her with an enlarged "love and prayer" for all humanity.

While the work of Christ stands out in John Wesley's Aldersgate experience ("I felt I did trust in Christ, Christ alone for salvation"), Charles Wesley's Pentecost experience highlights the work of the Spirit. In subsequent days, Charles prayed that his brother would come to a similar knowledge and, at one point, "almost believed the Holy Ghost was coming upon him."[18] Perhaps most significant, Charles's journal reveals that he expected to be filled with love as a direct result of his Pentecost experience. At one point, a vision of Christ's "broken, mangled body" left him speechless during the prayer of consecration. "Still," he claimed, "I could not observe the prayer, but only repeat with tears, 'O Love, Love!'"[19]

In the journals of two brothers, both written toward the end of May 1738, two distinct strands of Wesleyan theology emerge. Different reactions to these writings are not hard to imagine. Some could easily look back and declare: "See, what we really need is a heart-strangely warmed experience of conversion!" Just as easily, the response might be: "It's not enough to be saved, what we really need is a deeper experience of divine power!" For others, all this talk of conversion and tears only brings added confusion: "If I've never felt such an overwhelming sense of God's presence, then where does that leave me?" The range of possible responses is far wider than some might expect.

Susanna Wesley offered her own assessment of the situation: John and Charles had not finally converted but had become aware of an intense process of spiritual maturation. Writing in December 1738 to Charles, his mother explained that what matters most is not whether one knows the date of one's conversion but the knowledge of God's work in our hearts: "I think you are fallen into an odd way of thinking. You say that till within a few months you had no spiritual life nor any justifying faith. Now this is as if a man should affirm he was not alive in his infancy, because, when an infant he did not know he was alive. A strange way of arguing, this!"[20] Charles had come to a sensible awareness of God's love—so powerful that it seemed he had found new life in Christ. Whatever happened in May 1738, John and

Hymn singing quickly became a distinguishing feature of the early Methodist revival. Most congregations in the Church of England sang only metrical compositions from the Psalter, but the Wesley brothers encouraged hymn singing to bolster congregational unity and instruct members in Christian doctrine. In Georgia, John and Charles published *A Collection of Psalms and Hymns* (1737), the first hymnbook published for public worship in the United States. In subsequent decades the Wesleys published numerous other hymnbooks, most famously "a little body of experimental and practical divinity" titled *A Collection of Hymns for the Use of the People Called Methodists* (1780).

Charles Wesley each had experienced a work of God that deepened their faith in profound ways. Both men believed God *before* May 1738, and both men knew times of doubt and feelings of disconnect from God *after* May 1738.

Furthermore, recovering the story of Charles Wesley's Pentecost experience shapes our understanding of early Methodism. When Charles wrote hymns—no fewer than 7,300 over the course of his life—he wrote not from compulsion by a domineering brother or merely in support of a new vision of the church but out of his own experience of deeper faith in Christ.[21]

Consider, for example, one of Charles' most beloved hymns, "Wrestling Jacob" or "Come, O Thou Traveler Unknown":

Come, O Thou Traveler unknown,
    Whom still I hold, but cannot see,
My company before is gone,
    And I am left with Thee;
With Thee all night I mean to stay,
And wrestle till the break of day.

I need not tell Thee who I am,
    My misery or sin declare,
Thyself hast called me by my name,
    Look on Thy hands, and read it there;
But who, I ask Thee, who art Thou?
Tell me Thy name, and tell me now.

. . .

I know Thee, Savior, who Thou art,
    Jesus, the feeble sinner's Friend;

Nor wilt Thou with the night depart,
    But stay, and love me to the end;
Thy mercies never shall remove;
Thy nature, and Thy name is Love.[22]

The hymn, which John Wesley regarded as Charles's greatest composition, celebrates God's love in a first-person account of Jacob's wrestling with God in Genesis 32. Over and over again, the hymnist describes the meeting with God as an encounter with love personified. "'Tis Love! 'tis Love! Thou diedst for me; I hear Thy whisper in my heart," he cries. The theme of Pentecost-inspired love, witnessed to by the Spirit-filled heart, permeates Charles Wesley's writings.

Reclaiming Charles's story also reminds us of the collaborative relationship at the heart of early Methodism. What began as a small group of like-minded men at Oxford quickly developed into a movement of individual and social renewal throughout Britain and abroad. The Wesley brothers together guided a vast network of preachers and laity seeking deeper faith. They remained members of the Church of England, but their relationship with the established church grew complicated. The brothers

Figure 2.2. John Wesley "field preaching" outside a church

alike took up the controversial practice of "field preaching," a form of public evangelism they associated with Protestant dissent from the Church of England, and proclaimed renewal by God to several thousand people in market squares, public greens, and graveyards. The spectacle drew larger and larger crowds in the prosperous city of Bristol. During John's first month of preaching in Bristol, more than 47,000 listeners attended his sermons, and crowds of up to 15,000 gathered in subsequent months.[23] Charles, though initially suspicious of such reports, witnessed the same surprising attendance when he preached to more than ten thousand men, women, and children in the city. Preaching in the Church of England was an act typically reserved for well-educated and ordained ministers, but John Wesley began to assign untrained laity to the undertaking as well. Charles, on the other hand, thought renewal in the Church of England might better occur through a revival among the ranks of the clergy, but John sought single-minded devotion to evangelism across the nation through itinerant preachers who traveled in circuits that he personally organized and maintained. In the end, Methodism under the leadership of John and Charles Wesley together (though they differed in some significant respects) flourished in rapidly expanding cities where industrialization displaced families, and the Church of England had failed to respond.

Centuries later, Methodists may struggle to identify with Charles Wesley's story no less than that of his brother. Charles longed for a powerful work of God in his life. What he discovered transformed him entirely. Just as the disciples gathered on the day of Pentecost and were filled with God's Spirit, so, too, Charles found himself overcome by a divine power that overflowed in love. The result was profound. Three days before his brother's Aldersgate experience, Charles felt the power of God and recognized that God had worked a miracle in his life. Charles believed he was healed, his sins were forgiven, and his heart was assured of God's gracious favor. Yet Charles and John, for all their similarities, had two different experiences of God's work. John's Aldersgate experience focuses on the work of Christ and yields the impression that he has been born again. Charles's "Day of Pentecost," by contrast, emphasizes the renewing work of the Spirit. John's experience has stood as the representative case, the symbol of the ideal Methodist conversion, but Charles's influence was not ancillary. Instead, from very early on, the brothers found themselves in conflict over the leadership of what was still only disparagingly called Methodism. The small fissures in their relationship could easily be concealed, but, when John's actions effectively separated the Methodists from the Church of England at the end of their lives, Charles lamented that his brother had departed from the true ideals of the movement. But that is to get ahead of the story.

In the coming years, managing controversies—signs of a diverse, complicated, and vibrant network of Methodist belief and practice—became a major source of tension among the leadership of the rapidly expanding movement. Almost from the beginning, factions emerged within Methodism that divided the people. For while Methodism is most frequently associated with the lives, ministries, and writings of the Wesley brothers, other ordained ministers and lay preachers were also growing in popularity. Their names are largely forgotten or otherwise dissociated from the movement. As sociologists have explained, that's how *collective forgetting* works. In fact, if anyone not named Wesley appeared likely to lead Methodism in the earliest decades of the movement, his name was George Whitefield.

CHAPTER THREE

Perfect Love

ON AUGUST 30, 1769, LOOKING OUT OVER a crowd assembled in London, George Whitefield delivered a classic sermon on sin and salvation.[1] On this remarkable day he picked up his Bible, opened to the Gospel of John, and declared to all assembled, "My sheep hear my voice, and they follow me" (10:27). Whitefield was preparing to depart for America, where he would once again preach to throngs of listeners in New England. Before leaving, however, Whitefield spoke to the crowd, urging them to repentance. Christ divides the world into sheep and goats, he explained, for "there are but two sorts of people mentioned in Scripture; it does not say the Baptists and Independents, nor the Methodists and Presbyterians; no, Jesus Christ divides the whole world into but two classes: sheep and goats."[2] Whitefield's fiery voice, weathered by years of preaching to crowds in the thousands and even tens of thousands in England, Scotland, and Wales, and farther afield throughout the colonies of North America, called out to the people, urging them to contrition. "O sinner, sinner, you are come this morning to hear a poor creature take his last farewell," he implored, "see at what an expense of blood Christ purchased those whom he calls his own. . . . It was a hard bargain, but Christ was willing to strike the bargain that you and I might not be damned forever." In little more than a year, George Whitefield was dead.

The historian cannot know what Whitefield pondered as he stood in the pulpit that day, but few would be surprised if he thought back wistfully to his first acquaintance with John and Charles Wesley at Oxford. Whitefield joined the "Holy Club" in 1732 after meeting Charles Wesley and discovering a fellow Christian, like himself, earnestly seeking holiness. Charles had encouraged the younger Whitefield at Oxford, and at Charles's suggestion, he read several books on holy living. One stood out above all others: Henry

Scougal's *The Life of God in the Soul of Man* (1677). On reading Scougal, Whitefield realized his need for new birth:

> At my first reading it, I wondered what the Author meant by saying, "That some falsely placed Religion in going to Church, doing hurt to no one, being constant in the Duties of the Closet, and now and then reaching out their hands to give Alms to their poor Neighbours,"—Alas! thought I, "If this be not true religion, what is?" God soon showed me . . . "true religion was a Union of the soul with God, and Christ formed within us."[3]

Whitefield, aware of his need for new life in Christ, longed for holiness and a life completely devoted to God. He joined the Wesleys in close attention to personal discipline, including fasting, regular observance of the Lord's Supper, and ministry among the poor. Still, Whitefield yearned for something more. When deliverance came in May 1735—a conversion that liberated Whitefield from the weight of sin—the impact was drastic and lasting:

> One Day, perceiving an uncommon Drought, and a disagreeable Clamminess in my Mouth, and using Things to allay my Thirst, but in vain, it was suggested to me, that when Jesus Christ cried out, "I thirst," his Sufferings were near at an End. Upon which, I cast myself down on the Bed, crying out, "I thirst! I thirst!"—Soon after this, I found and felt myself that I was delivered from the Burden that had so heavily oppressed me![4]

Whitefield had experienced a profound change in his spiritual life. Soon he began preaching passionate sermons in parishes across the Church of England. Whitefield's methods, however, led to controversy wherever he went. He advertised through handbills that spread word of his appearances in advance, and when he spoke, he often excited the crowds with forceful words and tears flowing from his eyes. By the time the Wesleys returned from Georgia, wearied by their unsuccessful labors and largely

Figure 3.1. George Whitefield

uncertain of the future, Whitefield had spread word of revival far beyond Oxford and had begun organizing the earliest Methodists.[5]

Looking back nearly three centuries, Methodists today may find it difficult to imagine that Whitefield deserves a prominent place in the story of the early movement. Nonetheless, in 1738 Whitefield was a budding celebrity while John and Charles still waited for signs of divine assurance. Whitefield encouraged John Wesley to take up field preaching and oversee the movement. Meanwhile, Whitefield already had established himself as a leader esteemed by the masses. Wherever he went, he condemned ineffective clergy for failing to preach repentance from sin. Whitefield was innovative and entrepreneurial. He was also controversial. In America, he participated in what historians later called the Great Awakening with Jonathan Edwards, preaching to crowds so large that an incredulous Benjamin Franklin set about measuring the area in which the preacher's voice could be heard. In Philadelphia, Franklin estimated that no fewer than 30,000 people could hear Whitefield's address. He delivered more than 15,000 sermons in his lifetime, established orphanages in the colonies, and wrote extensively in correspondence and theological tracts. Yet Whitefield's notoriety also contributed to the widespread belief that Methodism was a dangerous sect that threatened to divide the Church of England by throwing the people into confusion and jeopardizing the unity of the nation.

Labeling a Methodist an "enthusiast" was commonplace at the time. The insult originated earlier in English history, but by the eighteenth century the term indicated someone who pretended to divine visions and individual revelation. Undoubtedly, some aspects of the revival under Whitefield and the Wesleys were outside the norms of life in the Church of England. Field preaching itself was born of necessity because clergy deemed Methodist preaching on the inward witness of the Spirit outside the bounds of national religion. Undoubtedly, too, some aspects of the revival were highly emotive affairs. Reports of bodily gesticulations and auditory responses accompanied the preaching of the Methodists. Enthusiasm certainly seemed an apt charge to level against such ministers.

John Wesley defended the Methodists against such an indictment but often to little benefit. John Wesley's sermon "The Nature of Enthusiasm," first preached in May 1741, warned against the errors of enthusiasm even as he challenged those who refused to wholly yield themselves to the work of

God's Spirit. Wesley refers to enthusiasm as "a religious madness arising from some falsely imagined influence or inspiration of God . . . or expecting something from God which ought not to be expected from him."[6] Some imagine that they have a *grace* of God that they simply do not have. Others claim *gifts* of God that they do not have. While all true ministry depends on the influence of the Spirit of God, some erroneously believe they speak words directed or even dictated by God, receiving guidance from God in even "the most trifling circumstances of life."[7] Yet, turning the label "enthusiast" on its head, Wesley also condemned what he deemed the most dangerous form of enthusiasm: the variety that arises among those who *neglect* the means of grace whereby God draws all people to a full and holy love of God. Against such neglect, Wesley urges Christians to "expect a daily growth in that pure and holy religion which the world always did, and always will, call enthusiasm; but which to all who are saved from real enthusiasm—from

Figure 3.2. Critics charged Methodists with religious "enthusiasm"

merely nominal Christianity—is the wisdom of God and the power of God . . . a fountain of living water, springing up into everlasting life!"[8]

John Wesley advised caution. In the sermon "Scriptural Christianity" (1744), commencing from Acts 4:31 ("And they were all filled with the Holy Ghost"), Wesley discouraged Methodists from prioritizing the extraordinary gifts of the Spirit above the fruit of the Spirit:

> Whether these gifts of the Holy Ghost were designed to remain in the church throughout all ages, and whether or not they remain in the church throughout all ages, and whether or not they will be restored at the nearer approach of the "restitution of all things," are questions which *it is not needful to decide*. . . . "Were all" even then "prophets?" Were "all workers of miracles? Had all the gifts of healing? Did all speak with tongues?" No, in no wise. Perhaps not one in a thousand. Probably none but the teachers in the church, and only some of them. It was therefore for a more excellent purpose than this that "they were all filled with the Holy Ghost."[9]

Wesley thought that far more important than the extraordinary gifts were the ordinary fruits that God assured would remain in every age. Christianity could not be identified with a special gift or a statement of beliefs but only with a way of life.[10]

In line with Whitefield's advice upon returning to England, the Wesley brothers began forming societies to organize those who responded to Methodist calls for repentance from sin and renewal by the power of the Holy Spirit. Although they remained members of the Church of England, they established meeting houses and chapels in Bristol and London, and some even registered these places under laws protecting Protestant dissent.[11] The Methodist societies had one rule for membership: "a desire to flee from the wrath to come, to be saved from their sins."[12] In practice, this single idea unfolded according to three general rules:

> Do no harm by avoiding evils such as Sabbath breaking, drunkenness, fighting, etc.
>
> Do good to all people by caring for the sick and imprisoned, practicing frugality, and taking up the cross daily.
>
> Attend the ordinances of God, such as public worship, reading the Bible, partaking of the Lord's Supper, and prayer.[13]

In time, three layers of Methodist meetings also emerged. Large gatherings of interested individuals met together in *societies*. John Wesley subdivided the societies into *classes* of about twelve people from common neighborhoods (males and females met together in the classes). The most mature believers met in small *bands* for rigorous accountability and examination. Bands met as small groups of like-minded men or women (members were separated by gender and marital status to maximize honesty and accountability). The bands gathered weekly for times of singing, prayer, and mutual confession. In

Early Methodism flourished through organization into three layers of community participation: **societies, classes,** and **bands**. *Societies* supplemented worship in local Church of England parishes and welcomed large groups of people interested in the movement. *Classes* divided all Methodists by geographical region. They were limited to twelve members and required a quarterly ticket, indicating good standing for participation. *Bands*, inspired by Moravian Pietism, provided a source of nurture and accountability for small groups of mature believers. These three divisions gradually fell into disuse in the nineteenth century, particularly through denominational growth and emphasis on Sunday schools.

an effort to establish complete transparency, five questions were asked of every individual at meetings:

What known sins have you committed since our last meeting?

What temptations have you met with?

How [were] you delivered?

What have you thought, said, or done, of which you doubt whether it be sin or not?

Have you nothing you desire to keep secret?[14]

As unfathomable as such practices may seem to some Methodists today, participation in classes and bands were hallmarks of the new movement. Such demanding expectations increased commitment among members but also bolstered the apprehension of fellow Anglicans who scorned Methodist preaching and teaching as little more than fanaticism.

Methodism quickly faced the prospect of division. As much as the Wesleys and George Whitefield were united in preaching repentance, conversion, and sanctification from sin, they differed substantially over the question of election and predestination. In brief, Western Christians had long asserted that sinners may be justified by God only by a work of divine grace. No amount of effort can make a person worthy of God. Among towering Christian theologians from Augustine in the early church to John Calvin in the Protestant Reformation, such an affirmation about grace meant that God must predestine some to salvation, since only God can provide the grace that transforms a person's life. The Church of England inherited this tradition, and the Thirty-Nine Articles of Religion (the doctrinal standard for Anglicans) declared that such a teaching "is full of sweet, pleasant, and unspeakable comfort to godly persons" (Article 17). George Whitefield heartily affirmed this teaching, but John and Charles worried that excessive emphasis on divine action might lead to a fatalistic determinism, leaving Christians in a state of spiritual apathy in the process.

> Calvinistic Methodism is most often associated with the preaching of George Whitefield and finds its roots in the theology of John Calvin (1509–1564), the French Reformer best known for his ministry in Geneva. Calvinism emphasizes the sovereignty of God in all things: God alone elects humans for salvation by an irresistible act of unmerited grace. Each individual is therefore predestined to life or death by God's eternal decree. The Wesleys, who quarreled with their friend George Whitefield in what is sometimes called the **"predestination controversy,"** rejected Calvin's theology and embraced Arminian theology, which claims that people are saved by grace on the basis of God's foreknowledge of their actions.

Despite their history, the former friends publicly disagreed over the doctrine in acerbic sermons and treatises that irreparably divided the movement. Whitefield had left the revival in John Wesley's care, but John advocated a measure of freedom that conflicted with George Whitefield's deepest belief in God's sovereignty. Moreover, John Wesley began teaching a doctrine of Christian perfection that some thought tantamount to salvation by works. Influenced by the theology of Jacobus Arminius (1560–1609), which called into question the doctrine of predestination, Wesley insisted that Christ alone is the cause of salvation, but Christians receive power to freely live and love by the Spirit. In part, John Wesley derived his teaching from early Christian sources that emphasized union with Christ. Those Eastern Christian sources contrast with Western traditions that underscored the legal aspect of justification.[15] Whitefield and others believed that the doctrine of perfection amounted to little more than righteousness by works, but the Wesleys claimed the doctrine's biblical basis, declaring that complete freedom from inward and outward sin is the proper goal of the Christian life. For John, perfection didn't mean liberty from ignorance or temptation but an instantaneous blessing or "entire sanctification" releasing the individual from pride, self-will, anger, and evil. Charles also claimed the doctrine but tended to emphasize the process that sanctification entailed. He theorized that suffering could gradually generate a state of sinless perfection and, immediately before one's death, the complete restoration of the *imago Dei*.[16] The emphasis on love borne of struggle appears in Charles's great hymn, "Come, O Thou Traveler Unknown," which reflects not only the Wesleys' dispute with Whitefield but also the subtle differences between John and Charles: "I stand and will not let Thee go, / Till I Thy name, Thy nature know."[17] At stake was the character of God: Charles referred to Whitefield's teaching of predestination as a "horrible decree" that blasphemed the love of an all-gracious God, and John compared the God of predestination to a divine tyrant who summons the prisoner to leave his cell while withholding the keys.

Since holiness cannot exclude active participation, the Wesleys promoted discipline fostered by societies, classes, and bands. Persistence in sin without repentance and amendment of life could lead to expulsion. When the brothers visited the societies, they took time examining members and expelling some for habitual offences ranging from drunkenness, idleness, Sabbath-breaking, and even carelessness.[18] Participation in the classes, similarly, required possession of quarterly tickets that certified the ticket-holder's desire to pursue inward and outward holiness. The Wesleys held Methodist preachers to an even higher standard. The episcopal inquiry, "Are you going on to perfection?" (a question that is still asked of Methodist ministers to the present day), probed not only

John Wesley's sermon on **"Christian Perfection"** (1741) explains one of his most controversial teachings: "Christian perfection therefore does not imply (as some men seem to have imagined) an exemption either from ignorance or mistake, or infirmities or temptations. Indeed, it is only another term for holiness. They are two names for the same thing. Thus everyone that is perfect is holy, and everyone that is holy is, in the Scripture sense, perfect."

a knowledge of the doctrinal standards but also an examination of life fitting of those committing their entire energies to leading others in the way of holiness.[19] Despite (or, some think, because of) such obligations, Methodism began to grow exponentially both in England and abroad.

In 1762, several events brought fresh scrutiny to the Methodist societies and John Wesley himself. In London, the movement had grown at a particularly rapid pace. According to John, "Many, who had hitherto cared for none of these things were deeply convinced of their lost estate. Many found redemption in the blood of Christ; not a few backsliders were healed. And a considerable number of persons believed that God had saved them from *all sin*."[20] Wesley claims that he recognized the potential dangers of the situation and took special measures to "apprize them" of the errors of "pride and enthusiasm." While he stayed in the city, the society remained stable and sober-minded, but, as soon as he left, enthusiasm reappeared. Some "began to take their own imaginations for impressions from God." Confusion spread rapidly. Soon others alleged unique spiritual gifts far beyond John Wesley's teaching: the end of all sinful temptations, gifts of prophecy, and discerning of spirits too. Wesley refused to name the individuals publicly, but manuscript letters and journals reveal that the "enthusiasts" in question were two of Wesley's own preachers. Thomas Maxfield, for one, began to teach that those who had received the gift of Christian perfection were superior to others in the society. George Bell, who had converted in 1758, claimed the gift of healing, began holding raucous meetings, and taught the rejection of the sacraments and the restored purity of Adam and Eve among the perfected.[21]

Wesley avoided a heavy-handed response. He hardly wished to hinder a work of God. However, the decisive break in what became known as the Maxfield-Bell schism occurred when Bell prophesied that the world would abruptly come to an end on February 28, 1762. Wesley, who had previously attempted compromise and urged moderation, now firmly rejected these teachers not only in private but even in public: "I warned the society, again and again, and spoke severally to as many as I could."[22] While John's labors meant that relatively few members of the society followed Bell and Maxfield in their break with the Methodists, still the damage was done: "they made abundance of noise, gave huge occasion of offence to those who took care to improve to the uttermost every occasion against me, and greatly increased both the number and courage of those who opposed Christian perfection."[23]

The Maxfield-Bell schism of 1762 created space for critics to attack the doctrine, discipline, and practice of Methodism anew. William Warburton, bishop of Gloucester, was one such opponent. Stirred by controversy in London, Warburton published a scathing rebuke of John Wesley and George Whitefield alike: *The Doctrine of Grace, or, The Office and Operations of the Holy Spirit Vindicated from the Insults of Infidelity, and the Abuses of Fanaticism* (1762). Warburton believed that enthusiasm results from the misuse of imagination and a propensity for superstition. Enthusiasm, Warburton thought, arises from hallmark Methodist doctrines including divine assurance, the inward witness of the Spirit, and the desire for Christian perfection: "their imagination grows heated . . . and they assume the airs, and mimic the Authority of Prophets and Apostles."[24] Enthusiasts allege direct access to divine power, healing and the working of miracles, speaking with tongues and prophecy, and inspired knowledge and discerning of spirits. All such miraculous claims, however, undermine the infallible authority of Scripture and the unerring rule given by God to the church.

The schism also prompted John Wesley to dissociate himself from claims to the extraordinary gifts of the Spirit once again. He warned against enthusiasm, encouraged biblical and rational reflection, and distanced himself from those who claimed spiritual knowledge by what amounts to imagination. He could easily have pointed to all the ways Methodists resisted enthusiasm in actual practice too. The societies and smaller classes alike stipulated not only personal but social holiness. They collected donations for the poor, sponsored small business loans, and taught exacting practices for the right use of money. John Wesley established the Kingswood School for underprivileged children in a time when education was often limited to Sunday schools on the day of rest from work. Wesley compiled the best practices in contemporary medicine in the *Primitive Physic* (1747), established free medical dispensaries, and created "The Poorhouse" to accommodate needy widows and children.[25] Wesley even encouraged lay preachers to gain knowledge of Christian doctrine, the history of Christianity, and the spiritual lives of Christian saints through inexpensive publications such as his fifty-volume *Christian Library*. Despite widespread denunciation of Methodism by critics, the pursuit of social holiness accompanied personal holiness at every turn.

While most Methodists in the world today are Wesleyan in their theology, there are still some **Calvinistic Methodists** in Wales and elsewhere. While most early Calvinistic Methodists were followers of George Whitefield, others were organized by Selina Hastings, Countess of Huntingdon (1707–1791). The Countess was a force in the early Methodist revival in Britain. Lady Huntingdon served as a patron of the societies, built numerous chapels, and established Trevecca College to educate Calvinist Methodist ministers. She organized a small but independent connection of chapels that continued after her death.

Figure 3.3. Selina Hastings, Countess of Huntingdon

Still, from the earliest years of the movement, the Methodists were plagued by controversy. The followers of Whitefield became known as Calvinistic Methodists, grew steadily in Wales (where they continue today as the Presbyterian Church of Wales), and counted supporters among the revival abroad.[26] John Wesley and George Whitefield eventually reconciled, but their disciples never embraced the settlement. In fact, when George Whitefield died in Massachusetts in 1770, little more than a year after his "Good Shepherd" sermon in London, John Wesley preached his funeral sermon, celebrating Whitefield's "unparalleled zeal, his indefatigable activity, his tender-heartedness to the afflicted, and charitableness toward the poor."[27] Still Calvinistic Methodists perceived a slight in the eulogy, objecting to Wesley's lurking doctrine of perfection in calls to "wrestle with God" for the same holiness as their own shepherd. Though troubles mounted in decade after decade of ministry, no single event proved as divisive—or as instrumental in the growth of the movement—as John Wesley's unilateral decision to ordain ministers for the work in America. Yet even here Wesley's self-defense contained a curious homage to the farewell sermon of his old friend George Whitefield: "If anyone will point out a more rational way of feeding and guiding those poor sheep in the wilderness, I will gladly embrace it."[28]

CHAPTER FOUR

....

Costly Obedience

IN THE CLOSING MINUTES OF THE twentieth-century film *John Wesley* (1954), the elder statesman of Methodism discusses the success of ministry in England with his colleague Dr. Thomas Coke. The year is 1784, and Wesley, about to depart on a preaching tour, exclaims, "How the tide has turned! . . . Why, I am become *respectable!*" The conversation shifts to Methodism in America. Coke notes that he will leave with Richard Whatcoat and Thomas Vasey next month. "Once, I too set out for America," Wesley muses. "The people there are hungry for the gospel, as Francis Asbury has found. He and his men are taking the Word into the very heart of the wilderness. Tom, I am sending you out as superintendent. I beg you, see that those you choose as helpers are in very truth the sons of God, that their teaching may not be mere words but have as its source the inward witness." Wesley then offers a final prediction: "It is my belief that a handful of men with their hearts alight with the love of God could set whole towns on fire. Not only towns but continents. Yea, the whole world."[1] In the final scene of the film, a crowd watches as Coke, Whatcoat, and Vesey slowly drift away in the Bristol Harbor. The onlookers share a hymn of commitment. Coke looks to Wesley, standing on the dock, and Wesley knowingly gazes back at Coke with Prayer Book in hand as the ship sails off in the distance.

The scene neatly summarizes a pivotal moment in the history of Methodism, but the actual events were even more remarkable. Earlier that year, Wesley had established a legal plan to secure the future of the Methodist conference. For decades, Methodism constituted a connection. Beginning in the early 1740s, the preachers gathered with John Wesley to discuss the standards of doctrine, discipline, and practice in the conference. By 1784, however, Wesley was eighty years old, and though he was still active in ministry, the future of Methodism seemed increasingly uncertain. Bolstered by Thomas Coke's encouragement, the Deed of Declaration was written to establish the legal existence of the conference, naming one hundred preachers (with their successors) as the lawful holders of the conference and providing the basis for transference of property and administration of the societies in the event of Wesley's death.[2]

Meanwhile, in America, the end of the Revolutionary War had left Methodists in a state of relative disarray. Since Church of England ministers operated under the authority of the crown, preaching by Anglican clergy was regarded as an inherently political act. Wesley had directed numerous preachers to perform the work of ministry in circuits along the eastern seaboard and into the expanding West, but almost all returned to Britain for safety during the conflict. Francis Asbury alone remained. Asbury's reports on the state of the societies in America were sobering at best: the absence of ordained ministers left children numbering in the thousands unbaptized and the Lord's Supper unavailable to countless others. All the while, the Church of England seemed unwilling to act, and early efforts to unite with the emerging Episcopal Church in America (that is, the Church of England separated from its national political authority) were stymied by Methodist commitment to Wesley's authority. Finally, John Wesley took matters into his own hands. In September 1784, he ordained ministers—Vasey and Whatcoat—and set apart Coke as superintendent for the work in America.[3]

> The **Deed of Declaration** (1784) made provision for the Methodists in the event of John Wesley's death while ensuring that the authority of John and Charles remained secure so long as they remained alive. The deed named one hundred Methodist preachers (the so-called **"Legal Hundred"**) who constitute the Methodist "conference." While many found reassurance in the deed, some others thought the document too exclusive: Francis Asbury, serving faithfully in America, was not named among the Legal Hundred.

Far from a decision made in haste, the determination to ordain ministers transpired following extensive reflection. In fact, as early as 1746, Wesley became convinced that the Bible did not forbid such an act, since he believed that presbyters possessed an authority equal to bishops.[4] Still, Wesley refused to proceed. Even when lay preachers clamored for the right to administer the sacraments among the societies, Wesley rebuffed their efforts. Unilaterally ordaining Methodist preachers, he knew, would be perceived as an act of schism. Wesley even published a treatise titled *Reasons Against a Separation from the Church of England* (1758) to clarify how separation would hinder the fruitfulness of Methodist ministry. Yet when Wesley finally decided to act on behalf of Methodists in America, there was no turning back.

John never consulted with Charles, so it is no surprise that his brother received the news in shock and dismay. Charles's most famous response challenged John's authority to ordain ministers without episcopal approval:

> So easily are Bishops made
>   By man's or woman's whim?
> W—his hands on C—hath laid,
>   But who laid hands on him?[5]

The friction between Charles and John was also interpersonal. Charles felt John had undermined their relationship and, after a lifetime of collaboration, the shared work of ministry:

> In infancy their hopes and fears,
> In youth, and in their riper years,
> Their hearts were to each other known
> Attuned in perfect Unison.
> No private End, no selfish art
> Did then the faithful Brothers part,
> No flatterer the Friends divide,
> Who each from each could nothing hide,
> Neither enjoyed a good alone,
> Or called what he possessed his own,
> Their good supreme with humble zeal
> To know, and do the Master's will.[6]

In one letter, Charles begged John to stop before the separation was complete, declaring that their downfall was at hand: "*Go to your grave in peace*: at least, suffer me to go first, before this ruin is under your hand. . . . I am on the brink of the grave. Do not push me in, or embitter my last moments."[7]

For his part, John Wesley remained steadfast. In personal correspondence with his brother, John insisted on his right to ordain as a minister of the gospel. He vowed that he had done nothing rashly, having maintained the same standards of discipline during forty years of ministry. As for the personal aspect, he only asked that Charles leave him to his business: "If you will go on hand in hand with me, do. But do not hinder me, if you will not help." He adds, in an act of fraternal rationalization, "Perhaps if you had kept close to me, I might have done better. However, with or without your help, I creep on."[8]

John Wesley also brought the matter to public consideration in a sermon on the meaning of schism. "I am now, and have been from my youth, a member and a minister of the Church of England," John declared, "and I have no desire nor design to separate from it till my soul separates from my body."[9] Wesley maintains that it is a matter of "indispensable duty" to remain within a church or society so long as that body "does not require me to do anything which the Scripture forbids, or to omit anything which the Scripture enjoins." His allegiance to the Church of England reflects a widespread loyalty to the national church; members of dissenting churches still faced significant social and political disadvantages at the time. On the other hand, Wesley professed, the Christian is "under an absolute necessity of separating" whenever a church requires acts of idolatry, lying, hypocrisy, or preaching doctrines that are contrary to the gospel. Despite such efforts, and although John Wesley insisted that his ordinations were only intended for work outside of England (so as not to undermine the well-being of the nation), all recognized that ordination apart from the authority of the episcopacy set the wheels of separation in motion.

At least part of the predicament resulted from a perceived vacuum in leadership. Charles had gradually stepped away from the rigors of itinerary and, though he remained active in managing the Methodists, had settled into a more stable pattern of ministry and family life ever since his marriage to Sally Gwynn in 1749. John thought he had found a suitable successor for he and his brother in Jean Guillaume de la Fléchère, a brilliant young man from Switzerland. John Fletcher (as he was better known in England) had studied classics at Geneva University before moving to England in 1750. Not long after, Fletcher experienced an evangelical conversion under the influence of the Methodists, pursued ordination in the Church of England, and served as a priest in a parish near Birmingham. Fletcher's wife, Mary Bosanquet (1739–1815), also received permission from John Wesley to preach under an "extraordinary call" and quickly emerged as one of the leading women in early Methodism. As partners in itinerant ministry, John and Mary shared alike in the joys and hardships of leadership. When trouble with the Calvinists revived in the 1770s (around the time of Whitefield's death), John Fletcher wrote incisive responses that reflected Wesley's own teachings and amplified Wesley's doctrine of Christian perfection through reference to the biblical notion of "baptism in the Spirit." Still, even Fletcher, whom John had attempted to convince on several occasions to succeed him, disagreed with Wesley's plan for America.

Figure 4.1. John Fletcher

Figure 4.2. Mary Bosanquet Fletcher

And so it was that in early September 1784, Wesley consecrated Thomas Coke as superintendent and ordained Richard Whatcoat and Thomas Vasey as deacons and then, the following day, as presbyters. All this was done without consulting the conference. Once the first ordinations were complete, little stopped John Wesley from performing more. Fletcher suddenly died after a brief illness the following year,[10] and Charles's death in March 1788 removed any obstacles that remained. In short, Wesley "crossed the Rubicon" and soon "advanced further into the forbidden territory."[11] Undoubtedly, whatever reasons he may have had, subsequent acts came in quick succession.

He ordained presbyters for Scotland and for the mission field in 1785 and 1786. And in 1788 and 1789 he ordained a few men for work in parts of England where the Methodists could not obtain the Sacrament, and consecrated one man Superintendent. In 1786 the Conference allowed Methodist services to be held at Church times in parishes where the minister was notoriously wicked or heretical, where there were not enough churches to contain half the population, or where there was no church within two miles.[12]

Once Wesley opened the door to separation, Methodists could opt in or out of Anglican parish practices at will. By the time of John Wesley's death in 1791, British Methodists found themselves in an unfamiliar territory: mourning the death of their founder yet ready for new life to begin.

―――――――――

The story of Methodism doesn't politely sail off to America at this point. British Methodism continued expanding and even flourishing for many years to come. Not long after Wesley's death, British Methodists faced the pressing questions that their founders had worked so hard to forestall. Ordination by vote (rather than laying on of hands, as with the Anglicans) brought ministers into full connection with the conference, and the Lord's Supper was allowed in Methodist chapels wherever a majority of trustees, church stewards, and class leaders agreed on the practice (the so-called "Plan of Pacification" of 1795). Some soon worried that the authority of ordained ministers had expanded to the detriment of the laity (a sign of a new democratic spirit), and in 1795 these members separated, forming the Methodist New Connexion. The remaining majority became known as the Wesleyan Methodist Connexion to further distinguish them from Whitefield's Calvinistic Methodists (in Wales) and various church bodies that began to form in the early nineteenth century. Others feared that the increasing respectability of Wesleyan Methodism had diminished the revivalist roots of the original movement; these individuals resumed the old practice of field preaching, held camp meeting revivals, and formed a new denomination called the Primitive Methodists. While Wesley had allowed some women to preach, gradually pulpits closed to all but men.[13] Another church split occurred in 1827, when the installation of an organ at the Wesleyan Methodist chapel in Leeds proved so controversial that, after the conference overruled the wishes of district preachers in favor of those wealthier trustees who backed the organ, some members separated and formed the so-called Protestant Methodists. These and other bodies engaged in various unions and associations (and still more separations) until the various branches of British Methodism finally merged in the formation of the Methodist Church in 1932.[14]

Long into the nineteenth century, British Methodists continued to follow John Wesley's practice of referring to the societies as "connections" rather than churches. The distinction provides an important reminder that British Methodists often embraced membership in the Church of England even if they also attended Methodist chapels. "Double allegiance" to the Church of England and Methodist chapel alike resulted from several factors. Above all, the practice of local parish attendance was a standard set by John and Charles Wesley. Methodist societies intentionally scheduled meetings at times that wouldn't conflict with parish ministry and undermine the Church of England. Moreover, many Methodists continued to value the liturgical practices of the church, so it is no surprise that even when the Lord's Supper might have been available in the chapel, various rites of passage related to the birth of a child (baptism), the coming into adulthood (confirmation, marriage), or the death of the body (Christian burial) were all memorialized in the established church. Membership in the national church also had certain political advantages for Methodists in Britain: the universities of Oxford and Cambridge

William and Catherine Booth founded the **Salvation Army** in 1865 while working in London's East Side. The Booths were members of the Methodist New Connexion but deeply influenced by American Holiness Movement teaching on entire sanctification. Although widely known for their social ministries, including soup kitchens, addiction treatment, and other relief services, the Salvation Army has become an international denomination composed of clergy ("officers") and laity ("soldiers") committed to helping others through both spiritual and social outreach.

Figure 4.3. Salvation Army home service campaign poster, 1919

did not open admission for degrees to Protestant dissenters until 1854 and 1856, respectively. Double allegiance, however, was less a sign of shrewd calculation than a mark of devotion. If church and chapel were both available for deliberation on matters of deep personal interest (namely, salvation and holiness), then why not attend both? At least part of the gradual dissociation between Methodism and Anglicanism seems to be the rise of Anglo-Catholic ritualism during the 1830s and 1840s, when the Oxford Movement brought the Church of England closer to Roman Catholicism in its beliefs about baptism, the Lord's Supper, and other aspects of order, discipline, and worship. Evangelical Anglicans, among whom numbered the Methodists, increasingly felt displaced by the trend toward formal liturgy.[15] In short, although Wesley's ordinations prompted an ecclesial separation, actual changes in church membership occurred only gradually.

> In England, the practice of **"double allegiance"** was common among Anglicans and Methodists well into the nineteenth century. Religious options were rapidly expanding, so attending a Methodist chapel could be a helpful supplement to Anglican spiritual life. Only in the second half of the century did this pervasive feature of Anglican practice decline.

British Methodism continued to have great leaders and noted critics in the years that followed the death of John Wesley. No single individual merits notice more than Jabez Bunting (1779–1858), the foremost British Methodist minister during the first half of the 1800s. Bunting served in every major leadership role among the Wesleyan Methodists, established the first theological college in 1818, and guided the Methodists through a period of sustained membership growth. Bunting embodied John Wesley's mind and heart alike, administering the Wesleyan Methodists with a similarly unyielding hand.[16] Over time, Methodists boasted influential Bible scholars such as Adam Clarke and the systematic theologian Richard Watson among their members too. Such scholars contributed to the growing reputation of British Methodism as a respectable denomination in the United Kingdom and abroad. Nonetheless, critics continued to repeat the old canards of Methodist enthusiasm. The radical journalist Leigh Hunt, for example, wrote a series of six scathing essays titled "An Attempt to Show the Folly and Danger of Methodism" (1808). Fanaticism, Hunt asserts, led Methodists to damn their neighbors while claiming divine favor in the most trivial aspects of life:

The most vulgar and insolent of the inspired are continually boasting of their union with the dear Jesus and the sweet Jesus. . . . If a man is too lazy to work for a dinner, he puts his faith in God, goes walking into the fields or road, and is sure to pick up a shilling somewhere. If he wants to go out of doors and the rain suddenly clears up, that is a miracle in his favor. If a preacher is going to a certain chapel and meets with a thunderstorm, that is a miracle to warn him against preaching. . . . In short, he cannot take a beefsteak or a walk, he cannot stumble upon a stone or a dinner, he cannot speak, look, or move without interesting the divine being most actively in his behalf.[17]

In time, such criticism took its toll, and British Methodists opted for stability over superstition. The earlier dynamism and discipline that once characterized the Methodists under John and Charles diminished. Holiness and piety gave way to a new formalism: "Class meetings began to decline in significance, as did the influence of the class leader. Wesleyan Methodists now faced the problem of the mixed church, consisting of some who were fervent believers and others who were Wesleyans only by virtue of being born into a Methodist family."[18]

Jabez Bunting (1779–1858) was among the most significant, if controversial, trailblazers in the Wesleyan Methodist Church during the nineteenth century. Bunting served as secretary of the conference twice (1814–1819 and 1824–1827), though splits with the Protestant Methodists and Wesleyan Association illuminate the widespread perception of his dictatorial inflexibility. Bunting's leadership facilitated significant advances in world missions, the role of the laity, and the training and ordination of ministers in the Wesleyan Methodist Church.

Figure 4.4. Jabez Bunting

The subsequent history of British Methodism may seem archaic and remote to some Methodists around the world today, but understanding the afterlife of the movement in Great Britain contributes to our appreciation of the breadth of the global connection. Changes in the movement can be illustrated with a closer look at a simultaneously theological and practical idea: the Sabbath. Observance of Sunday as a day of rest had a long political history in England—that it might seem a matter of individual preference today is itself a reminder of the nature of religious change. In England, Sabbath practices were governed by law. In the 1600s, both James I and Charles I each took English Puritans to task for their exacting expectations for English citizens. Against the Puritans, the "Declaration on Sports" (1618/1633) allowed for only "lawful recreations and honest exercises upon Sunday and other holydays." King Charles later sanctioned that dancing (for men or women), archery (for men), or "leaping, vaulting, or any other such harmless recreation" should be permitted throughout the land, so long as such activities were pursued after church services.

John Wesley, not surprisingly, had his own opinions on the topic. In his sermon "On the Sabbath" (1730), Wesley explained that the Sabbath was, at its core, an act of obedience and imitation of God.[19] Wesley offered three guidelines to Christian Sabbath-keeping: (1) what we must, (2) what we may, and (3) what we may not do on Sunday. First, one must dedicate much of the day to prayer and praise. Second, because God did not want to over-burden body and soul with excessive labors of devotion, God also allows that the individual may perform various works of mercy (such as feeding cattle, etc.). However, one may not do works that "neither necessity nor mercy requires" or work that could be performed on another day without loss or pain to one's neighbor. To those who could not heed the commands of God, Wesley's advice was simple: given a choice between work and play, choose work—for then at least the Sabbath-breaking act will be profitable! Wesley's commitment to Sabbath observance continued in later writings as well, whether in the condemnation of those who seek amusement in un-necessary distractions or in the neglect of fruitful work.[20]

Yet, as circumstances changed and the memory of John Wesley's advice slowly faded, the Methodists gradually transformed Sabbath observance from a strictly theological to a broadly social issue for the good of society. Sunday schools were increasingly regarded as centers of basic academic learning (since education was often limited to the privileged) rather than training in righteousness—so much so that Jabez Bunting began to fear that Sunday schools were displacing the honor due to God alone. The Methodist theologian Richard Watson addressed the meaning of Sabbath observance in his widely studied *Theological Institutes* (1823–1828), but, unlike Wesley,

Watson gave wider latitude for observance and stated that the matter required a measure of prudence and charity. The differences between Wesley and Watson ought not be overstated, but a subtle shift was already becoming apparent. For Wesley, Sabbath observance was based on the obedient repetition of divine commands toward the goal of interior and exterior holiness. For Watson, by contrast, individual conscience dictates the form of Sabbath observance rather than a strict imitation of biblical commands.

Still, in 1852, when British politicians first considered opening the Crystal Palace in London on Sundays, Methodists rallied against the change with gusto. The *Primitive Methodist Magazine* maintained that the move "would be as plainly a sin as to legalize drunkenness, lying, and stealing. It would be to set God's law at utter defiance, to spurn his authority, and to upset his government."[21] Yet Methodist leaders could no longer depend on the nation to enforce Sabbath observance on strictly theological grounds, so increasingly they contended for its observation for the well-being of the nation.

For example, William Arthur (1819–1901), an eloquent and well-known Irish Methodist, claimed that participating in amusements on the Sabbath undermined its true purpose: rest. While the mechanic who devotes Sunday to rest and worship is "found refreshed in body, sober in mind, and cheerful in heart for his Monday's work," the one who fills his time with pleasure ends up "jaded, unhinged, and in want of more excitement."[22] By maintaining the Sabbath based on universal principles of order and arguing for the well-being of workers, Arthur participated in a broad reconceptualization of Sabbath observance from an act of moral duty and Christian obedience to a matter of civic religion.

While many associate Methodism almost exclusively with individual piety, the leadership of **Hugh Price Hughes** (1847–1902) represented a fresh emphasis on the social aspect of the early Wesleyan movement. Hughes spoke on behalf of the "nonconformist conscience" in Britain, calling for greater concern in the churches for social problems such as temperance, gambling, and inadequate housing for the poor. A marked ecumenicity led Hughes to serve as the first president of the National Council of the Evangelical Free Churches.

The gradual evolution of British Methodism becomes even clearer a generation later in the writings of one of its most respected twentieth-century voices: John Scott Lidgett (1854–1953). Lidgett, sometimes called "the greatest Methodist since Wesley," established the Bermondsey Settlement in southeast London to provide social and educational services for the poor. Lidgett, however, wasn't only a devoted worker but also a theologian. He penned major works and fostered the unity of Methodism through participation in the ecumenical movement. While Lidgett drew deep from the well of Wesleyan theology, he did so in decidedly modern terms. Thus he founded Bermondsey with the express interest in bringing people together for positive social action apart from any sectarian (that is, denominational) concern, and his theological beliefs reflect a wider departure from historic Christian doctrine through the influence of German and British Protestant liberalism.[23] When Lidgett mentioned the Sabbath in his writings, he emphasized observance not in terms of the imitation of God (as for Wesley) or the need for rest (as, in different ways, with Watson or Arthur) but the exercise of universal human values. In earlier days, "the Sabbath [was] an institution which at the time was held in superstitious reverence, and fenced round by artificial and childish regulations that destroyed the great spiritual ends for which it was ordained."[24] Was John Wesley's practice of Sabbath keeping similarly superstitious? Lidgett doesn't say. Still, he thought the life and ministry of Christ

Figure 4.5. John Scott Lidgett

demonstrates that external authority cannot be depended on, a truth he believed John Wesley surely had learned in his Aldersgate experience.[25] Lidgett thought that Wesley's commitment to the Spirit of Christ was so steadfast, whether in matters of Sabbath observance or ordination, that he felt the need to break with authority as "an act of costly obedience to God."[26] Lidgett's Wesley was a radical—whether or not Wesley would have agreed is another matter entirely.

Wesley's bold decision to ordain ministers for the work in America altered the course of Methodism. Yet had he refused to act, Methodism still would not have remained the same. In the decades that followed Wesley's death, preachers and theologians alike wrote for new generations faced with new challenges. They wrote in acts of faithfulness amidst difference, for Wesley's sermons, appeals, and thoughts on the Christian life continued to serve as foundational resources for Methodist societies. In his day, Wesley had turned the movement outside the walls of the church to promote a message of holiness among an increasingly urban populace: "One feels the chill of the early morning air, the push of crowds and the rigor of rutted roads; there were rioting mobs and contagious religious conversions."[27] Later, British Methodism—under the leadership of preachers such as Watson, Arthur, and Lidgett—returned to the sanctuary, to the formality of the chapels, and regained the admiration of the Anglican communion. British Methodism had indeed become respectable, but by the beginning of the twenty-first century, the membership rolls had dwindled considerably in the face of a widely secular society. All the while, looking back on Wesley's fateful decision in 1784, the movement was expanding rapidly across the Atlantic under the indefatigable leadership of Francis Asbury.

PART TWO

THE *Growth* OF NORTH AMERICAN METHODISM

CHAPTER FIVE

Revival Fire

ON WEDNESDAY, SEPTEMBER 4, 1771, a young man of twenty-six years set sail from a port near Bristol, England, bound for the city of Philadelphia. Several days into the journey, Francis Asbury (1745–1816) reflected on the task at hand, posing a series of questions to himself: "Whither am I going? To the New World. What to do? To gain honour? No, if I know my own heart. To get money? No: I am going to live to God, and to bring others so to do. . . . If God does not acknowledge me in America, I will soon return to England."[1] Asbury's journal reveals his openness to God on the cusp of a new and dangerous mission but also his unconscious desire for success and personal achievement. He added, "I know my views are upright now; may they never be otherwise." Francis Asbury served the people in America for more than four decades. He never returned to the land of his birth.

Just three years earlier, Asbury had been received into the Methodist connection and assigned to a preaching circuit along the east coast of England. He faced persecution in some areas but persisted in the work where others grew disheartened. Away from home and the parents he loved, Asbury devoted himself to Methodist preaching as a faithful worker. He later thought the trials of these years were given by God as a means of preparation for the larger challenges he would face overseas. In August 1771, Asbury had attended his first and only annual conference in Bristol, a central hub of Methodist activity in the southwest of England. He listened as reports from America were conveyed to the preachers and felt stirred by stories of ministry and opportunity.

America had revealed itself as a land of promise. Methodist ministry there already had expanded under the influence of the Irish Methodist Robert Strawbridge in Maryland, Barbara Heck and Philip Embury in New

York, and Captain Thomas Webb in New York, Philadelphia, and Baltimore. By 1770, John Wesley had appointed four regular preachers for the mission at the annual conference: Richard Boardman, Joseph Pilmore, Robert Williams, and John King. These ministers discovered fields ripe for harvest in the burgeoning centers of American life. In some regions, the lack of preachers left otherwise willing hearers hungry for opportunities to attend sermons, and some waited several months or more for access to baptism or the Lord's Supper. America was ostensibly a free religious market in most of the colonies. Anglican ministers were also there, but Methodist lay preachers soon established their own identity. Methodists built chapels and formed societies that deepened faith among Anglicans and members of other denominations alike. Yet one worry persisted. Some thought the lack of ordination would undermine ministry in Word and sacrament, threatening the stability and longevity of the movement in a land of opportunity.

> The terms **connection** and **conference** are widely used to indicate the discipline that governed the Methodists. From the earliest years of the revival, they used the term *connection* to describe the network of Methodist societies throughout Britain. John Wesley helped the itinerant preachers maintain contact across the connection by means of *holy conferencing*, which allowed him to address doctrinal questions, provide guidance on disciplinary matters, and promote right Christian practice.

At the annual conference in Bristol, Asbury responded to John Wesley's call for volunteers. He spoke his mind to the gathered preachers and offered to join the work overseas. His foremost biographer, John Wigger, perfectly describes the match: "Asbury was both dependable and expendable."[2] He had already proven himself as a capable preacher, willing to withstand the challenges of ministry in difficult circumstances, and yet he was not among Wesley's closest advisors. Five volunteered. Two were chosen. Within a month, Asbury set sail.

Upon arrival, Asbury quickly set about establishing a pattern of life focused on preaching, discipline, and administration. Preaching consumed Asbury's life. Over the course of the next decade, he established a habit of itinerancy that brought him through New York, New Jersey, Pennsylvania, Delaware, Maryland, West Virginia, Virginia, North Carolina, and South Carolina. He led prayers in public, preached outdoors, faced opposition from settled ministers for urging repentance in their parishes, and busied himself in private to strengthen himself in public. In one entry, Asbury describes his routine:

> My present mode of conduct is as follows—to read about a hundred pages a day; usually to pray in public five times a day; to preach in the open air every other day; and to lecture in prayer meeting every evening. And if it were in my power, I would do a thousand times as much for such a gracious and blessed Master. But in the midst of all my little employments, I feel myself as nothing, and Christ to me is all in all.[3]

When Asbury arrived in New York, he soon discovered that American Methodist leadership lacked the sort of discipline he had come to expect among Methodists in England. Sermons were delivered regularly, but, rather than itinerating as their peers in Britain, Pilmore and Boardman had begun to settle in large cities such as New York and Philadelphia. Class meetings, too, weren't organized effectively, and Asbury feared that Methodist disciplines had gradually fallen off. For his part, he devoted hours each day to private prayer and sought divine guidance for the future.[4]

Figure 5.1. Francis Asbury

The more time Asbury spent among Methodist societies, the more he discovered that American Methodism lacked the sort of unity and organization that would make the mission fully effective. Lay leadership brought conversions and formed new societies, but they suffered from John Wesley's absence. Asbury recognized that most of the growth occurred in the South, despite tensions between ordained Anglican ministers and Methodist lay preachers. Anglican ministers in the colonies tended to view Methodist lay preachers much as had their counterparts in England: Methodist preachers were uneducated enthusiasts who divided the flock in the name of self-interest. American Methodists, by contrast, regarded many Anglican ministers as slothful, inattentive, and inadequate to the task. Still, where the Church of England thrived, Methodism prospered. By 1776 more than half of all Methodists in America resided in North Carolina or Virginia alone.[5]

The astounding growth of early American Methodism owes much to the tireless work of the laity. Lay preachers often asserted the need for repentance to avoid eternal damnation, and many responded to their counsel with striking accounts of transformation. Rebecca Ridgley's report of her conversion under Captain Webb in 1774 illustrates how extraordinary experiences of renewal became commonplace:

> O, how I began to weep. I saw that I was the very person who had neglected the call of God: a lost, poor, undone creature. O, how I fell on my knees and prayed to the Lord to call me once more and how I would run [to God]. It then was a shame to kneel before the people, but O I thought, what is all the world to me if I must lose my soul? . . . At length [I] came home with no peace . . . and [I] seemed to give myself up as lost. I [then] felt something come as an arrow out of a bow into my heart. "O," said I, "what is this?" I had scarcely said this then I found it was the holy baptism. I was then baptized with the Holy Ghost and with fire.[6]

Those listening to Methodist preaching often responded with visible, emotional reactions. Some wept over sin or shouted aloud, others fell to the ground in prayer, and a few were reported to lay on the ground as if in a trance.

While their sermons focused on familiar Protestant themes such as repentance, justification, and sanctification, lay ministers relied on class

Figure 5.2. Thomas Webb

meetings and love feasts to foster a sense of community. Influenced by the Moravians, the Wesleys developed love feasts from a recovery of early Christian spirituality. Love feasts encouraged communal witness and thanksgiving and, unlike the celebration of the Lord's Supper, did not require administration by clergy. Members (as opposed to seekers or the merely curious) gathered to share a "feast" of bread and water with hymns, prayers, offerings for the needy, and testimonies of divine grace. Asbury's account of one love feast held at a quarterly meeting intimates a revival reminiscent of Pentecost:

> As soon as it began the power of the Lord came down on the assembly like a rushing mighty wind; and it seemed as if the whole house was filled with the presence of God. A flame kindled and ran from heart to heart. Many were deeply convinced of sin; many mourners were filled with consolation; and many believers were so overwhelmed with love, that they could not doubt but God had enabled them to love him with *all* their heart.[7]

Some, such as Robert Strawbridge, ignored tradition and administered the sacraments without ordination, but most American Methodists prior to the Revolution followed the established rule of observing the sacrament at Anglican churches. In this way, American Methodism combined passionate evangelical preaching, the Anglican standards of church order, and the doctrinal principles of John and Charles Wesley.[8]

For his part, Asbury worked to organize the Methodists wherever he traveled. He instituted quarterly meetings just as Wesley had established in England and gathered lay preachers throughout the circuits for common order, unity, discipline, and spiritual guidance. When controversy arose—as when the Virginia Methodists unilaterally began ordaining and administering sacraments during the war—Asbury successfully saved the connection through negotiation, compromise, and a cautious reconciliation.[9] Asbury read constantly and found wisdom and comfort in the works of John Wesley, Joseph Fletcher, and other ministers and scholars both inside and outside the movement. In all his years of ministry, he never owned a home or engaged in romance but trekked from town to town on horse or by carriage through untrammeled wilderness, disease-infested woodlands, and perilous

John Wesley revived the practice of the ancient Christian **love feast** among Methodists as a means of Christian fellowship, thanksgiving, and prayer. Wesley first learned of the practice while serving among Moravians in Georgia and considered the meal an imitation of early Christian practice. Although similar to the Lord's Supper in the sharing of food, the two meals should not be confused. Most important, the Lord's Supper requires an authorized minister, while the love feast may be led by any Christian and practiced freely in ecumenical settings.

rivers. Asbury devoted himself to the work in America by appointing new preachers to the circuits, moderating appeals for sacramental authority, and planning for new class meetings, chapels, and revivals. In the process, Asbury earned an unparalleled reputation.

Sunday, November 14, 1784. Thirteen years after his voyage to America, Francis Asbury reached Barratt's Chapel in Delaware. An assembly had already gathered for public worship. The two men who guided the service, Dr. Thomas Coke and Richard Whatcoat, had only recently arrived from England by way of New York. Coke preached, and soon after—to Asbury's complete astonishment—Whatcoat assisted in the sacrament, taking up the cup in the administration of the Lord's Supper. Until that moment, Asbury had no idea that John Wesley had ordained Whatcoat for the work of ministry. Later that

The Methodist preacher **James O'Kelly** (1757–1826) was born in Ireland before emigrating to North America in 1778. O'Kelly led one of the most significant schismatic movements in early Methodism when in 1792 he proposed that preachers should have the right to object to the appointment made by Francis Asbury and, with the support of the conference, be reassigned. The motion failed to gain the approval of the conference, but his departure from the denomination led many preachers into the short-lived Republican Methodist Church.

Figure 5.3. O'Kelly Chapel, c. 1910

day, Coke explained Wesley's plan to organize the Methodists into an independent episcopal church. Asbury prudently agreed, on one condition: "If the preachers unanimously choose me." In his journal, Asbury confided, "It may be of God."[10] Those present agreed to take up the matter at a general conference six weeks later in Baltimore. The energetic young preacher Freeborn Garrettson immediately rode out to gather the connection; Asbury and Coke set out on a preaching tour, where they journeyed through Delaware, Maryland, and Virginia in the weeks leading up to the conference.[11] Despite unfamiliar hardships, little could dampen Coke's enthusiasm: "Perhaps I have in this little tour baptized more children and adults than I should in my whole life, if stationed in an English parish."[12]

Asbury's cautious response reflects the political spirit of early American Methodism.[13] Neither Coke nor Wesley had fully recognized that Methodism across the Atlantic succeeded in a land where the language of liberty and individual rights opposed the specter of corruption and tyranny. In England, support for the crown was the norm among Methodists who sought respect from the government no less than their neighbors. In America, by contrast, John Wesley's leadership could easily be mistaken for ecclesial control by a foreign sovereign. Asbury previously had warned Wesley that any preachers assigned to circuits in America must be governed by one who is "always out among them."[14] Asbury's solution was simple: John Wesley must return to America and serve until the day of his death (just as George Whitefield had). Wesley rejected Asbury's proposal. Instead, a year before Coke's arrival, Wesley directed Asbury to serve as his general assistant "and to receive no preachers from Europe that are not recommended by him, nor any in America, who will not submit to me."[15]

Wesley's response did little more than confirm the position that Asbury had already attained among Methodists in every circuit. If Wesley hoped the move would shore up his own authority among American Methodists, he had gravely miscalculated. Unlike so many other preachers whom Wesley assigned to America, the two men had less a personal relationship than an intellectual affinity. Asbury was still a young man when he volunteered for service abroad. While his journal often stresses the depth of wisdom he discovered in Wesley's writings, he never shared in ministry by his side through long days of rugged and cheerless travel or the bonds of friendship cultivated

The American Revolution left the colonies without ordained ministers from the Church of England. In response to this crucial need, Wesley ordained Richard Whatcoat and Thomas Vasey, directing them to go to America with Thomas Coke. At Lovely Lane Chapel in Baltimore, meeting late in December 1784, a general conference known as the **Christmas Conference** approved Wesley's plan for liturgy, doctrine, and practice in the formation of the Methodist Episcopal Church.

Figure 5.4. The ordination of Francis Asbury at the Christmas Conference, 1784

through shared community. Rather, Asbury had become increasingly American in outlook and temperament, and once he even refused to leave when Wesley had suggested he might return home.[16] When the preachers Wesley had assigned to America fled the colonies during the dangerous years of the American Revolution, Asbury alone remained and supervised the Methodists from a place of relative seclusion in Delaware.[17] When Wesley chastised the Americans for their revolutionary spirit (a rebellion that destabilized the proper order of society), Asbury cheered the victory as an accomplishment blessed by God: "I heard the good news that Britain had acknowledged the Independence for which America has been contending— may it be so! The Lord does what to him seemeth good."[18] And so it was that with the arrival of Coke and Whatcoat, American Methodism and Wesley's preeminence came to a watershed moment, revealing a deeper divide in the movement than John Wesley could have imagined.

The general conference gathered over the course of two weeks at Lovely Lane Chapel in Baltimore. On December 24, the first day of the illustrious Christmas Conference of 1784, the preachers who were close enough to attend resolved to form the Methodist Episcopal Church in the United States (MEC). The preachers, honoring John Wesley's guidance, unanimously elected Coke and Asbury as their first superintendents. With the new church established, Coke ordained Asbury deacon on Christmas day. The following day Asbury was ordained elder. Finally, on December 27, Asbury was consecrated superintendent, with Thomas Coke, Asbury's friend William Otterbein (the German minister and founder of the United Brethren), Richard Whatcoat, and Thomas Vasey assisting.

The Christmas Conference of 1784 established a new church with simultaneously Wesleyan and Anglican characteristics. John Wesley produced a revised liturgy, articles, and discipline for the American Methodists. *The Sunday Service of the Methodists in North America* was little more than an abridgement of the Anglican Book of Common Prayer. Wesley shortened some services and eliminated language he regarded as confusing or potentially misleading (such as terminology that implied infant baptismal regeneration).[19] Wesley also revised the Thirty-Nine Articles of Religion, omitting fifteen articles and clarifying some phrasing that savored of Reformation-era controversies. The conference pledged fidelity to Wesley's authority during his lifetime and Methodists abroad thereafter: "We acknowledge ourselves his Sons in the Gospel, ready, in matters belonging to church government, to obey his commands; and we do engage after his death to do everything that we judge consistent with the cause of religion in America, and the political interests of these States to preserve and promote our union with the Methodists in Europe."[20]

> John Wesley established a standard of doctrine in the Methodist Episcopal Church through a revision of the Anglican **Thirty-Nine Articles of Religion**. He originally emended the articles to twenty-four by eliminating obedience to the British monarch (unfitting for the newly established nation) and adjusting some theological language. The Americans approved the articles at the Christmas Conference (1784) with one addition: on the sovereignty of the delegated authorities of the United States government.

Wesley's move to ordain had set off controversy in Britain, but the act preserved the Anglican character of Methodism in the United States.

Around the time of the Christmas Conference, the leaders of the nascent Protestant Episcopal Church attempted to merge the two movements, but Methodist commitment to Wesley's authority and teachings proved an impassible obstacle to the union.[21] Yet, in the years that followed the formation of the MEC, Wesley's preeminence quickly came into question. Asbury's prior concern that Wesley might attempt to rule the Methodists from across the Atlantic was soon shared by his ministerial colleagues, who already felt like second-class citizens in the Methodist hierarchy; though no American Methodist had the reputation of Francis Asbury, his name had not even been named among the so-called "Legal Hundred."[22] As a result, when Wesley called for a general conference in America in 1787 to name Richard Whatcoat as superintendent alongside Asbury (Coke had returned to England in June 1785, leaving administration of the new church to Asbury), the Americans refused. Some thought Wesley intended to replace Asbury, but, whatever the reason, the sharp tone of Asbury's letters reveals his growing frustration. He complained to one fellow Methodist, "There is not a man in the world so obnoxious to the American politicians as our dear old Daddy [Wesley], but no matter, we must treat him with all the respect we can and that is due to him." Respect, in a matter of sentences, could easily give way to anger:

> I write you as my confidential friend: my real sentiments are union but no subordination, connexion but no subjection. I am sure that no man or number of men in England can direct either the head or the body here unless he or they should possess divine powers, be omnipotent, omniscient and omnipresent. That one thousand preachers traveling and local; and thirty thousand people would submit to a man they never have nor can see, his advice they will follow as far as they judge it right. For our old, old Daddy to appoint conferences when and where he pleased, to appoint a joint superintendent with me, were strokes of power we did not understand.[23]

Asbury's complaints were apparently not isolated to a single trusted advisor either. To one correspondent, John Wesley complained that he had seen letters from Asbury that objected to his abortive interference with the American Methodists. From another associate, Wesley learned that Asbury had quipped, "Mr. Wesley and I are like Caesar and Pompey: he will bear no equal, and I will bear no superior."[24] When Wesley heard that Asbury now referred to himself as "bishop" (the new church had been dubbed an *episcopal* body), Wesley's anger boiled over. Wesley wrote condescendingly to "my dear Franky" in a futile attempt to reverse the course of history:

> I am a little afraid both the Doctor [Coke] and you differ from me. I study to be little: you study to be great. I creep; you strut along. . . . How can you, how dare you suffer yourself to be called Bishop? I shudder, I start at the very thought! Men may call me a knave or a fool, a rascal, a scoundrel, and I am content; but they shall never by my consent call me Bishop! For my sake, for God's sake, for Christ's sake put a full end to this![25]

Still, for all the tensions that crept into their friendship, when Asbury learned of John Wesley's death in 1791 he lamented, "I feel the stroke most sensibly," and "I shall never read his works without reflecting on the loss which the Church of God and the world has sustained by his death."[26]

Years earlier, John Wesley had looked in vain for a trustworthy individual to lead the Methodists after his passing. Charles had settled in marriage. John Fletcher was unwilling. He outlived them both besides. Unbeknownst to Wesley, his legitimate successor already was itinerating across the ocean. Although they only had spent a few hours together, no Methodist expanded the work as faithfully as Bishop Francis Asbury. Ironically, like John Wesley, Asbury so embodied early American Methodism that no single individual could replace him. In later years, as his health began to decline, Asbury gradually ceded control to William McKendree, who took a more "committee-oriented" approach to church administration.[27] Still Asbury, even in a reduced role, continued to minister to the end. Men carried him into the Richmond, Virginia, church where he delivered his final sermon from a chair. Yet unlike his forebear in England, Asbury left no collection of sermons or compilation of treatises when he died on March 31, 1816. He only left a journal that testifies to his extraordinary perseverance. "I live in God from moment to moment," he wrote in one of his final journal entries.[28] Yet, for all the ways that Asbury sought to unify the American Methodists, the issue of slavery threatened to divide the movement almost from the start.

CHAPTER SIX

Everlasting Freedom

For sixty years American Methodism prospered. All the while, hostility over race and slavery destabilized the unity of the church. Then, in 1844, the church could hold together no longer. Years before the nation divided in Civil War, the MEC developed a plan of separation that formally divided American Methodism for almost a century. Rumors that one of the five bishops of the church owned slaves by marriage led to an investigation, admission of facts, weeks of debate, and, finally, a vote directing the offending bishop to discontinue ministry immediately. Protests followed, and plans for separation emerged. These were days of crisis. The real story of separation, however, began not in the sensational events of 1844 but much earlier in a series of acts, allowances, and compromises that surrounded two African American preachers whose captivating lives reveal as much about American Methodism as they do about the nature of early American Christianity.

The dramatic growth of early American Methodism owes a great deal to African American membership. From the beginning of the denomination, leaders of the Methodist Episcopal Church (MEC) condemned slaveholding and supported abolitionism. The stance made the MEC a welcoming place for African Americans, and, in turn, black Methodists fundamentally shaped the mission, evangelism, and discipleship of the fledgling church. In 1786, when the churches first began listing black and white members separately on the rolls, African American Methodists accounted for nearly 10 percent of the church. By 1790, African American membership swelled to 20 percent of the entire denomination. In some regions, such as the Delmarva Peninsula (a region along the east coast occupying portions of Delaware, Maryland, and Virginia), black membership accounted for upward of 30 percent of the church during these pivotal years of growth.[1] In short, free and enslaved black members formed a critical component of early American Methodism.

Although he has largely slipped from memory, one of the most well-known preachers in early American Methodism was a former slave named Harry Hosier (c. 1750–c. 1806). "Black Harry," as he was widely known, traveled with Francis Asbury as a horse groom. But there was more. Asbury's journal verifies that Hosier went to Virginia with Asbury in 1780 to advance the gospel among the black population.[2] Occasionally, Hosier preached to

Harry Hosier (c. 1750–c. 1806) was among the earliest black preachers in the Methodist movement. Many believe Hosier was born in slavery on an American plantation. He served as a groom for Francis Asbury and often preached to great acclaim in meetings organized by the likes of Thomas Coke and Freeborn Garrettson. Hosier was one of only two black Methodists (with Richard Allen) who attended the Christmas Conference of 1784.

Figure 6.1. Harry Hosier

the crowds that gathered after Asbury had completed a service. Asbury's journal also indicates that Hosier gained notoriety through his addresses and that some listeners "came a great distance to hear him." Yet while Asbury was an opponent of slavery, his journal also implies an element of mistrust for his colleague. Not only blacks but also many whites heard Hosier preach, and though he was illiterate, his commanding style and prophetic voice undoubtedly left many listeners uneasy. One of his most popular sermons was on the parable of the barren fig tree, with its uncompromising moral: "Except ye repent, ye shall all likewise perish" (Lk 13:3). "Certain sectarians are greatly displeased with him," Asbury explained, "because he tells them they may fall from grace, and that they must be holy."[3] Preaching on the fall from grace was the bread and butter of Wesleyan doctrine, but for a black man to call crowds to repent from sin or risk damnation pushed the envelope further than many white Americans could handle.[4]

When Dr. Thomas Coke and Francis Asbury toured in preparation for the Christmas Conference (1784), Harry Hosier's preaching stood out. Coke discovered a man with unique talents and uncommon charm: "I have now had the pleasure of hearing *Harry* preach several times. I sometimes give notice immediately after preaching, that in a little time *Harry* will preach to the blacks; but the whites always stay to hear him. Sometimes I publish him to preach at candle-light, as the negroes can better attend at that time."[5] Coke had traveled with many of the greatest evangelists of the revival in Britain and abroad, but he still dubbed Hosier "one of the best preachers in the world." He was astounded by the "amazing power" that attended his speaking, despite Hosier's inability to read. Notwithstanding such unparalleled gifts, Coke discerned in Hosier an uncommon modesty, avowing that he was "one of the humblest creatures I ever saw."[6]

Coke's assessment of Hosier's character challenges allegations made by some of his contemporaries. The large crowds that amassed to hear Hosier speak certainly attracted attention—undoubtedly one of the foremost reasons that he was encouraged to preach—but may have left some less-charismatic Methodists (such as Asbury, who was known for an "energetic" but "plain and simple" style) feeling uncertain about the rise to fame of a poor black man.[7] As early as 1781, Asbury complained that Hosier resisted his supervision and feared that "his speaking so much to white people in the city has been, or will be, injurious; he has been flattered, and may be ruined."[8]

By contrast, when Hosier traveled New England with Freeborn Garrettson, word spread of larger and larger crowds—and no complaints from his companion. Rather, Garrettson's journal repeatedly praises Hosier, describing the "admiration," "fondness," and "applause" of listeners who responded to Hosier's exhortations. Though he was treated uncivilly by some crowds, Hosier preached to more than one thousand in Providence, Rhode Island, and, shortly after, Garrettson declined a speaking engagement in favor of Hosier in Hudson, New York. The sermon was so well received—even across denominational lines—that the Quakers thought he preached by immediate inspiration.[9] Despite such acclaim, Hosier never advanced to ordination in the ranks of the Methodist Episcopal Church on the dubious grounds that he had "backslid" from pride.[10]

Hosier's case is a reminder that many Methodists were progressive in their opposition to slavery, but their treatment of men and women of African descent often reflected cultural prejudices. First, Asbury and other preachers were not immune to bias. While Methodists such as Asbury

Born in Maryland to an Anglican family, **Freeborn Garrettson** (1752–1827) established a legacy as one of the pioneers of American Methodism. He preached widely throughout North America, ardently opposed the practice of slavery, and called the Methodist preachers to the Christmas Conference (1784). Later, Garrettson served as missionary to Nova Scotia and a presiding elder in New York, where his wife, Catherine Livingstone Garrettson (1752–1849), provided hospitality for numerous Methodist preachers traveling in the region.

Figure 6.2. Freeborn Garrettson

sanctioned Hosier's exhortations, his sermons were delivered after the service or in a separate location. Second, American Methodists such as Asbury thought freedom of the body was subordinate to the freedom of the soul. Asbury admired the Quakers in their abolitionism and even believed that Methodists must follow suit or "the Lord will depart from them." Still, Methodists were not Quakers.[11] Third, the early American Methodist emphasis on spiritual liberation over political liberation led many to compromise with slaveholders for the sake of evangelism. They condemned the institution of slavery but limited their remarks in some places in order to secure access. While there is no doubt about Asbury's firm opposition to slavery, he often worked pragmatically.[12] In some ways, even this approach risked the appearance of impropriety among his peers. In one letter, Asbury notes that he visited a vicious and "tyrannical old Welshman" who treated enslaved men and women like animals. While some Methodists might avoid any contact with such a man, Asbury responded, "that would be just as the devil would have it." Over the course of a year, he found that the man's heart had softened, and he finally permitted the entire plantation to worship together. He did not, however, emancipate the men and women, which calls into question Asbury's glowing remarks on the Welshman's change of heart. "What now can sweeten the bitter cup like religion?" Asbury asked. "The slaves soon see the preachers are their friends, and soften their owners towards them. There are thousands here of slaves who if we could come out to them would embrace religion. It is of vast moment for us to send the news far and wide. It hath its influence."[13] In short, while it is tempting to look back on Methodists and imagine a sterling example of uncompromising abolitionism, northern and southern Methodists both failed to practice full inclusion in church life.

Nonetheless, Asbury's abolitionism contrasts sharply with the practices of the Church of England's missionary arm, the Society for the Propagation of the Gospel in Foreign Parts (SPG). In 1710 the SPG received a charitable bequest that made the society the owner of a plantation and its slaves in Barbados. As more and more critics agitated for abolition and an end to the slave trade, the SPG sought guidance on the moral ramifications of slaveholding. The society even invited William Knox (1732–1810), a prominent government consultant and owner of a large plantation in Georgia (including 122 slaves), to provide direction on the issue. Knox argued that, whatever the legality of slaveholding, instruction in religion is essential to the well-being of an American plantation: "No planter is so grossly barbarous as not to wish to have his Negroes do his work with a good will; and very few would be so brutal or ignorant as not to perceive, that were their Negroes instructed in religion, and taught to serve their masters for conscience sake, that they would be much better served by them."[14] Although he feared the possibility of insurrection, Knox advocated evangelism as the basis of pacification. The SPG was complicit in the slave system.

When the noted Quaker abolitionist Anthony Benezet (1713–84) challenged the practices of the SPG, arguing that love of neighbor forbids slavery, the society responded by reasserting the need to treat all people with care and kindness. "But they cannot condemn the practice of keeping slaves as unlawful," Knox explained, "finding the contrary very plainly implied in the precepts given by the apostles, both to masters and servants, which last were then for the most part slaves."[15] The society reasoned that the Bible supports slavery, and so could not be opposed. If Benezet and others proved successful in their campaign against the slave system, then grave consequences would result: slaveholders would gradually restrict access, enslaved Africans would inevitably revolt, and bloodshed would ensue.

John Wesley, whose missionary work in Georgia may have been sponsored in part by the SPG, condemned the slave system in no uncertain terms. Even during his time in America, Wesley had contact with men and women of African descent and lamented their cruel treatment. After witnessing firsthand the treatment of black men and women in South Carolina, Wesley appealed to the language of the prophet Isaiah: "O earth! How long wilt thou hide their blood? How long wilt thou cover thy slain?"[16] Wesley's most public statement, however, came in *Thoughts upon Slavery* (1774), an accessible revision and republication of Anthony Benezet's *Some Historical Account of Guinea* (1772). Wesley wrote and appended "a little application" at the conclusion of his edition that called for an end to the slave system. He rebuked all captains of vessels who abused men and women with "souls immortal as your own," merchants blinded by the prospect of wealth, and American plantation owners who subsidized the entire system: "Thy hands, thy bed, thy furniture, thy house, thy lands are at present stained with blood . . . accumulate no more guilt: spill no more the blood of the innocent!"[17] Wesley offered a stark, uncompromising judgment on all who dishonored men and women of African descent.

Early American Methodists initially followed Wesley's guidance. At the Christmas Conference, the founders of the MEC not only established the new denomination but also formed a plan to eradicate slaveholding from the church. They justified the plan on the dual authority of the Bible (namely, the law of love of neighbor "on which hang all the law and the prophets") and the political principles of national independence.[18] American Methodists didn't simply condemn the practice, they warned that slaveholders who refused to emancipate their slaves risked expulsion from the church. Still, even in this, Methodists refused to make a clean break, allowing for a gradual process of emancipation. Legal deeds of manumission had to be produced and recorded by local preachers within one year, though the timeline for actual liberation varied by age (for example, enslaved men and women under twenty years old had to be emancipated by the age of twenty-five).[19] Selling slaves to avoid the rule (and profit in the process) could also lead to expulsion from the church.

Tragically, American Methodists failed to implement the rule. Although Coke and Asbury both supported legislative petitions and even broached the subject in a meeting with President George Washington, they confronted their stiffest opposition in the very places where Methodism was numerically strongest. Asbury preached cautiously against slavery in Virginia and North Carolina but sometimes avoided the subject altogether or skipped visits to some cities in order to remain free from legal troubles or threats of violence. Coke faced indictments for abolitionist preaching in two Virginia counties.[20] Other preachers faced imprisonment or acts of aggression. Meanwhile, local discipline varied considerably, and the issue does not appear again in general conference minutes until 1796. In some conferences, slaveholding could result in expulsion from the church, while in other conferences the matter could not even be raised without contention.

Steadily, American Methodist practice adapted to local culture. Slaveholders embraced Wesleyan doctrines such as justification and sanctification while ignoring the social teachings that accompanied the foundation of the denomination. Some Methodists in the South supported abolitionism, but their inability to eradicate or even diminish the practice led to what amounts to the "troubled conscience" of American Methodism: "Later reformers easily envisioned a past more radical than it had been and construed their own contemporaries and the ambivalences about racial matters of that latter day as betraying the Methodist heritage."[21] The case of Harry Hosier, with his rise to fame offset by distrust among colleagues in ministry, exemplifies the ways that prejudice coexisted with abolitionism. Methodism expanded in America but always with small and seemingly insignificant compromises that gradually divided the denomination.

However, Harry Hosier wasn't the only black Methodist to face scrutiny in these early years. In fact, two African Americans attended the Christmas Conference of 1784: Harry Hosier and Richard Allen (1760–1831). If Hosier represents the archetypal evangelist of early American Methodism, Allen carried the mantle of prophetic leadership. Born into slavery in Philadelphia, Allen lived most of his youth in Delaware. He describes his master, Stokeley Sturgis, as an unconverted but "tender, humane man." Allen undoubtedly suffered. Among other adversities, his mother and siblings were sold off in a time of economic distress. At twenty, Allen came alive to religion and first felt the weight of his sin. He sought mercy in his prayers and, as with so many Methodists before him, feared he would find no relief. "I thought hell would be my portion," he wrote in his autobiography. After several days of struggle and inner turmoil, Allen had a powerful experience of conversion: "I cried unto Him who delighteth to hear the prayers of a poor sinner, and all of a sudden my dungeon shook, my chains flew off, and, glory to God, I cried. My soul was filled. I cried, enough for me—the Saviour died."[22]

Thereafter, Allen began to evangelize his friends and neighbors. He joined a Methodist society and attended class meetings in the forest at night. Eventually, even Sturgis discovered his own need for Christ under the preaching of Freeborn Garrettson. Yet unlike so many Methodists who accommodated the practice of slavery, Sturgis became convinced that he needed to release his slaves (though only after they had worked off the price of their freedom).[23] By 1783, some five years after Sturgis's conversion, Richard Allen gained his liberty. Soon Allen began preaching and traveling with many of the leading Methodists of the era.

Richard Allen (1760–1831), the founder of the African Methodist Episcopal Church (AME), was born in slavery in Philadelphia but secured his freedom in 1783. Allen attended the Christmas Conference of 1784 as a nonvoting representative of black American Methodists. Alongside other black preachers such as Absalom Jones (1746–1818), Allen formed the Free African Society and, after conflict with white Methodists at St. George's Church in Philadelphia, established Bethel AME with the support of Francis Asbury.

Figure 6.3. Richard Allen

Allen's inimitable leadership emerged most clearly in a series of events at St. George's Church in Philadelphia. Allen had settled in Philadelphia in 1786 and began preaching regularly to other black Methodists there, often twice a day or more. He soon formed a society of African Americans who met with white Methodists at St. George's. Their numbers increased, and gradually Allen determined that the society required a separate meeting place to accommodate the needs of African American Methodists. When Allen approached the district elder with the idea, he was rebuffed with abusive language. Abolitionism aside, American Methodists still refused to ordain African American men (or women, for that matter). So with Absalom Jones (1746–1818), Allen formed the Free African Society in 1787 to encourage aid for fugitive slaves and establish special gatherings for prayer and exhortation.

Despite the setback, many members continued to meet for worship at St. George's. Though white and black members coexisted in the congregation, some white Methodists resented the growing proportion of African Americans at the church. At first, black members were moved to the outer wall, but the solution proved unsatisfactory. In 1792 white officials directed a gallery to be built above the main level to accommodate the crowds that filled the noisy sanctuary. Black members completed many improvements on the property, and the gallery itself was the fruit of their labors, but when they attended worship, they were treated as subordinates.[24]

The decisive moment came soon after the completion of the new balcony.[25] When several members of the Free African Society came to worship, the black congregants were directed not to their regular seats on the main floor but upstairs to the gallery. They dutifully moved above their former seats and knelt in prayer. Without warning, one of the church trustees pulled Absalom Jones off his knees, demanding him to get up. Jones only replied, "Wait until prayer is over," but the impertinent man insisted, "No, you must get up now, or I will call for aid and force you away." Jones remained and soon faced further abuse. Allen's terse record indicates their humiliation: "We all went out of the church in a body, and they were no more plagued with us in the church."[26]

From this time, Allen and the others determined to establish a separate body, but Allen remained committed to the Methodists through it all. The presiding elder in Philadelphia, John McClaskey, threatened to "read them out" of the church if they continued plans to meet separately. Allen refused to submit. They refurbished a building as a temporary meeting place and began raising money for a more suitable edifice. Many in the society thought the group should join up with the Episcopalians—a move that would likely have made Allen the first ordained African American in the nation—but Allen declined, noting,

> I was confident that there was no religious sect or denomination would suit the capacity of the colored people as well as the Methodist; for the plain and simple gospel suits best for any people; for the unlearned can understand, and the learned are sure to understand; and the reason that the Methodist is so successful in the awakening and conversion of the colored people, [is] the plain doctrine and having a good discipline.[27]

Records indicate that some white members of St. George's were embarrassed by the gallery incident, but there was little hope for lasting change. When yellow fever overwhelmed the city, Allen mobilized the black community to carry out the most dangerous work of providing medical aid and burying thousands of infectious corpses, but even then, white Methodists refused to treat black Methodists as equals.[28]

Francis Asbury recognized the problem. He moved McClaskey to Baltimore, though he had been in Philadelphia for only a year, and replaced him with none other than Freeborn Garrettson as presiding elder, hoping that Allen's society might prosper without severing its connection to the MEC. Eventually, Allen broke ground on newly purchased property, and, in June 1794, Asbury preached at the opening service of Bethel Church, noting in his journal that the congregation would "be governed by the doctrine and discipline of the Methodists."[29] Despite such efforts, resistance to black leadership and governance at Bethel continued with requirements for white oversight of the church. Five years after the founding of the "house of God,"

Leaders of the **African Methodist Episcopal Church (AME)** and **African Methodist Episcopal Zion Church (AMEZ)** formed new denominations in response to racial discrimination among Methodists in cities such as New York, Philadelphia, and Baltimore. The two denominations quickly grew throughout the United States and, through the work of foreign missions, into parts of the Caribbean and Africa. Leading AME and AMEZ church members include Bishop Henry McNeal Turner, Rosa Parks, Alexander Walters, Stephen Gill Spotswood, and James Cone.

Figure 6.4. The current Mother Bethel AME in Philadelphia was built in 1890 on the same property as the first AME church

Asbury ordained Richard Allen the first African American deacon of the Methodist Episcopal Church.[30] Subsequent elders remained hostile to the work at Bethel nonetheless: they treated members disrespectfully, required exorbitant financial support, and demanded access to the pulpit against the wishes of the trustees. On April 9, 1816, little more than a week after the death of Francis Asbury, Allen met with other black church leaders to establish the African Methodist Episcopal Church (AME). He served as bishop until his death in 1831.[31] The formation of the AME remains one of the most significant events in the history of American Christianity.

—————

The practice of slavery threatened to divide American Methodists over the course of the early nineteenth century. In both northern and southern churches, laity and clergy alike felt the weight of the issue but couldn't muster a unified voice. While other black preachers labored and new black denominations formed, including James Varick's African Methodist Episcopal Zion Church in New York (1821) (AMEZ), the ministry of Harry Hosier and Richard Allen symbolized the tensions between race and faith that imperiled American Methodism throughout the early nineteenth century.

Annual conferences enforced the discipline but unevenly at best. Methodists consistently held to the rule against buying and selling slaves, but expulsion for violating the rule was rare. More often, preachers denounced the practice while simultaneously urging better treatment of slaves by their Methodist masters. When slaves came into the possession of a Methodist, conferences became complicit in the evil by facilitating contracts for their freedom after a designated period of work (based on their perceived value). Others who violated the rule were quickly reconciled with acknowledgement of the evil act. Methodists condemned slavery and exhorted masters to benevolence but compromised in hopes of bringing change over time.[32]

While most American Methodists favored gradual emancipation, the strategy failed to curtail the practice. Increasingly, abolitionists demanded the immediate emancipation of slaves, condemning the purchase, sale, and holding of enslaved people as incompatible with the gospel. By the general conferences of 1836 and 1840, some began agitating for more radical changes in the church. The bishops, unable to reform the MEC, urged silence. Many feared schism. In 1843, Orange Scott of the New England Conference grew weary of waiting, establishing the Wesleyan Methodist Connection in protest against MEC inaction.

At the General Conference of 1844, two prominent cases brought the MEC to the brink of separation. Delegates first dealt with an appeal originating from the Baltimore annual conference. Francis Harding, an elder in the church, refused to emancipate several slaves he had acquired through marriage after ordination. The Baltimore conference had suspended Harding's membership, and the general conference refused his appeal for reinstatement.[33] The suspension of Harding's membership showed the willingness of conference delegates to act against ministers associated with "this great evil."

They next took up an even more controversial and bewildering case. The general conference, having become aware that one of the bishops was connected to slavery, directed the Committee on Episcopacy to investigate.[34] The committee's report focused on James O. Andrew, one of the five superintending bishops of the MEC. Andrew explained that two slaves had previously been bequeathed to him: one girl from an elderly lady in Augusta, Georgia, whom he was instructed to either send to Liberia or, if the girl refused her consent, manumit to the best of his ability. Since the laws of Georgia forbade emancipation, Bishop Andrew established a home on his property in which the girl could live without any service to him or his family. The second slave, a boy, came into Bishop Andrew's property after the death of his first wife. The boy had previously been left to his wife by her mother, and his wife's subsequent death without a will brought the child into Bishop Andrew's estate. The bishop explained that the child would be free to leave the state once the boy was capable of caring for himself.[35] Despite these accommodations, both remained his property and would pass to his heirs in the event of his death.

The **General Conference** of 1844, held in Louisville, Kentucky was the most divisive conference in the history of American Methodism, resulting in the schism of the Methodist Episcopal Church. The discovery that Bishop James Andrew (1796–1871) and his wife owned slaves by inheritance, despite claims that he had renounced any legal claim to these individuals, led to a resolution that he stop exercising the duties of his episcopal office. Southern Methodists objected, and, after the Plan of Separation formed the Methodist Episcopal Church, South, Bishop Andrew continued in his office.

Bishop Andrew's acknowledgement of two slaves by inheritance immediately tarnished his standing, whatever his justifications, but his further ownership of more than a dozen slaves by a recent remarriage revealed the full extent of his culpability. Bishop Andrew protested that (1) the slaves were his wife's property (though under Georgia law the marriage automatically gave him property rights), (2) the slaves were legally attached to her by a deed of trust (a sign of calculation that neglected to admit the benefits he continued to receive from their labor), and (3) he could not emancipate them in the state of Georgia (a common defense of southern slaveholding that subsequent historians have called into question).[36] In light of this additional information, conference delegates moved that Bishop Andrew immediately resign his episcopal office, since he had only been elected to the episcopacy with the understanding that he would remain free from all associations with slavery.

The conference debated the matter for nearly two weeks, often with Bishop Andrew guiding the proceedings from the chair. The bishops, sensing the potential for schism, urged delegates to postpone action until the next general conference, "to prevent disunion, and to promote harmony in the church."[37] Finally, refusing to allow the bishop's behavior to go unaddressed, the delegates approved a substitute resolution (by a vote of 110 to 68) that called for Bishop Andrew to immediately "desist from the exercise of his office so long as this impediment remains."[38] Objections from members of the southern conferences quickly ensued, including a lengthy protest that refused the resolution as contrary to a longstanding legal compromise that held the church together.[39] These events had brought the MEC to a watershed moment: while the formal division required years to effect, the separation of the Methodist Episcopal Church was a *fait accompli*.

The great schism of American Methodism preceded the Civil War by little more than a decade, serving as a bellwether of religious life in the nation. Southern delegates convened to form the Methodist Episcopal Church, South (MECS), in Louisville in 1845 and gathered in Virginia for the first general conference of the new denomination one year later. Bishop Andrew, for his part, continued as a bishop in the new church. Although the two bodies originally hoped to maintain a kindly and familial relationship, they soon descended into an antagonistic struggle that took nearly a century to repair. In the meantime, Methodists had begun to grapple with the corresponding issue of holiness with the assistance of John Wesley's teaching on Christian sanctification.

CHAPTER SEVEN

Holy People

"How Methodists Invented Your Kid's Grape Juice Sugar High."[1] The provocative magazine title is a reminder of an oft-repeated bit of Methodist lore. As the story goes, a Methodist minister named Thomas B. Welch (1825–1903) combined prohibitionist-style teetotalism with an equal share of American entrepreneurialism and single-handedly replaced wine with grape juice at communion tables across the country. Blame Welch for the demise of the Lord's Supper, some say; blame Methodists for the misguided politics of American Prohibition, claim others. Now add one more to the list: blame holier-than-thou Methodists for your child's sugar rush.

One problem: the familiar story of Welch, Methodism, and the substitution of grape juice for communion is misleading in several significant respects.[2] Above all, the move away from wine and alcohol generally had begun much earlier. By the 1830s, American Methodist papers began publishing articles about the use and abuse of alcohol and offering guidance on the need for reform.[3] Alcohol consumption in the United States was remarkably high in the 1800s—far higher than at any other time since. The situation confronting Methodists and clergy across denominations is truly remarkable: "Consumption peaked at 7.1 gallons of absolute alcohol per person per year in 1810 and again in 1830. Early nineteenth-century temperance efforts focused on abstaining from whiskey and other distilled spirits. But by the 1840s, more and more reformers—clergy, scientists, politicians, and concerned citizens—began to urge total abstinence from wine and beer."[4]

In part, Methodists and other temperance advocates relied on an innovative (if somewhat questionable) interpretation of the Bible. According to their reading, whenever the Bible mentioned alcohol consumption in a positive light, the text referred to unfermented grapes; but whenever the Scriptures mentioned alcohol in a negative light, the text implied fermentation. Armed with this "two-wine theory" of biblical interpretation and a growing body of medical literature warning against the dangerous effects of alcohol abuse, more and more Methodists began to favor total abstinence from alcohol. Their efforts paid off: alcohol consumption steadily dropped from 7.1 gallons to just 1.8 gallons of absolute alcohol per person between 1830 and 1845.[5]

Temperance advocates were fighting—and winning—a battle against drunkenness and alcohol consumption long before Welch "invented" grape juice in 1869. As a young man, Thomas B. Welch had been a minister in the Wesleyan Methodist Connection (a body founded in 1843 on opposition to slavery *and* support for the temperance movement), but he stopped preaching in the church due to vocal problems and began practicing dentistry instead. By the time Welch applied the newly discovered pasteurization process to unfermented grapes, Methodist churches were already recommending unfermented grape juice for communion—they just didn't have a dependable way to regularize the practice. Welch, who had moved to Vineland, New Jersey, and joined the Methodist Episcopal Church, was merely innovating from a felt need in the wider community. Yet "Dr. Welch's Unfermented Wine" wasn't a success in the churches until 1893, when Welch's son Charles revived the business and launched Welch's Grape Juice Company to compete with others who were also selling the product. The rest is history.

The story of how grape juice replaced wine at American Methodist altars belongs to a broader conversation about the search for holiness in the nineteenth and early twentieth centuries. American Methodists struggled with the question of slavery but also the damaging effects of alcoholism—reports from the general conferences are replete with references to temperance and abolitionism alike in the 1800s. The boundaries of holiness are sometimes blurry, though, as Methodists from different regions and backgrounds defined the marks of holiness each in their own ways. While some Methodists labored for change on what they deemed to be pivotal personal and societal concerns—including temperance, gambling, amusements, the rights of women, race relations, and the treatment of indigenous Americans—other Methodists disregarded or diminished the moral (and often biblical)

The
Children's Beverage
It's Welch's

All children know "what's
good." They all love Welch's
and older folk know that Welch's
is not only a delicious treat, but

Figure 7.1. Advertisement from Welch's grape juice emphasizing domesticity and moral purity, 1913

significance of these same issues. Gradually, new rifts appeared in the rapidly expanding family tree of American Methodism.

Preaching on personal and social holiness is as old as Christianity, of course, but Methodists in Britain and North America alike excelled in the custom. John Wesley regularly admonished listeners to pursue both justification (forgiveness and reconciliation with God) and sanctification (holiness in life). In the sermon "On Sin in Believers," Wesley explained that believers are regenerated when they trust in Christ, but the work is, in some sense, incomplete. The flesh "still remains," requiring a fuller work of grace by the Spirit.[6] Other Methodists followed his example. For example, the British Methodist preacher and biblical scholar Adam Clarke (1762–1832) denounced the widespread use of tobacco in the church as a form of slavery: "When many of the tobacco-consumers get into trouble or under any cross or affliction, instead of looking to God for support, the pipe, the snuffbox, or the twist is applied to with quadruple earnestness. . . . What a comfort is this weed in time of sorrow! What a support in time of trouble! In a word, what a god!"[7] Such preaching reflected a deeply held Wesleyan belief that prayer, reading the Bible, and receiving the Lord's Supper were each various "means of grace" that keep a Christian's love of God from growing cold.[8] Reliance on tobacco indicated moral confusion at best. John Wesley similarly thought the "drunkard" risked damnation by trifling with sin that had the potential to lead even the most devout astray. "You have forced the Spirit of God to depart from you," Wesley claims, "for you would take none of his reproof; and you have given yourself up into the hands of the devil, to be led blindfolded by him at his will."[9] American Methodists inherited these teachings but struggled to maintain them consistently in a context where alcohol and tobacco use had become staples of the national economy. Still, many American Methodists linked the call to preach on individual sin and salvation with a broader message of social reform.

Race, for example, continued to complicate narrow thinking about holiness. In works originating in the MECS, calls for the holy life accompanied a *defense* of the morality of slavery. Moses Henkle's *Primary Platform of Methodism* (1851), for example, strained out a gnat in its meticulous opposition to swearing, criticizing, fighting, usury, dancing, card playing, fiction reading, theater, horse racing, and the circus, but swallowed a camel in his indiscriminate defense of slaveholding ("a subject of great difficulty and delicacy").[10] By contrast, Bishop Matthew Simpson, president of Garrett Biblical Institute in Evanston, Illinois, conducted Abraham Lincoln's funeral and honored the nation's leader with the call to finish his work: "Let us vow, in the sight of Heaven, to eradicate every vestige of human slavery; to give every human being his true position before God and man; to crush every form of rebellion, and to stand by the flag which God has given us."[11] Yet while Simpson confidently venerated Lincoln as a martyr before God, others thought he instigated "diabolical mischief." In 1863 Bishop James Andrew, along with sixteen other bishops, elders, and dignitaries in the Methodist Episcopal Church, South, were among the signers of a declaration against Lincoln's Emancipation Proclamation:

> The South has done more than any people on earth for the Christianization of the African race. . . . We regard abolitionism as an interference with the plans of Divine Providence. It has not the signs of the Lord's blessing. It is a fanaticism which puts forth no good fruit; instead of blessing, it has brought forth cursing; instead of love, hatred; instead of life, death—bitterness and sorrow and pain and infidelity and more degeneracy follow its labors.[12]

During postwar reconstruction, despite extensive missionary outreach to the black community, African American membership declined precipitously in the MECS (and rose dramatically in the MEC). By the end of the century, no mixed-race conferences remained in the MECS, as African American Methodists moved to AME and AMEZ churches or formed separate conferences in the Colored Methodist Episcopal Church (originally supervised by white bishops from the MECS).[13]

Race also factored into Methodist attitudes toward Native Americans. Methodists who opposed the prejudicial treatment of African Americans often failed to see how the westward movement of settlers threatened the wellbeing of those who already inhabited the land. In one sense, Methodists energetically resisted the neglect of Native Americans in their midst. Backed by funding from the federal government for the education and "civilization" of Native Americans, the MEC established several schools in the 1820s. The MEC also commissioned resident missionaries for work among indigenous peoples such as the Wyandotte in Ohio. Such outreach proved successful, in part because the Methodists professed the work of the Holy Spirit in all people.

Figure 7.2. William Apess

For example, William Apess (1798–1839), a member of the Pequot tribe living as an indentured servant in Massachusetts, discovered a sense of self-worth among the Methodists that he hadn't found in other denominations. In *A Son of the Forest* (1829), among the first autobiographies written by a Native American, Apess describes how some discouraged him from attending Methodist meetings. They claimed that associating with the Methodists risked a "stain" on his character: "But it had no effect on me. I thought I had no character to lose in the estimation of those who were accounted great. But what cared they for me. They had possession of the red man's inheritance, and had deprived me of liberty; with this they were satisfied, and could do as they pleased; therefore I thought I would do as I pleased."[14] To his surprise, Apess found the Methodists very much to his liking: they sang "sweet" music, gathered in an orderly fashion, and listened attentively to trustworthy ministers. In this, he sensed the blessing of God. The people "shouted for joy," "sinners wept," and "the Spirit's influence was felt at every meeting."[15] Although he experienced persecution (particularly among fellow Methodist Episcopal Church members) and faced the challenge of alcoholism, Apess eventually received ordination in the Methodist Protestant Church and ministered from a deep conviction that "Christ died for all mankind . . . sect, colour, country, or situation made no difference."[16]

Still, American Methodists repeatedly undermined their own ministry among Native Americans.[17] The education of indigenous people often amounted to efforts to wash away ethnic heritage in the name of Christ. Moreover, while early missions work among Native Americans proved successful, some conferences too quickly expanded the circuits, diluting

John Wesley's concern for **Native Americans** began in his ministry in Georgia and remained evident even late in his life, as in a letter he wrote to Asbury in 1787: "How few of these have seen the light of the glory of God since the English first settled among them! And now scarce one in fifty of them among whom we settled, perhaps scarce one in a hundred of them are left alive!"

Figure 7.3. John Wesley preaching to Native Americans

ministry effectiveness in the process. In Georgia, where Methodist missionaries opposed civil rights violations by the state against the Cherokee, missionaries faced arrest, imprisonment, and even hard labor for their unwillingness to swear oaths of allegiance to the government.[18] The conference refused to support these courageous acts of solidarity, however, and declined even to consider resolutions in support of the Cherokee people, claiming, "As a body of Christian ministers, we do not feel at liberty, nor are we disposed, to depart from the principles uniformly maintained by members and ministers of our church in carefully refraining from all such interference in political affairs."[19] The statement is little more than a pious invention: no such apolitical stance existed in Methodism.

In fact, although the General Conference of 1844 set out a strategy for evangelism in the formation of the Indian Mission Conference, dangerous stereotypes persisted. While it may seem unfair to suggest that the acts of a few individuals outweighed the good of so many others, there can be little doubt that Methodist action *and* inaction hampered the witness of the church. Most notoriously, two American Methodists were principally responsible for the massacre of some 150 peaceful Cheyenne and Arapaho people at Sand Creek in November 1864. Many of the victims were women and children. The territorial governor of Colorado, John Evans, whose policies brought about the slaughter, was a prominent Methodist layman, while the commanding officer who carried out the attack, John M. Chivington, was formerly a presiding elder of the Rocky Mountain District of the Methodist Episcopal Church.[20] American Methodist commitment to holiness during the period cannot be assessed without reference to the benefits received from policies of westward expansion and the forcible removal of Native Americans. In short, American Methodists preached the universality of the Spirit's work but often failed to enact this in practice.

Whatever their shortcomings, American Methodists devoted themselves to preaching, teaching, and writing about holiness throughout the nineteenth century. No American Methodist proved more influential than the MEC revivalist Phoebe Worrall Palmer (1807–1874). Beginning in New York and then traveling widely throughout the US, Canada, and Great Britain, Palmer developed and adapted John Wesley's teaching on entire sanctification by claiming that the work of grace was instantaneous rather than gradual. As with John Wesley's associate John Fletcher, Phoebe Palmer

One of the most popular American revivalists in the nineteenth century was the Holiness Movement leader **Phoebe Worrall Palmer** (1807–1874), who promoted the so-called "higher Christian life" teaching through her renowned Tuesday Meetings for the Promotion of Holiness in New York City. An energetic social reformer working in New York's Five Points Mission, Palmer advocated a widely accepted model of entire sanctification that influenced not only many Methodists but also political and cultural figures across American Protestantism.

Figure 7.4. Phoebe Worrall Palmer

believed that entire sanctification could be identified with the biblical idea of "baptism in the Holy Spirit." Holiness signifies divine empowerment. Rather than a gradual work over the course of a lifetime (perhaps only to be fulfilled in the afterlife), Palmer thought entire sanctification came instantaneously and marked the commencement of a fully Christian life. John Wesley had, in fact, theorized the possibility of such an instantaneous work, rousing congregants in his sermon "The Scripture Way of Salvation" to "expect it *by faith*, expect it *as you are*, and expect it *now!*"[21] Yet what John and Charles Wesley preached as a possibility and a goal, Palmer taught as a necessity and a beginning.

At the heart of Palmer's theology of sanctification was entire devotion to God through what she called the "altar covenant." This "shorter way" to sanctification required a three-step process that the Christian could follow with as much certainty as depending on Christ alone for salvation. First, the believer determines to make a careful assessment of personal life in an act of *entire consecration*. No stone remains unturned in the formation of a complete and rigorous inventory of every aspect of daily life; the individual should even ask God to reveal anything that might remain hidden and hinder complete devotion. Second, the Christian seeks God in an act of *faith*.

Here, the individual depends on God's promises in the Bible rather than feelings or emotions related to self-worth, or outward signs that might cloud the sure and trustworthy assurance of God. Finally, the individual testifies to the work of God in an act of *witness*. The proper response to God's assurance is confession, sharing God's good gift with others for the sake of spreading scriptural holiness throughout the world.[22] For Palmer, then, holiness involves not striving to become like God but dependence on the promised blessing of God's declaration: "Let me assure you, dear friend, that as surely as you need holiness *now*, so surely it is for you *now*. . . . Are you commanded to be ready for the coming of the Lord *now*? Then holiness is a blessing which it is now your privilege and also your duty to enjoy."[23]

Entire sanctification brought not only the duty of holy living but also the expectation of active Christian service. Consider Palmer's own life as an example. Although she had extensive responsibilities with young children at home, Palmer labored among the poor throughout her many years of teaching and writing. She formed one of the earliest American prison ministries in the New York "Tombs" and gave support for orphanages and alcohol rehabilitation. Palmer also served as Founding Directress of the Five Points Mission in New York, working to provide food, clothing, housing, and spiritual resources for the poor on the lower east side of Manhattan.[24] Yet these acts of social concern were neither aspects of a growing responsibility or spiritual ascent to God, nor an effort to remake social institutions or advocate for political gain. Rather, Palmer believed that service to the needy results from a prior work of divine grace in the individual's heart.

Across America, Methodist bishops, local pastors, and laypeople alike studied Palmer's writings and came to hear her speak at the "Tuesday Meeting for the Promotion of Holiness" held in New York or revivals in the United States or Great Britain. Palmer's influence was extraordinary. Yet as more and more

> The **Holiness Movement** flourished in North America through the preaching and teaching of women and men such as Phoebe Palmer, Charles Finney, and Hannah Whitall Smith. These figures countered a perceived complacency among Protestants by teaching that Christian perfection occurs in an instant. Holiness camp meeting revivals spurred widespread public interest and led to the formation of numerous associations and denominations, including the Church of the Nazarene, the Church of God (Anderson, Indiana), and varieties of Pentecostalism.

churches began to approve of Palmer's teachings, holiness doctrine became divisive. While many within the MEC and MECS subscribed to the Holiness Movement as a work of reform from within Methodism, disputes over sanctification contributed to a growing rift between the churches.

In Britain, the Wesleyan Methodist Connection was the first to formally endorse the doctrine of entire sanctification as an "instantaneous and subsequent work to regeneration"—against the increasing worldliness they perceived among other Methodists.[25] In 1860, American advocates of holiness formed the Free Methodist Church to protest similar trends among MEC congregations. Derisively labeled "Nazarites" by their opponents, Free Methodists sought freedom from the world through entire and instantaneous sanctification by the Holy Spirit. In addition to their opposition to slavery, Free Methodists lamented the formalization of worship, dependence on "pew rents" to finance building projects (a sign of an increasingly middle-class membership), the proliferation of secret societies such as the Masons, the decline of camp meetings, and the popularity of organs and choirs—all signs of accommodation to bourgeois American culture.[26] Although numerous theologians attempted to mediate the growing controversy over sanctification by suggesting that Wesley primarily emphasized the gradual nature of the work, more and more churches followed the path to independence, including the Church of God (Anderson, Indiana) and the Church of God (Holiness).[27] Eventually MEC and MECS leaders formally disavowed holiness teachings and marginalized ministers who advocated for holiness doctrine and practice.

In the MECS Episcopal Address of 1894, the bishops explicitly bemoaned the increase in holiness meetings, preachers, and associations. The risk of sectarianism and potential for disparaging the "stages of spiritual growth" in

> American Methodists, as with Anglican Methodists before them, routinely observed the **baptism of infants**. From the mid-nineteenth century, however, several American Methodist denominations began to incorporate the language of "dedicating" children to God's service in their rites of baptism. Holiness churches gradually made this concept a separate and parallel act: the Church of the Nazarene introduced infant dedication as an alternative in 1936, while Free Methodists made the two practices practically interchangeable. In the UMC, the official statement *By Water and the Spirit* (1996) formally rejected the practice as incompatible with Wesleyan teaching on the sufficiency of God's grace.

the Christian life gave reason for caution: "We do not question the sincerity and zeal of these brethren; we desire the church to profit by their earnest preaching and godly example; but we deplore their teaching and methods in so far as they claim a monopoly of the experience, practice, and advocacy of holiness, and separate themselves from the body of ministers and disciples."[28]

Perhaps the most significant division within American Methodism that originates from this movement began in response to criticism of holiness teaching in California. During the 1890s, holiness doctrine began to spread as part of a broad evangelistic effort by several MEC churches. However, when Phineas Bresee (1838–1915) inaugurated holiness revivals in Southern California, he fell into disfavor with Bishop John H. Vincent, who wanted to bring Methodism into a position of greater social influence in the region. The bishop removed Bresee from his position as presiding elder, refused his request for an appointment to mission work in the city, and transferred him to a wealthy congregation known for its opposition to the Holiness Movement. In 1895, frustrated by his bishop's actions, Bresee founded an independent congregation to minister to the poor in Los Angeles. He named the new ministry the "Church of the Nazarene" after "the toiling, lowly mission of Christ."[29] Nearly ten years later, Bresee's group joined with other Holiness churches from around the country to form the Church of the Nazarene.[30] From the beginning of the movement, the Church of the Nazarene identified with the doctrine of entire sanctification, commitment to personal holiness, and witness through missionary work around the world.[31]

> The **Church of the Nazarene,** founded in 1907, was formed through a merger of churches active in the Holiness Movement in California, New York, Tennessee, and Texas. The denomination quickly gained national and international prominence through promotion of the doctrine of entire sanctification, work in higher education, and devotion to foreign missions in Africa, Asia, and many other parts of the world.

Holiness leavened the American Methodist loaf, especially through the national crusade against alcohol. Although significant gains against alcohol consumption had been made during the century, temperance laws gradually fell into disuse in the years after the Civil War. Women, long a mainstay of the churches, waged public battles against alcohol sales, taking to the streets and protesting at saloons. Through national organizations such as the

Women's Christian Temperance Union (WCTU), Methodists such as Frances Willard (1839–1898) rose to national prominence and demanded an equal voice in the public square.[32] Women faced the problem of alcoholism directly in the home, but they soon realized that only public and legislative action would bring about lasting change.

In turn, Willard and other Methodist women found themselves in unanticipated positions of conflict. Although Methodism depended on women for seemingly innumerable areas of ministry, their presence remained unwelcome in the highest positions of leadership in the church. The influence of women such as Phoebe Palmer might have led to more progressive thinking on the issue, but Holiness churches tended to embrace a dynamism in worship that allowed women a stronger voice than in many MEC and MECS congregations. When the WCTU asked that Willard be allowed to address the MEC General Conference in 1880, her presence was rebuffed by many who had warmly invited her to speak elsewhere. After her own annual conference (the Rock River Conference of Illinois) elected her as a delegate to the MEC General Conference of 1888, she received opposition along with other women who had similarly been elected to represent their annual conferences. Among Methodists, it soon became apparent that the mistrust of women's leadership in the church ran parallel to the struggle over women's suffrage in the nation, only now some questioned whether the leadership of women contradicted biblical teaching. This came as a shock to many: women regularly exhorted their fellow Methodists at class meetings, camp meetings,

In her book *Woman in the Pulpit* (1888), **Frances Willard** (1839–1898) concluded that Methodist women ought to ordain for themselves if male clergy refused to acknowledge the gifts God had given them: "These noble women should knock only once more at the doors of the Methodist General Conference, and if their signals and entreaties are again uncivilly disregarded they should never knock again."

Figure 7.5. Frances Willard

love feasts, and Sunday services alike. Still, in the gradual cultural shift toward respectability among Methodists, the notion that women might provide leadership in the highest decision-making assembly of the church seemed impossibly problematic. Willard and others fought back, maintaining that the predominance of male leadership had left the hearts of the world cold: "It is men who have given us the dead letter rather than the living Gospel. The mother-heart of God will never be known to the world until translated into terms of speech by mother-hearted women. Law and love will never balance in the realm of grace until a woman's hand shall hold the scales."[33] The MEC General Conference of 1904 finally permitted women to sit as lay delegates, years after Willard's death, but controversy over women's roles would continue for decades to come.[34]

By the end of the nineteenth century, the Wesleyan Holiness Movement had permanently shaped the landscape of American Methodism. Doctrinally, the teaching instigated a wide discussion among Methodists on the meaning of entire sanctification. Practically, holiness contributed to the national conversation on a host of social issues. If holiness wasn't something that people gradually worked their way into, then moral purity could be expected of all who claimed to be Christian. Much as in early Methodism, when John Wesley exhorted listeners to become "altogether" Christians by leaving aside the pleasures of this world, American Methodists influenced by the Holiness Movement called into question the sanctity of those who hoped to gradually leave aside the desires of the flesh.

Holiness had gone mainstream. In 1916, when the MEC required that all churches use grape juice at the celebration of the Lord's Supper, they only formalized a practice that had been in the works for nearly a century. The move was hardly a radical innovation. Yet far more significant than whether or not Methodists foisted grape juice on the churches—or the public, for that matter—are the ways American Methodism had changed. In the century that had passed, the Methodists constituted one of the most powerful religious bodies in the nation. They even had a president in the White House: Rutherford B. Hays received his education in Methodist schools and attended Foundry Church in Washington, DC, with his wife, Lucy (who gained her nickname "Lemonade Lucy" for advocating temperance in the White House).[35] Although the Methodists had suffered losses in the separation of 1844 and saw their members locked in armed conflict during the

Civil War, American Methodists enjoyed unprecedented prosperity during the late 1800s, making Francis Asbury's life on horseback seem little more than a distant memory. In the century ahead, the Methodists would celebrate the reunion of churches long separated, but they quickly discovered that questions of holiness threatened to tear the church apart yet again.

CHAPTER EIGHT

....

United Ministry

In Harold Frederic's celebrated novel, *The Damnation of Theron Ware* (1896), a young American Methodist minister passes from innocence to experience as he unexpectedly discovers a world beyond the narrow confines of his church. Reverend Theron Ware, the novel's protagonist, expects the bishop to assign him to one of the most influential congregations in the conference—a step up in status, to be sure—but he ends up assigned to a congregation in a provincial town instead. When the young minister and his wife move into the church parsonage, they quickly discover that their every move is monitored by members of the congregation. The parishioners demand an unreasonable degree of frugality and simplicity. Although the Wares imagine themselves devotedly serving in "the hands of the Lord," the pressure to maintain the support of the wealthiest members of the congregation presses their faith to the edge. Soon Theron Ware meets others in town, including a fascinating group of Irish Roman Catholics, and finds himself attracted to their independent thinking, thirst for knowledge, and openness to the pleasures of the world. Ware soon descends into despair. He questions the authority of the biblical text, his belief that revival is the work of God, and his call to Methodist ministry. Only the shrewd maternal pragmatism of a fundraising evangelist keeps Ware from self-destruction. Undone by a desire for knowledge and pleasure, Ware experiences an eventual transformation from childlike faith to worldly knowledge that mirrors the conversion of a sin-sick soul: "It was apparent to the Rev. Theron Ware, from the very first moment of waking next morning, that both he and the world had changed over night. . . . He lacked even the impulse to turn round and inspect the cocoon from which he had emerged. Let the past bury the past. He had no vestige of interest in it."[1] He now recognized that the

....

success of the church was less a matter of overcoming the devil than the implementation of shrewd political measures. In the process, Ware lost the heart religion that made him such a promising clergyman in the first place and discovered that he must leave the ministry or live in hypocrisy.[2]

American Methodists entered the twentieth century in a position of strength. Thriving churches across the nation gathered each week in towering edifices symbolizing the vast wealth and influence of Methodism throughout the nation. Union and cooperation were the watchwords of the times; still, as the reach of the church extended around the world, the threat of schism remained as powerful as ever. In this chapter, I will focus on the ways that Methodists looked to develop leadership in the transformation of the church from a scattered connection to a united, global communion.

Everything was changing, and nothing was changing. Education, for example, had long been a hallmark of Methodism. John Wesley had urged his lay preachers to devote themselves to learning and published his *Christian Library* in hopes that they would gain insight from outstanding sources of Christian history, biography, and theology.[3] American Methodists followed Wesley's example. When Coke and Asbury first met to discuss the formal establishment of the MEC, they also set plans for a school to educate the children of ministers and the poor. Although Cokesbury College in Maryland failed to thrive during its brief tenure (1787–1795), other colleges and seminaries soon opened wherever annual conferences met: McKendree College in Illinois (1828), Randolph-Macon in Virginia (1832), Dickinson in Pennsylvania (1833), Emory in Georgia (1836), and Indiana Asbury (now DePauw) in Indiana (1838). By the time of separation in 1844, the MEC had already founded more than a dozen colleges; by 1860 there were forty-nine Methodist colleges throughout the nation.[4] John Wesley and the early Methodists often had suffered ridicule for sending uneducated lay preachers into itinerant ministry, but by the early twentieth-century, Methodists were establishing themselves as among the most educated Christians in the nation.[5]

The history of Methodist educational institutions serves as a bellwether for the changing shape of American Methodist ministry. If American Methodists had divergent views about the future of the church, so too did the educational institutions they founded. As Methodist universities and colleges proliferated, rival institutions formed to inculcate the values of other strands of belief within the broader Wesleyan movement. Pressures from outside the church matched pressures within: colleges and universities became contested spaces for church and national politics. For instance, in Georgia, Emory College forced the resignation of a classics professor after he condemned the practice of lynching African Americans.[6] Public outcry could create immense pressure on an institution; so long as a school belonged to the church, the work of the classroom remained a matter of ecclesial concern. American Methodist educators didn't simply reiterate the teachings of John Wesley or, for that matter, later systematicians such as Richard Watson either. Rather, they offered new perspectives on Christian faith with an openness to the latest research in biblical studies, philosophy, and the sciences. Some Methodist educators introduced ideas and methods from outside the church, too, questioning whether cherished beliefs about biblical inspiration, miracles, or human origins could meet the demands of life in the modern world.[7]

Candidates for Methodist ministry often found themselves caught between opposing forces. Seminaries trained pastors with the latest theological and philosophical tools for ministry, but their students served congregations largely unprepared for the answers they provided. One of the most influential

Methodist commitment to **education** can be seen from the earliest years of the movement, when John Wesley and George Whitefield first established Kingswood School for children near Bristol, England. When Wesley reorganized the fledgling institute in 1748, he formed an impressive and demanding curriculum for students that emphasized routine and self-discipline. In North America and elsewhere, the Methodist emphasis on education may be discerned in the organization of Sunday schools, publishing houses, and the founding of numerous colleges, universities, and seminaries.

voices of the early twentieth century was the Methodist theologian and philosopher Borden Parker Bowne (1847–1910) of Boston University. Bowne, raised by Methodist parents persuaded by the Holiness Movement that swept the nation during the 1800s, had studied in Germany and discovered in post-Hegelian philosophy a possible avenue for thinking about God's work in history through individual "feeling." Some Methodists worried that "Boston Personalism" denied the transcendence of God—and undercut doctrinal commitments to the Trinity, miracles, and the atonement in the process.[8]

Amid such charges, the MEC General Conference unsuccessfully tried Bowne for heresy in 1904. In turn, Bowne's liberal vision of Christian faith—Wesleyan in piety but unabashedly modern in character—shaped generations of Methodist theologians and clergy. His acquittal, put positively, demonstrated that American Methodism would approach theological education with an openness to inquiry and innovative systems of belief, but, put negatively, the inability of the church to form doctrinal boundaries implicitly undermined its commitment to historic orthodoxy. Some agitated for changes in the Methodist Articles of Religion, while others questioned whether Wesley's teachings remained relevant to the needs of the modern church. In time, some Methodist colleges and universities began looking to other funding sources entirely or simply distanced themselves from the church to preserve academic freedom.[9]

> **Boston Personalism,** a philosophical and theological movement, regards the human person as the fundamental basis of all reality. The movement, spearheaded by Borden Parker Bowne (1847–1910) at Boston University, influenced a significant number of American Methodists in the twentieth century, especially through Bowne's book *Personalism* (1908). The movement also influenced Martin Luther King Jr., who studied under Personalists while at Boston University.

Despite such tensions, the call to equip new leaders remained at the forefront. In a period of extraordinary optimism, the task of mobilization gave rise to one of the most visionary trailblazers of the twentieth-century. John R. Mott (1865–1955) grew up in Iowa, where he attended Methodist class meetings with his mother and showed signs of academic promise as a youth. When it was time for college, he moved to Ithaca, New York, where he attended Cornell University and experienced a spiritual and vocational conversion. Subsequently, Mott changed his plans from a career in law to ecumenical leadership and advocacy for world evangelism. He took a position with the YMCA, gained public recognition as a national speaker, and advocated for international cooperation and humanitarianism.[10]

In one of his most prominent books, *The Future Leadership of the Church* (1908), Mott argued that the formation of a new generation of leaders is the foremost task of the churches. Leadership is no accident. "No society," Mott claims, "can realize great objects without thoroughly qualified leaders."[11] In successive chapters, Mott addresses essential aspects of leadership for churches that hope to address the needs of a modern, global society. Mott believed that the sharp decline in ministerial candidates was an urgent problem that needed to be corrected. Without the church, the world suffers, so the church must concentrate its energies on identifying the most capable individuals and encouraging them to pursue ordination and full-time Christian ministry. The problem, Mott thought, is that a "secular and materialistic spirit of the age" had undermined self-denial and service among potential candidates for ministry. The solution would require total commitment on the part of the church. Ministers should actively encourage youth to consider ministry, denominational schools ought to promote high academic standards, revivals (though falling into disuse) might still awaken an interest in full-time service, and families could prayerfully promote ordination as an esteemed calling. In this way, the church would raise up a new generation of leaders.

Figure 8.1. John R. Mott

Mott's work captured a deeply felt need in American Methodism and, indeed, the nation. More than sixty reviews of his book appeared in the papers, and President Theodore Roosevelt publicly endorsed Mott's call for heroic Christian leaders, claiming, "The call of duty to undertake this great spiritual adventure, this work for the betterment of mankind, should ring in the ears of young men who are high of heart and gallant of soul, as a challenge to turn to the hard life of labor and risk, which is so infinitely well worth living."[12] Mott's dream of forming leaders of the highest caliber undoubtedly participated in a vision of masculine, "muscular Christianity" that could hamper the development of otherwise gifted ministerial candidates, and yet he identified a broad plan for leadership that fostered a high respect for Christian ministry.

Mott's hopes for the future of the church came to an abrupt halt with the onset of the Great War. While the churches had grown accustomed to singing the sweet hymns of the Methodist lyricist Fanny Crosby (1820–1915), whose "Blessed Assurance" (1873) and "To God Be the Glory" (1875) were already cherished tunes, war raged abroad.[13] Christian optimism could hardly stand in the face of intolerable slaughter. World evangelism, a major objective for

Mott and others at the turn of the century, now seemed an impossible ambition. Instead, the churches sought cooperation. Ecumenism, in which Christians dialogue and work toward common mission rather than competition, brought churches together in times of limited resources. In America, two international wars divided by a period of sustained economic depression left many denominations in a position of unprecedented vulnerability.

The optimism for world evangelism soon transformed into an eagerness for united church structures. Financial need hastened the process. In 1939, the formation of The Methodist Church (MC) from the MEC, MECS, and the Methodist Protestant Church ended nearly a century of division. Similarly, in 1946, the Evangelical Church and the United Brethren Church formed the Evangelical United Brethren (EUB).[14] The Methodists and the EUB, of course, weren't exceptional in this move toward union: Protestant churches across America and around the world engaged in similar mergers at mid-century to strengthen mission in a time of diminished resources. Methodists were prominent contributors to global ecumenism, too, with membership in the World Council of Churches, the Federal Council of Churches, and the World Methodist Council.[15] Church unions strengthened the work of ministry, bringing a host of national agencies and international missions under a single denominational banner. The formation of the MC allowed one body to regulate dozens of prestigious universities, seminaries, and colleges.[16]

Union required compromise, which brought resistance. Members of the Methodist Protestant Church came to union through a gradual process—acceptance of the episcopacy and agreements that an equal number of lay and ordained delegates would represent every annual conference proved essential. Several churches in the MPC remained dissatisfied and, in turn, established the Fundamentalist Methodist Church (1942) in protest.[17] The MC also institutionalized segregation by establishing a Central Jurisdiction to represent African American Methodists. Instead of integrating the conferences, the MC deepened the division. Even so, other Methodists remained unhappy with the plan: some members of the MECS thought reunion with the North made concessions with modernism and established the Southern Methodist Church (1940) in response.

Women suffered acute losses in church unions. From the earliest days of Methodism, women had provided substantial leadership and service in the

Influenced by German and Swiss Methodists, the Deaconess Movement in North America arose out of an increasing awareness of urban growth and poverty. Among the most prominent early leaders of the Methodist deaconesses was **Lucy Rider Meyer** (1849–1922), whose Chicago Training School for City, Home, and Foreign Missions educated thousands of women during her lifetime. The Methodist Episcopal Church officially recognized the contribution of deaconesses in 1888, and similar orders were soon established in the Wesleyan Methodist Church (1890), the United Methodist Free Churches (1891), and the Primitive Methodist Church (1895).

Figure 8.2. Lucy Rider Meyer

churches. In the 1700s, Methodist societies typically had a two-to-one ratio of female to male membership. Women, especially Methodist preachers' wives, were often responsible for leadership roles in the sexually segregated band meetings and regularly visited the sick and needy. Wesley affirmed and even encouraged women to speak publicly through exhortations and testimonies during love feasts or meetings of the societies. Wesley thought Mary Bosanquet Fletcher (1739–1815) had an extraordinary call to preaching—a gift she frequently used, including one occasion when she preached to several thousand listeners in September 1776.[18] In America, early Methodist women often led class meetings and even suffered public abuse (Mary Thorn was "pelted in the streets, and stoned in effigy" for leading multiple classes in association with the Methodists).[19] By 1800, however, women's leadership roles had rapidly declined. Methodist women continued to give testimonies and spiritual advice, but a renewed emphasis on submissiveness and domesticity predominated. In time, women regained visibility: popular orators such as Phoebe Palmer, writers including the former slave Amanda Berry Smith and the social reformer Frances Willard, and courageous deaconesses and members of the Woman's Foreign and Woman's Home Missionary Societies all made significant contributions to the churches.

In the twentieth century, the Methodist Georgia Harkness (1891–1974) emerged as a leading voice for women in ministry.[20] Harkness, the first woman to teach in a mainline Protestant seminary in the United States, never sought ordination but advocated change through the inclusion of women to positions of authority throughout the church. Ordination, she thought, was an important step but "not the final goal."[21] In fact, long before the formation of the MC in 1939, many American Methodists already affirmed women preachers: in the Methodist Protestant Church, women were licensed to preach as early as 1871, while the MEC had allowed women to be licensed in 1920 and serve as "local elders" in 1924.[22] Despite this illustrious history, at the Uniting Conference of the MC, full ordination rights for women was defeated by a vote of 371 to 384.[23] Appallingly, nearly two decades passed before the denomination returned to its heritage and finally granted women full clergy rights in 1956.[24]

In fact, the church depended on a wider vision of leadership than many Methodists recognized. Georgia Harkness, among others, challenged the predominant belief that laypeople are merely "non-ordained Christians whose function is to help the clergy do the work of the church."[25] Instead, Harkness proposed that the work of God belongs to *all* people in *every* sphere of life. Piety, worship, learning, and fellowship belong to *all* Christians. While Harkness rejected the notion that the laity could carry out ministry without partnering with the clergy, she thought laity and clergy

The ethicist and theologian **Georgia Harkness** (1891–1947) stands out as one of the foremost educators in twentieth-century American Methodism. Born in New York and educated at Cornell and Boston Universities, Harkness eventually taught at Garrett Biblical Institute in Evanston (1939–1950) and Pacific School of Religion in California (1950–1961). She wrote more than thirty books on social issues such as racism, depression, and war, often in an accessible style that appealed to clergy and laity.

Figure 8.3. Georgia Harkness

could serve together for the good of others: "So, let no Christian whether clergyman or layman think lightly of his calling! . . . It is through a fidelity born of trust in the power of God and the Lordship of Christ that the Church has survived many crises in the past and has come to the present day of challenge and opportunity."[26] In this, Harkness's vision for laity in active service belonged to an enduring theology of ministry: the body of Christ united in worship and service for the good of the world.

In 1968, after years of planning, reflection, and ecumenical engagement, the MC and the EUB formed The United Methodist Church (UMC).[27] The new denomination established a global communion of churches. At the Uniting Conference, Rev. Albert Outler, who spearheaded the renewal of Wesley and Methodist studies for the latter half of the century, compared the new denomination to the birth of the church in Acts:

> After years of consultation and planning, **The United Methodist Church (UMC)** was established in 1968 in the merger of the Evangelical United Brethren (EUB) and the Methodist Church (MC) in Dallas, Texas. Although the founders of the Evangelical Church and the United Brethren had close ties to the Wesleyan movement in North America, the merger left many of the EUB's nearly 800,000 members worldwide worried that their own piety and heritage might be lost in the process. The UMC is the largest branch of worldwide Methodism today.

> Pentecost is rightly remembered as the day when the Christian church was launched on its career *in* history, *for* the world. In every age, her performance has been scandalously short of her visions and dreams—and her plain imperatives. And yet also in every age since the first Pentecost, it is the Christian church that has marked off the crucial difference between man's best hope and his genuine despair.[28]

Outler claimed the event was less the celebration of an achievement than a moment when "the real work" begins. The goal, he suggested, was nothing less than the formation of a church truly catholic, truly evangelical, and truly reformed. By this, Outler meant that the UMC ought to be open to all who claim faith in Christ, persist in teaching the fullness of the gospel, and listen to God's judgment and renewal. In response, the UMC quickly worked to refocus the ministries of the church. Delegates ended the Central Jurisdiction (which had institutionalized racial segregation), embraced dialogue

with other Christian denominations, and reorganized global UMC conferences in Africa and elsewhere.[29] Their efforts, designed to promote a more
Christ-centered vision of a just society, also resulted in landmark shifts in
episcopal representation.[30]

While the formation of the UMC brought unity to broad swaths of
American Methodists (and members of the MC and EUB congregations in
nations around the world), subtle divisions almost immediately threatened
to throw the UMC into disarray. No issue proved as challenging as the
subject of sexuality.[31] In the wake of the 1960s, a time of social upheaval in
America, the UMC quickly discovered that changing beliefs about human
sexuality sharply divided American Methodists. Matters of justice had long
been a concern of Methodism: the Methodist Episcopal Church adopted its
first Social Creed in 1908 in support of the rights of laborers in American
factories. While Methodists have often divided over matters of political significance, the Social Creed has continued to serve as a guide to matters of
ethical concern. Yet no issue since slaveholding proved as acrimonious as
the introduction of language into the Social Creed of the UMC declaring
homosexuality to be "incompatible with Christian teaching."[32]

The origin of the story centers on a United Methodist pastor named Gene
Leggett (1935–1978). A magnetic personality, Leggett seemed destined to rise
through the ranks of Methodism in Texas, but he maintained a secret life in
the gay community unknown to his wife and children. In 1965, when word
of his sexuality reached the senior pastor of his church, Leggett faced a
choice: either resign and locate in non-parish ministry, or face dismissal and
public recognition of his sexuality. Although he chose to resign quietly,
Leggett's marriage soon dissolved. The following year, he began working in
the gay community in Dallas through a new ministry he named "The House
of the Covenant." Five years later, Leggett decided to reveal his secret life to
his annual conference. The Board of Ministry moved to revoke his ordination—this despite Leggett's belief that he continued to work faithfully in
Christian ministry: "I do not feel that I am unacceptable to the work of the
Ministry . . . [rather] I am in a unique position to carry on a ministry which
is unprecedented in the field of Christian witness in this conference."[33] When
the annual conference met in May 1971, activists disrupted the meetings to
resist UMC ministerial policies on sexuality. Still, by a relatively narrow
margin, the clergy affirmed the Board's decision. Leggett was suspended.

Leggett's case indirectly influenced the discussion of human sexuality at the UMC General Conference of 1972. One aspect of the conference's work was the creation of a new statement of Social Principles. The UMC originally published both the EUB and MC statements on sexuality in the new *Book of Discipline* (1968). The statements offered little guidance on homosexuality, but the UMC Committee on Christian Social Concerns sought language that would protect civil rights in a time when many in the gay community faced legal and economic discrimination. In addition to language affirming that "homosexuals no less than heterosexuals are persons of sacred worth," the original draft claimed, "We insist that homosexuals are entitled to have their human and civil rights ensured." Gene Leggett attended General Conference in protest of his suspension, and the committee agreed to hear a statement from him calling for stronger language affirming sexuality as "a gift of God" regardless of "sexual preferment." The pivotal moment came during debate at general conference, when one of the same Texas delegates who had witnessed firsthand the confusion over Leggett's suspension introduced a pivotal emendation to the proposed Social Principles. The final wording asserted that "all persons are entitled to have their human and civil rights ensured, though we do not condone the practice of homosexuality and consider the practice incompatible with Christian doctrine." The new language, presented with the hope of strengthening the UMC, instead became a lightning rod for controversy and "the most divisive event in the church" since the MEC split over the question of slavery.[34]

American Methodism, from the days of Francis Asbury to the present, has faced continual controversy in what may be described as a gradual movement from innocence to experience. The formation of the UMC, only one among many denominations in the American Wesleyan family, didn't result in massive growth but brought the churches together for more effective ministry worldwide. Along with almost every other mainline denomination in America, including many other Methodist and Wesleyan churches, the UMC has witnessed a steady decline. Yet if the future of the movement seems uncertain to many American Methodists today, at least part of the problem is a persistent myopia. In America, Methodism forges on, but the church grows exponentially in foreign lands. To understand why, we must return to May 1814, as stunned onlookers watched a lifeless body drop into the ocean.

PART THREE

THE *Expansion* OF WORLD METHODISM

CHAPTER NINE

Round Tables

WHEN THEY ENTERED THE ROOM of Dr. Thomas Coke, his body lay motionless on the floor. The minister, who had been unwell for several days prior, had died of a "fit of apoplexy"—what we now call a stroke. On this day, May 3, 1814, Coke was not at home in England, where he had attended Jesus College, Oxford, and later served as a parish priest in the pastoral Somerset region of southwest England. Nor was Coke traveling in Virginia, the Ohio Valley, or the expanding frontiers of North America, where John Wesley had once sent him to ordain Francis Asbury and serve together as the first superintendents of the American Methodists (to Wesley's annoyance, they soon styled themselves "bishops"). Rather, Thomas Coke died alone in a room on board a vessel in the Indian Ocean, bound for Ceylon (today Sri Lanka) via Bombay, India (today Mumbai).

For the grieving and now-leaderless missionaries who gathered around Coke's body as it dropped to its final resting place in the rough waters of the

Thomas Coke (1747–1814) is remembered as the father of Methodist missions. He attended Jesus College, Oxford, and served as curate of a Church of England parish in Somerset before the influence of Methodism led to his service as one of John Wesley's most faithful assistants. John Wesley named Coke one of the founding "superintendents" (bishops) of the Methodist Episcopal Church (MEC), but Coke devoted most of his energy to worldwide evangelism.

Figure 9.1. Thomas Coke

Indian Ocean, this surely seemed the demise of their mission—the last in a series of failures for Coke.[1] When he first came under the influence of Methodist preaching in the mid-1770s, Coke approached John Wesley about joining his growing ranks of ministers. Wesley demurred, advising him to remain in his current parish. Coke's exuberant support for Methodist teaching, however, soon led to conflict. In time, he left his position and emerged as one of Wesley's most trusted advisors, but his role in the ordinations for American Methodists left many of his Methodist colleagues, including Charles Wesley, irritated. The American Methodists, for their part, never trusted Coke as they did their beloved Asbury. There could have been little surprise that when news of John Wesley's death spread to America in 1791, Coke quickly departed for London, hoping to lead the next generation of Methodists back home. Then the unexpected happened. The British Methodists didn't elect Coke to assume Wesley's role. In fact, six long years passed before the British Methodists finally selected him to the annual presidency. And so it was that one of the great Methodists of the eighteenth and early-nineteenth centuries found himself surprisingly itinerant, always traveling to the next preaching appointment, and curiously forced into global service by the providence of unpopularity.

In this chapter, I look at three Methodists who were associated with ministry in India and Sri Lanka: Thomas Coke, E. Stanley Jones, and D. T. Niles. These three ministers, each figures of repute, influenced how Methodists think about the church outside of Great Britain and North America. Through a closer look at their lives, a portrait of the opportunities and challenges faced by Methodists living in the majority world comes into view.[2] Methodism wasn't simply transplanted into new lands, like a potted plant brought to a new climate. Rather, much as with Methodism in America, Methodist witness to Christ abroad required translation for the people and culture of the local soil.

The introduction of global Methodism rightly begins with Dr. Thomas Coke. A decade before the great Baptist minister William Carey penned his famous appeal for missionaries to enter foreign service,[3] Coke published *A Plan of the Society for the Establishment of Missions Amongst the Heathen* (1783/84). In subsequent years, Coke penned more than fifteen other treatises, reports, and histories on different aspects of missions and missionary service abroad. Wesley thought Coke's designs for a global church might hinder the work in America, but Coke resolutely pressed forward. In 1786, having finally earned Wesley's support, Coke set sail for Newfoundland and the West Indies, hoping to establish Methodist societies in Canada and the Caribbean. The seas conspired against the plan, and the captain turned the ship south. The group landed on the tiny island of Antigua in the Caribbean on Christmas morning.

Imagine Coke's disbelief when he and his fellow missionaries discovered that Methodism had already begun to flourish through the work of the West Indian planter Nathanael Gilbert (1721–1774). Gilbert had previously heard John Wesley in London, preached the same message of grace to his slaves, and founded a Methodist society on the island. The work was continued after Gilbert's death, and Coke heard of some 1,500 other Methodists already growing in faith on the island. The following month, Coke visited other nearby islands, leaving preachers in stations along the way; and in subsequent years British Methodists sponsored missionaries and churches throughout the islands. By the time Coke sailed toward India and Ceylon, Methodist preachers served 17,000 members in twelve circuits throughout Caribbean islands such as Barbados, Jamaica, and the Bahamas.[4]

Coke knew more about the expansion of Christianity around the world than almost anyone alive, yet despite such knowledge, he left England in a state of uncertainty. After returning from the exciting new work in the West Indies, he dedicated himself to fundraising. While the Missionary Committee that subsidized his travel to India and Ceylon remained watchful of what some regarded as his exorbitant spending on supplies for fellow missionaries, Coke worried that the committee's cost-cutting would stymie progress and frustrate the effort to recruit new laborers to the field.

Although he was approaching seventy and less fit for arduous travel on the high seas, Coke made the journey and intended to remain in Ceylon and India for at least two years while the missionaries settled into their work.[5] Not surprisingly, Coke's sudden death left his team in a state of disbelief. When they arrived in Bombay, the immensity of the task overwhelmed them all, for they had anticipated his guidance in the formative years of ministry. Rather than falling into despair, however, the missionaries rose to the occasion. On hearing early reports from the field, one noted, "The death of Dr. Coke, instead of proving the ruin of the Mission, seems to have been overruled greatly for the furtherance of it."[6]

The missionaries who finally arrived in Ceylon would have failed if not for the assistance of a court interpreter named Andrew Armour. Once again, the arrival of missionaries to a foreign field was welcomed by a fellow Methodist already active in the work. Armour, a former soldier, helped the missionaries to understand the complicated religious and social landscape of the island. Most of the Ceylonese people were Theravada Buddhist, but Hindu Tamils formed a majority in the North. The missionaries decided to settle in different areas of the island, quickly forming schools wherever they went.

Armour also provided an essential link to the expansion of Methodist ministry in India. By law, Anglican clergy could only serve as chaplains to employees of the East India Company, so formal evangelism among the people was forbidden. As a soldier, however, Armour had already established a Methodist society at Madras. When the Madras society heard news of the Methodist missionaries in Ceylon, they requested additional support. One of Coke's fellow missionaries, the Irish Methodist James Lynch, responded to the call, founding Methodism in India in 1817.

> **The Methodist Church of India** originates in the work of the Methodist Episcopal Church. In 1856, the missionary William Butler (1818–1899) arrived, and by 1870, the new church began to see the fruit of their labors. The work in India succeeded through the energy of tireless workers from home and abroad, including several women associated with medicine and education. In 1870, Isabella Thoburn (1840–1901) and Clara A. Swain, MD (1834–1910) were sent to join the work in India as two of the first missionaries appointed by the Woman's Foreign Missionary Society.

British Methodists were not alone. Other churches began sending missionaries to the region to evangelize the poor and provide facilities for education. The American Methodists soon joined the work as well: the MEC sent its first missionaries to India in 1856.[7] Among the most influential American missionaries to the region was a young man named E. Stanley Jones (1884–1973). Jones attended Asbury College in Kentucky and originally planned a career in law before recognizing a call to missions. In 1907 the Methodist Board of Missions accepted his application, gave him "a Hindustani grammar, forty pounds in British gold, a ticket to Bombay via Britain, a handshake," and sent him off to work.[8] At Lucknow, Jones advocated a strict message of Wesleyan-Holiness piety, served as district superintendent, and supervised a boarding school. By 1915, however, Jones was exhausted. Overwhelmed by his work among the poor, he suffered a mental breakdown and returned to America for a furlough, entertaining the possibility that he might never go back.

With rest and study at home, Jones discovered a new vision for evangelism abroad. He resumed life in India with an eye to reach not only the poor but also the elites by taking seriously Indian religious virtues, culture, and identity. Soon Jones began publishing some of the most influential works on Christian evangelism and mission of his generation, including *The Christ of the Indian Road* (1925), *Christ at the Round Table* (1928), and *The Christ of Every Road* (1930), advocating a new approach to witness that centered on Jesus rather than the transmission of Western culture. "We want the East to keep its own soul—only thus can it be creative," Jones maintained. "We are not there to plaster Western civilization

Figure 9.2. E. Stanley Jones

upon the East, to make it a pale copy of ourselves. We must go deeper—infinitely deeper—than that."[9]

Jones believed that Jesus alone could shape the hearts and minds of Indians, transforming the nation with a message that cut across conventional lines of division. Confessions of faith were not inconsequential, but the reality of the living Christ was greater than any system: "I weave my formulas about him and he steps out beyond them!"[10] The experience of Christ reveals a profound knowledge of the human condition, and Christ knows the condition of the Indian people because he understands "toil and pain and sorrow and enters in and feels with them."[11] Christ walked in sympathetic understanding alongside others, entering their sufferings: "He could feel the darkness of the blind, the leprosy of the leper, the loneliness of the rich, the degradation of the poor, and the guilt of the sinner."[12]

Evangelism, then, requires not teaching *about* Christ so much as introducing people *to* Christ. To this end, Jones founded Christian ashrams, combining elements of Methodist class meetings with characteristics of Indian religious communities formed by his friend Mahatma Gandhi.[13] Ashrams allowed Christianity to flourish in a distinctly Indian context.[14] Participants were expected to live according to the same standards (across racial or economic lines), wear Indian clothes, eat a vegetarian diet (since Hindus would regularly participate in the community), and study the Bible in the light of India's heritage and national life.[15] In this way, participants encountered the living Christ of the Gospels without the entrapments of Western culture.

When E. Stanley Jones called Christians to "go deeper" in their witness to the living Christ, he insinuated a major Wesleyan theme. In the sermon "Catholic Spirit" (1750), John Wesley rejected not only the tendency toward dogmatism that divided Christians but also the indifference to matters of faith that could easily lead to confusion:

> Every wise man therefore will allow others the same liberty of thinking which he desires they should allow him; and will no more insist on their embracing his opinions than he would have them to insist on his embracing theirs. He bears with those who differ from him, and only asks him with whom he desires to unite in love that single question. "Is thine heart right, as my heart is with thy heart?"[16]

The statement is more than a little surprising given Wesley's willingness to enter controversy. What, then, did Wesley mean by the union of hearts implied in the provocative title "catholic spirit"? Wesley's answer did not imply that matters of historic Christian doctrine were inconsequential.[17] Wesley assumed a total commitment to the love of God and enjoined that all who follow Jesus Christ will reject evil, live holy lives, and demonstrate love of neighbor by doing good to all. Yet while Wesley remained steadfast in these beliefs, he allowed for latitude. As a lifelong Anglican, Wesley affirmed historic structures of church government, traditional forms of public prayer, and sacramental practices according to the order of the church. Nonetheless, Wesley recognized that other believers may disagree and ought to have liberty of conscience to practice their faith accordingly (and even he had appealed to a wider understanding of ordination to set apart ministers for

America than his fellow Anglicans thought appropriate). The greatest error was indifference:

> Observe this, you who know not what spirit ye are of, who call yourselves men of a catholic spirit only because you are of a muddy understanding; because your mind is all in a mist; because you have no settled, consistent principles, but are for jumbling all opinions together. Be convinced that you have quite missed your way: you know not where you are. You think you are got into the very spirit of Christ, when in truth you are nearer the spirit of antichrist. Go first and learn the first elements of the gospel of Christ, and then shall you learn to be of a truly catholic spirit.[18]

Wesley's strident language, in a work ostensibly encouraging charity amongst Christians, disallows any suggestion that a "catholic spirit" might be conflated with apathy or disinterest.

What might this mean for Methodists in India? By reorienting evangelism around the goal of introducing Christ, Jones encouraged Indian Christians to discern for themselves the difference between what is essential to faith and what belongs to local culture. Of course, talk of encountering the "living Christ" may sound like a vague and wooly mysticism, but Jones thought this idea was directly connected to the message of Acts 2. In the many tongues of Pentecost, Christ becomes recognizable in every language and culture— truly catholic. In turn, as individuals meet Christ by the power of the Spirit, Christ becomes "entirely dominant in the soul" and transforms social, racial, and economic relationships.[19] This, he thought, was the true meaning of "entire sanctification." Jones was so committed to this belief that upon election to the episcopacy by the mission board in 1928, he declined consecration; two years later, Indian Methodists had their first

> Life in India reshaped how E. Stanley Jones thought about Christian faith and practice, as he describes in *The Christ of Every Road* (1925): "The people called Methodists believe in **entire sanctification**—at least their standards say they do! . . . Entire sanctification would be the life of Christ entirely dominant in the soul. I have no quarrel with this. My only quarrel is that the sanctification, as usually presented, has not been sufficiently entire. If it is to be entire, it should begin at the individual man and go as far as his relationships— social, economic, racial, and international—extend. Then, and then only, would it be entire sanctification."

indigenous bishop. "I went to India through pity," Jones wrote. "I stay through respect."[20]

Meanwhile, as Jones worked in India, a young man was studying in Jaffna, Ceylon, at a school established little more than a century earlier by the Irish Methodist James Lynch (one of Thomas Coke's fellow missionaries). Daniel Thambyrajah Niles (1908–1970) was a member of the minority Tamil Christian community whose paternal great-grandfather and maternal great-great grandfather were two of the first converts from Hinduism of the American Mission in Jaffna. Niles's grandfather, with whom he lived until he was eight years old, was a Methodist pastor, so he unsurprisingly received ordination to ministry in 1936. Niles began as a district evangelist and a local church pastor but soon found himself bridging Sri Lanka and the world in prominent speaking engagements at the International Missionary Council in Madras (1938), the first session of the World Council of Churches (1948), and through the presidency of the Methodist Church in Sri Lanka.[21]

The Sri Lankan evangelist and theologian **Daniel Thambyrajah Niles** (1908–1970) was a Methodist who influenced Christians around the world. Ordained in the Methodist Church in 1936, Niles served as a local evangelist and pastor while also serving national and international organizations. In *That They May Have Life* (1951), Niles writes of the universal need for the bread of life and famously describes evangelism as "one beggar telling another beggar where to get food."

Figure 9.3. D. T. Niles

Few Methodists today recognize D. T. Niles by name, though his influence may still be felt in churches around the world. Niles wrote numerous hymns and translated many others, most notably through his work as editor of the *East Asia Christian Conference Hymnal*. Moreover, Niles's address on evangelism (1954) to the World Council of Churches at Evanston, Illinois, inspired one of the most well-known sermons of the twentieth century. Niles, relating the biblical story of the persistent friend (Lk 11:5–13), boldly declared,

There are those who are knocking at the door of the Church; and they are not merely the hungry, the homeless, the refugee, the displaced person, the outcast; there are at the Church's door, also, every type of community—nations, races, classes, political groupings—knocking for different reasons. Some are asking for bread, others simply ask what kind of people live in this house in which a light shines at midnight, and still others come just to shake their fists in the faces of those who keep a light burning but have no bread.[22]

Martin Luther King Jr. outlined his famous sermon "A Knock at Midnight" on a personal copy of Niles's address, and only months after King was assassinated, the World Council of Churches called on Niles to take King's place as the opening speaker at the assembly of the World Council of Churches in Uppsala, Sweden (1968).

While Niles shared the Methodists' commitment to ecumenism, he insisted that longstanding patterns of evangelism risked stunting the growth of younger churches in the majority world. Rather, a truly united church requires fully indigenous churches that are each unique: "national in its expression, spontaneous in its growth, and local in its colouring."[23] To accomplish this end, Niles believed that the West must create space for the younger churches to develop their own voices. Such a bold move would require openness and trust. As with E. Stanley Jones before him, Niles believed Christianity would only flourish as the message of Christ was appropriated by local Christians.

> **The World Council of Churches** (WCC) is an ecumenical agency based in Geneva, Switzerland. Although founded in 1948, the origins of the WCC spring from the Edinburgh World Missionary Conference (1910) and interdenominational working groups that continued to meet in subsequent years. Methodist churches have a long history with the WCC. The Methodist John Mott was named the honorary president at its founding, while the noted Bishop G. Bromley Oxnam (1891–1963) served as one of its first presidents (1948–1954).

Words alone, however, would never suffice. Too often Niles heard Christians abroad speak about Jesus Christ as little more than a man or an event in the distant past. In his book *Who Is This Jesus?* (1968), Niles records what he calls a "strange experience" in which a group of theological students discussed Christ as "a historical point of reference around whom a body of doctrine and ethics had been built." The students identified only "a bare skeleton of events" related to Jesus and "denied that it was possible really to know what Jesus Christ was like or said or did when he walked the earth in the flesh."[24] The students, though committed to Christian proclamation, seemed to have little sense of how the living Christ related to them today or how a transcendent God might confront and challenge them to obey through an immediate encounter with Christ.

Niles gave witness to Christ in what amounts to a contemporary enactment of Wesley's "catholic spirit." As a Tamil Christian, a minority religion within a minority ethnic group, Niles wrote from a position of vulnerability. He knew the experience of persecution, government disruption of educational institutions, and the distrust of his neighbors. A friend to major Christian leaders in the West, Niles could see that they were insulated from the challenges that accompanied minority status in a context of religious pluralism.[25] While Western Christians worked to encourage active participation among a largely nominal Christian populace, Niles ministered within a pluralist society among people who had never heard about the uniqueness of Jesus Christ. Niles could see God at work in the questions that his non-Christian neighbors asked him, in the provision for widows and orphans through the work of local churches, and the lasting witness of Christians in an often-hostile community.

> The merger of several Protestant denominations, including British Methodists, Anglicans, and other ecclesial bodies in the formation of the **Church of South India** (1947) and **Church of North India** (1970) has widened the influence of Methodism in that region of the world. These churches include more than five million members and administer numerous schools and hospitals. Due to their historic ties to Methodism, the churches are members of the World Methodist Council.

These themes were, of course, familiar to both Methodists and members of other denominations as well. Perhaps because of these challenges, Niles thought it strange that many Methodists in Britain and the United States felt greater kinship to Methodists across the world than to the Anglican, Baptist, or Presbyterian next door.[26] Niles therefore advocated for greater autonomy of local churches within denominations, increased participation by the laity, and the eventual union of the denominations within a nation. Christians in India had already witnessed just such a union when in 1947 the British-related Methodists joined Anglicans, Presbyterians, and Congregationalists in the formation of the Church of South India. Later, in 1970, a similar union was formed in the creation of the Church of North India.[27] Niles worked to achieve the same for the churches in Sri Lanka under the belief that denominations furthered difference rather than cooperation: "The finality of Jesus Christ is a standing judgment on denominational separateness. He alone is enough."[28] In 1963 the British Methodists granted autonomy to the Methodist Church of Ceylon. The following year, Niles was named president. Still, despite his efforts, political obstacles impeded plans for a union of churches in Sri Lanka during his lifetime and continue to hinder such a union today. Yet Niles, as with Coke and Jones in different ways before him, recognized that the future of the church depended on an encounter with the living Christ and the freedom to live out that experience.

The death of Dr. Thomas Coke appeared to mark the failure of Methodist missions, but the growth of Methodism never depended on the work of any one minister, lay preacher, or church. Methodism flourished because Christians preached the living Christ and recognized the active work of the Spirit in the hearts of those who believed. But letting go of control, as the next chapter reveals, is easier said than done.

CHAPTER TEN

Outstretched Hands

"THE EARTH SHALL BE FULL OF the knowledge of the Lord, as the waters cover the sea" (Is 11:9). For many Africans, Isaiah 11 is not a platitude but a promise. Yet had you visited some parts of Africa during the seventeenth or eighteenth century, you might have found their faith difficult to imagine. Consider Cape Coast Castle, sitting along the Gulf of Guinea in the West African nation of Ghana, where the slave trade prospered at the expense of Africans who passed through the "door of no return." Before making the passage across the Atlantic to the Americas, men and women were chained in cramped and filthy conditions in the Castle dungeons. Their captors regarded Africans as pagans, treating them without regard for their dignity or respect for their customs. Immediately above the dark and suffocating dungeon, however, European Christians could gather for worship in the bright, open chapel. Songs offered in praise to the Almighty drowned out the cries of the enslaved below, while alternately Portuguese, Dutch, or British clergymen ministered to Castle personnel nearby.

How is it possible that Christianity could succeed in a place with such a painful history? In this chapter, I take a closer look at the advent of Methodism in Africa. Although Africa is a vast continent incorporating a range of languages, customs, and beliefs, Methodism brought hope and dignity to Africans. While Christianity can easily be associated with the West, Africans made Methodism their own. Today, there are nearly as many Methodists in Africa as in the United States, and far more Methodists in some African countries than in Great Britain. Yet African Methodism cannot easily be linked to any single Wesleyan body or denomination. Instead, the founding of Methodist churches resulted from uniquely British, American, Canadian, and, above all, local influences. In fact, as the Ghanaian Methodist theologian Mercy Amba Oduyoye has suggested, there is good reason to believe that the success of missionary work in Africa resulted from the evangelists' willingness to be "Christians first and Europeans second."[1]

Long before the arrival of Thomas Birch Freeman (1809–1890), the pioneering Methodist missionary to West Africa, Christianity already showed signs that it might one day flourish there. While previous efforts to evangelize the continent had been associated with the slave trade, the spread of the gospel along trade routes north gradually led several Ghanaian Fantes to seek God together as an indigenous African community. Under the leadership of Africans such as Joseph Smith and William De Graft, the Fante "Bible Band" (c. 1831) affirmed the authority of the Bible as "the best rule a Christian ought to observe."[2] The earliest minutes of their meetings show them engaged in communal readings of the sacred text:

> A portion of scripture was then read by the most competent person present and explained in the Fante language, after which they concluded their service by singing part of another psalm and used another prayer from the [Anglican] liturgy. At 11 A.M. they attended divine service in the [Cape Coast] Castle, and at 3 P.M. they again had a service conducted in the same manner as that held early in the morning.[3]

Through contact with the captain of a British merchant vessel, De Graft and the Fante Bible Band requested Bibles for use in their meetings. When a Wesleyan Methodist missionary named Joseph Rhodes Dunwell arrived in 1835 with Bibles in hand, the Bible Band welcomed him with open arms. Dunwell stood out among European ministers, since he was not sent to work primarily as a chaplain to merchants but as a minister for Africans.[4]

Missionaries to West Africa rarely survived long. Dunwell endured only six months before succumbing to illness. Other Methodist missionaries soon arrived, but again and again these men and women died. George Wrigley, who reached West Africa only fifteen months after Dunwell's death, wrote home in desperation, "Come out to this hell if it is only to die here." The words echoed those of so many Methodists before him, but the calling seemed little more than a death sentence.

By the time the Fante Bible Band had formed, Methodists were already active in West Africa due to events first set off by the American Revolution of 1776. When in 1786 Thomas Coke set sail with missionaries bound for

Black **British Loyalists** during the American Revolution served as some of the earliest missionaries and founders of African Methodism. After briefly relocating to Nova Scotia, black Americans such as Moses Wilkinson and Boston King moved to Sierra Leone with the hope of sharing the good news. Although there are multiple Methodist church denominations in the region, the memory of these missionaries continues to be cherished today in the Methodist Church in Sierra Leone.

Figure 10.1. "Am I Not a Man and a Brother?" medallion by British abolitionist Josiah Wedgwood

Newfoundland, Canada, he probably didn't realize just how far Methodism had already begun to spread. The Irish Methodist (and Anglican clergyman) Lawrence Coughlan (d. c. 1784) was already at work evangelizing in the area.

In a strange series of events, Canadian Methodism further increased when, during the Revolutionary War, the British promised freedom to anyone of African descent who took up arms in the struggle. As the British left the American colonies, they followed through on their pledge. The British recognized that abandoning freed men and women of African descent in the colonies put them at renewed risk of enslavement. After the war, the British brought some three thousand Loyalist slaves who had escaped and sought refuge with them to Nova Scotia.

Among the Loyalists was a blind and lame Methodist named Moses ("Daddy") Wilkinson, who had led a group of fellow slaves from Virginia to freedom in New York. Wilkinson, who was illiterate, became known for his ecstatic preaching and the visible effects of God's presence among his listeners. Once he had arrived in Nova Scotia, Wilkinson resumed preaching but, as with other settlers to the area, found the harsh climate difficult to bear. In 1792, Wilkinson and more than one thousand other black Nova

Scotia settlers left Halifax for Sierra Leone in West Africa. Wilkinson established the first black Methodist church in Settler Town.[5]

Other Methodists of African descent made the journey with Wilkinson. Boston King (c. 1760–1802) was born in slavery on a planation in Charleston, South Carolina. Like Wilkinson, King escaped from a brutal master when he heard the British offer of freedom. After the war, King and his wife, Violet, moved to Nova Scotia with other Loyalists. Violet King was the first black Loyalist at Birchtown to encounter Christ, and she promptly emerged as a decisive figure in the Methodist movement there: "The joy and happiness which she now experienced, were too great to be concealed, and she was enabled to testify of the goodness and lovingkindness of the Lord, with such liveliness and power, that many were convinced by her testimony, and sincerely sought the Lord."[6] Boston King, reluctant to embrace Christianity at first, was eventually set free from doubt, fear, and unbelief.

> For this purpose I went into the garden at midnight, and kneeled down upon the snow, lifting my hands, eyes, and heart to Heaven; and entreated the Lord, who had called me by his Holy Spirit out of ignorance and wickedness, that he would increase and strengthen my awakenings and desires, and impress my heart with the importance of eternal things . . . and received a sense of his pardoning love.[7]

Soon after, King began itinerating as a Methodist preacher, and though he managed to find enough work to support a family in Nova Scotia, he and his wife resolved to emigrate to Sierra Leone. He left "not for the sake of the advantages I hoped to reap" but rather to contribute "in spreading the knowledge of Christianity in that country."[8] Upon arrival in West Africa, King continued preaching, despite considerable hardships and the death of his wife, Violet. Fellow Methodists were so impressed by his abilities as a teacher that they sponsored his attendance at the Methodist Kingswood School near Bristol, England, for two years. King later returned to Sierra Leone and, alongside his second wife, ministered among the interior Sherbro people for the remainder of his life.

George Wrigley's gloomy plea to the Methodists, "Come out to this hell if it is only to die here," brought Methodists face to face with the selfless sacrifice required to take up ministry in Africa. Few were willing, but one Englishman stands out for his unparalleled resolve: Thomas Birch Freeman.[9]

The son of an African man and an English woman, Freeman worked as a gardener and student of botany before joining the Methodists as a class leader and local preacher. At the age of twenty-eight, Freeman applied to serve as a Wesleyan Methodist missionary in response to Wrigley's appeal.

> Woe is me if I preach not the Gospel and woe is me if I am not prepared to forsake home, and friends, and all that I hold dear to me to preach that Gospel to the heathen . . . If I hesitate to go to a sickly clime at the command of the Lord of Hosts, because in so doing, I may risk the shortening of my days in this life, cannot He, who bids me so, strike me here, while surrounded with the advantages of this sea-girt isle?[10]

The son of an African father and English mother, **Thomas Birch Freeman** (1809–1890) was born and raised in England before serving as a Wesleyan Methodist missionary to West Africa. His wife, Elizabeth Booth Freeman, died soon after their arrival, but he pressed on to found mission stations in Ghana, Benin, western Nigeria, and Togo.

Figure 10.2. Thomas Birch Freeman

Before departing, Freeman married Elizabeth Booth (since marriage was a prerequisite for the mission) and prepared for the journey. Personally accompanied by the Fante Bible Band leader Joseph Smith, Freeman and his wife traveled to the Cape Coast of West Africa, where the African Methodists enthusiastically greeted them in early January 1838. Unbeknownst to them, Wrigley had died only months before their arrival. Six weeks later, Elizabeth Freeman succumbed to illness too.

Unlike so many missionaries in West Africa before him, however, Freeman embraced African culture and empowered local leadership. He immediately began training sessions to educate the laity, accepted the African Methodist William De Graft as a candidate for ministry, and commenced construction of the first chapel in Ghana that wasn't built to support the European forts.[11] One year after his arrival, Freeman traveled deep into the interior, where no missionaries had successfully ministered before. The journey was arduous and required patience:

in each village, he was welcomed by local chiefs, offered prayers and sermons for the people, and established new churches. When Freeman finally reached Kumasi, the seat of the Ashanti kingdom, a crowd of 40,000 people welcomed him. Freeman developed a good relationship with the king during his two-week visit and even baptized a convert in the presence of many of the Ashanti people, but he was unable to establish a church before the looming rainy season forced his departure. Though he suffered the loss of a second wife (Lucinda, who was pregnant at the time) and faced criticism from his sponsors for his financial management of the mission, Freeman worked in the region for the rest of his life.[12] In this way, Thomas Birch Freeman's ministry confirmed what he already recognized at the close of his first visit to the Ashanti: "Surely Ethiopia is stretching out her hands to God."[13]

John Wesley would not have been surprised to learn of Freeman's labors. In his sermon "The General Spread of the Gospel" (1783), Wesley paints a dire portrait of the spiritual state of the nations: "In what a condition is the world at present! How does darkness, intellectual darkness, ignorance, with vice and misery attendant upon it, cover the face of the earth!"[14] Relying on the best resources available at the time, Wesley surmised that only one in six people throughout the world was a Christian. The rest were lost and, he imagined, literally consumed each other like ravenous beasts in the field. Still, though brutality and ignorance reigned, Wesley optimistically believed that God had already begun a great work that would one day canvas the whole world. The enormity of the task hardly discouraged him. Not only *could* God transform whole nations by his grace, but the task *would be as easy* for God as the conversion of a single soul.[15] Wesley thought that God had raised up the Methodists as a leavening influence, offering true religion, the experience of grace, and the marks of inward and outward holiness for every person on earth. In this way, the work of God "will silently increase wherever it is set up, and spread from heart to heart, from house to house, from town to town, from one kingdom to another."[16]

Wesley's vision of organic growth certainly applies to the progress of Methodism in Africa. Little more than two decades after Wesley's death, the first Methodist missionaries arrived in Southern Africa. Once more, Methodists were already there. British soldiers stationed on the Cape had previously celebrated love fests and formed class meetings for their fellow soldiers. The most influential early Methodist minister in Southern Africa was William Shaw (1798–1872), who arrived in 1820. Shaw established Methodist class meetings, offered the sacraments of baptism and the Lord's Supper, developed a circuit for Methodist missions, and engaged both European settlers and Africans alike in teaching and preaching.[17]

Shaw recognized the transforming power of God even when the people responded in ways that many fellow Methodists at home would have thought indecorous. "We neither prayed for nor strove to produce these outward manifestations," he explained, but God alone chooses whether to "work by the 'still, small voice of His Spirit,' or by the thunder and lightning and earthquake of His power."[18] Shaw ministered in the Wesleyan belief that Christ died for all people, regardless of race or ethnicity. The message of liberty was for all—whether white or black, European or Asian, American or African—and all alike could proclaim "a free, full, and present salvation."[19]

Methodist missionaries followed the longstanding practice of offering the sacraments wherever they shared the gospel. From the earliest days of Methodism, John Wesley taught that participation in the **Lord's Supper** (or Eucharist) was a duty enjoined by God, a means of forgiveness of sins, and a source of spiritual nourishment. In his sermon, "On the Duty of Constant Communion" (1787), Wesley counters the commonplace hesitation to receive the sacrament due to unworthiness, stating, "All the preparation that is absolutely necessary is contained in those words, 'Repent you truly of your sins past; have faith in Christ our Saviour.'"

Yet while Africans performed much of the pioneering work of Methodist witness and mission, they were increasingly excluded from the unity of the connection in Southern Africa. Much as in North America, discriminatory treatment led to schism. For example, though all contributed to the establishment of the church, Africans and European colonists often worshiped in separate church buildings, and African Methodists were continually frustrated in their attempts to secure suitable worship spaces from church leaders when existing options were repurposed without adequate alternatives for their needs. The Wesleyan emphasis on God's pardon and assurance of the Spirit had bolstered the dignity and self-worth of the African, but Methodist administration of the churches left African Christians unable to fully express their gifts in ministry. In short, Methodist practice often failed to embody Wesleyan belief.

The case of Mangena Mokone (1851–1931) exemplifies the consequences of segregation in Southern Africa. Ordained in 1887, Mokone was a Wesleyan Methodist (Britain) minister and educator at a time when the segregation of ministers at district meetings was commonplace. He protested that he and other African ministers and ministerial candidates were often treated unfairly. Some African candidates for ministry were unjustly deemed unfit, and African ministers received lower wages and other financial support than their peers.[20] In 1892, Mokone resigned from Wesleyan Methodist ministry and established the Ethiopian Church in South Africa, bringing other African ministers and laity who had experienced similar mistreatment with him in the process.

Not long after, Mokone and other leaders of the new church learned of the African Methodist Episcopal Church (AME) in North America. Impressed by reports of the church and their commitment to black leadership, Mokone and the Ethiopian Church chose to merge with the AME, which was equally inspired by similarities between the Ethiopian Movement and the origins of the AME.[21] Encouraged by testimonies of the growing church movement, Bishop Henry McNeal Turner visited South Africa, where he received an unprecedented welcome. Some Africans traveled hundreds of miles to hear Turner's stirring message. Given the increasing authority of Christianity in Africa, some regarded this bold and prophetic individual as something of a messianic figure.[22] Many white South Africans, by contrast, thought Bishop Turner inspired only unrest and discontent. Ironically, some ministers eventually left the South African district of the AME to form new independent churches, since the church refused to establish an African as bishop in the region until 1956.[23] Though no longer bearing the name Methodist, these independent congregations belong to the family tree of Methodist denominations.[24] Mangena Mokone, the trailblazer of the Ethiopian Movement, remained active in the AME until the end of his life.

Mangena Mokone (1851–1931) received ordination with the Wesleyan Methodists in 1887, but practices of racial discrimination hindered support for African leadership. In 1892 Mokone formed the Ethiopian Church. After a visit from Bishop Henry McNeal Turner in 1898, Mokone and other members of the Ethiopian Church supported a merger with the African Methodist Episcopal Church. As an African, Mokone was ineligible to be named bishop by church law, but he remained active in the church for the remainder of his life.

Figure 10.3. Bishop Henry McNeal Turner

As the sordid history of race and ministry in Southern Africa reveals, Western missionary societies often struggled to see African Christians as equals. Still, there is another side of this problem that emerged again and again in the effort to transition from a missionary church to an autonomous church: culture. The emergence of Methodism in East Africa sheds light on this perennial problem.

In 1862 the first Methodist missionary arrived in Kenya. Little more than a century later, the Methodist Church in Kenya became fully autonomous (1967). The path to independence wasn't easy. Thomas Wakefield (1836–1901) belonged to the small United Methodist Free Churches in England (yet another reminder of the diverse wellsprings of African Methodism). Early Methodist evangelism in Kenya focused on the Galla (or Oromo) people, but few missionaries could tolerate the tropical climate, and many found that their susceptibility to disease limited travel in the region.[25] To be clear: it is a mistake to believe that missionaries only furthered colonial interests. In fact, they often made great sacrifices. When Maasi warriors raided a village in 1886, Methodist missionaries suffered martyrdom—but just as significantly, so, too, did their new African converts.[26] Women also served with remarkable faithfulness at personal loss. Wesleyan Methodist deaconesses, for example, actively served throughout Africa during the twentieth century, engaging selflessly in the work of ministry through medicine and education: "They were not so much fleeing from the wrath to come as constructing the new society envisioned in the gospel."[27]

Missionaries sometimes advocated against the policies of colonial power. Tensions mounted, for example, as the British East Africa Company (founded 1888) tolerated the ubiquity of Muslim slave trade in the region. One missionary wrote of the latent hypocrisy:

Wherever I go, I see and hear the same horror that prevailed years ago—chained gangs, manacled and fettered individuals; the clank, clank, clank of irons, the grip of the stocks, the thud of the stick, the screams of the afflicted fall upon the ear every day. Unmentionable cruelties are perpetrated, and the victims suffer, bleed and die; yet England is congratulating herself upon her wonderful philanthropy and persuading herself that slavery is no more.[28]

The British East Africa Company abided a culture of slavery while missionaries stood in solidarity with the African people.[29] Still, the sacrifices of African Methodist converts, who served and gave their own lives alongside these individuals, often go unrecognized.

By the end of the nineteenth century, however, the Methodist effort to evangelize the region may be regarded as a failure. The reasons reveal the complicated relationship between Western missionaries and the African people.

- Africans often associated missionaries with colonial administrative power.

- Missionaries were unable to protect either the Africans or themselves from violent incursions.

- Missionaries often failed to distinguish between local custom and religious commitment, hastily condemning traditional cultural practices as incompatible with the gospel.

- Africans feared that missionaries intended to steal their land. (The Tana River mission alone acquired six thousand acres for agricultural use and support of the mission.)

- The missionaries often lacked adequate resources, including sufficient workers and financial support for expansion in the region.[30]

These problems hindered the growth of Methodism, but Christianity still flourished wherever African laity shared the gospel in their daily lives.[31]

Despite gradual successes, Methodist missionaries struggled with fundamental questions about the relationship between Christianity and culture during the twentieth century. While attention to the slave trade had predominated in the nineteenth century, contentious issues subsequently arose that threatened to unravel decades of progress. The practice of female circumcision, for example, proved particularly challenging. Clitoridectomies were abhorrent to Western missionaries, since the custom caused permanent damage to women's bodies. In the eyes of the missionaries, stopping the practice was a matter of justice. However, the attempt to prohibit the rite among African Christians arose not from African believers but white missionaries. Women who rejected such customs faced exclusion from social opportunity and advancement, since they lived in highly communal societies.

Failure to participate in African cultural customs—initiation rites involving male and female circumcision or animal sacrifice, the commonplace practice of polygamy for economic reasons, or various rituals related to life and death—had real social consequences for African Methodists.[32] Participation could lead to expulsion from the church; failure to participate in public rituals left African converts marginalized from the community. To complicate matters even further, African Methodists read in Scripture that polygamy was common among many of the heroes of faith (such as Abraham, Isaac, and Jacob), yet the churches often demanded that men with multiple wives needed to renounce all but one wife to receive baptism and gain admission to the church. In the eyes of the missionary, polygamy was a sin rooted in lust and greed, but to the Africans the practice belonged to economic security, the provision for widows, and the good of the community. Some Africans argued that Methodists might allow baptism for polygamists on the condition that no additional wives be taken, but a compromise proved difficult to achieve. In some regions, local African preachers allowed polygamists to enter the church quietly, but more often the impact of church policy was to prevent many of the most wealthy and respected members of the community from participation in the church.[33]

> Methodist and Wesleyan presence in Africa includes representatives of numerous international and national denominations. The **Free Methodists** have sent more than 150 missionaries to six nations in Africa in over seventy-five years of ministry through medicine and education. The **Church of the Nazarene** began ministry in Southern Africa and expanded to thirty-four countries in Central, Eastern, and Western Africa. In Nigeria, Wesleyan Methodists and Primitive Methodists first arrived from Britain and eventually formed the autonomous Methodist Church Nigeria, while other Nigerian churches associated with **The United Methodist Church** originated in the work of various Evangelical and United Brethren missionaries.

When Methodist missionaries failed to divest themselves of cultural expectations, Africans tended to reject their message. One (Ghanaian) Asante ruler told a Wesleyan missionary, "The Bible is for the White man, the Muslims have another book, and we the Asante have our own religion. We know and keep all God's commandments and have no need for Christianity."[34] But as Africans assumed more and more responsibility for leadership and policymaking, the Methodist churches began to thrive and expand. Whenever missionaries attempted to keep "African collaborators on the leash," as Oduyoye claims, they stunted the growth of Christianity in African soil.[35] Paternalism limited the maturation of the African churches.[36] Where Africans could freely organize societies in the connection without interference, Methodist churches grew with deep roots in biblical faith. In turn, the people increasingly regarded Methodist educational and medical facilities as trusted resources rather than potential instruments of manipulation or misappropriation. Worship changed too. Instead of singing exclusively English hymns in the style of Western Christians, African Christians allowed their own faith to respond freely to the work of the Spirit. Consider the development of Methodist worship in Zimbabwe:

> One of these hymns, *Kuita basa rake pano* ("To do his will"), was particularly popular. The women would follow the original tune for seven verses. Then, creatively, they would start to sing *Ndindindi ndindi, ndindi vanamai imi* ("Oh, oh, oh you mothers") with movement and ululation in the process. The women's faces would light up with joy and expression. New verses would be invented, reflecting with deep emotion the particular needs of the community and the situation.[37]

Improvisation meant older hymns could be taken up, modified, and expanded as prayers reflecting the needs and interests of the people. African worship yielded truly African Methodism.

John Wesley's view of the world was simultaneously dim and hopeful. Throughout the nations, people lived without Christ and without hope. Yet Methodism had been raised up by God, he thought, to bring about a gracious renewal across the earth. To the farthest corners and remotest regions, the good news would spread until God had reestablished "universal holiness and happiness, and caused all the inhabitants of the earth to sing together, 'Hallelujah! The Lord God omnipotent reigneth!'"[38] But the great work

Wesley anticipated—and Methodists worked so tirelessly toward—depended just as much on the labors of those whom they hoped to reach. Methodism depends upon all parties in the Wesleyan connection. Yet as with so many other places around the world, African Methodism flourished only so far as the people saw Christ at work in and through the culture in which they lived, fulfilling the biblical promise, "Surely Ethiopia is stretching out her hands to God." Despite the exponential growth they witnessed in Africa, however, early twentieth-century Methodists devoted almost all of their attention to a region of limitless possibility: Asia.

CHAPTER ELEVEN

....

Spiritual Conquest

On a Thursday evening, June 23, 1910, in the city of Edinburgh, a young Methodist layman stood to speak at the lectern before one of the most significant gatherings in modern Christian history. Careful planning had set the stage. In the years leading up to the conference, the organizers collected data from churches in every region where Christian workers ministered so that a systematic and scientific assessment of the status of world Christianity could be made. Instead of approaching the problem in an atmosphere of competition, all agreed to work in concert, sharing plans and coordinating efforts around the world. At the Edinburgh World Missionary Conference, church leaders and missionaries assembled to discuss a plan to reach every nation of the world with the gospel in their generation.

As the distinguished American stepped to the lectern, dressed formally in a dark suit and tie, those listening surely felt the gravity of the moment. Edinburgh, with its palatial environment and distinguished history of Christian evangelism, captured the spirit of romance that imbued the room. After more than a week of meetings, with attendees working in committees on a host of problems, those gathered were prepared to enact what they hoped would result in a global revival. They had set the agenda, devoted themselves to prayer, and expected nothing short of a new Pentecost. Hundreds of delegates from societies based in Britain, North America, and continental Europe dominated the conference, but significant contributions also came from representatives of younger churches in Korea, China, Japan, India, Australia, and South Africa.[1] Those seated around the room waited eagerly as the American Methodist layman John R. Mott prepared to speak. In a clear voice, the man pronounced words that would shape global Christianity during the next hundred years: "The end of the conference is the beginning of the conquest."

Mott's militant language perhaps shakes us today, with its allusion to crusading powers conquering foreign lands, and yet his "Closing Address" that night in Edinburgh captured the sense of urgency that inspired representatives to risk their lives for the sake of the gospel. Mott followed his powerful opening statement with a series of questions, skillfully crafted to bolster confidence as each delegate pondered the work that remained:

> The end of the planning is the beginning of the doing. What shall be the issue of these memorable days? Were the streams of influence set in motion by God through this gathering to come to a stop this night, the gathering would yet hold its place as truly notable in His sight. Has it not widened us all? Has it

The **Edinburgh World Missionary Conference (1910)** included more than a thousand delegates from over 150 Protestant missionary boards and societies. Representatives from Great Britain, Europe, and North America were heavily represented in the gathering, but they focused on evangelism in non-Western regions, especially Asia. The first World War disrupted their plans, but their work established the foundation for later ecumenical developments, such as the International Missionary Council (1921) and the World Council of Churches (1948).

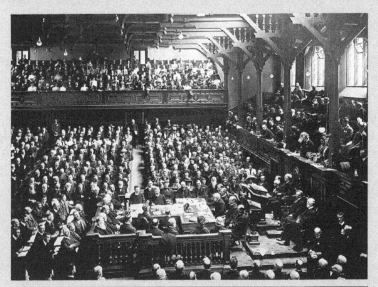

Figure 11.1. World Missionary Conference, University of Edinburgh, 1910

not deepened us all? Has it not humbled us increasingly as we have discovered that the greatest hindrance to the expansion of Christianity lies in ourselves?[2]

Mott's rhetoric dazzled the crowd, capturing the sense of urgency and determination felt by all. Only one question remained: Who will allow this extraordinary opportunity, a divine appointment if there ever was one, to slip away?

The Edinburgh Missionary Conference focused its attention on prospects in Asia more than any other region of the world. The organizers ruled out evangelism in Latin America from the beginning: while Roman Catholics did not participate in the Edinburgh conference, the organizers determined not to expend limited resources in areas where the name of Christ was already known. Further, though delegates from South Africa were among the attendees of the conference, most of the African continent appeared strangely inaccessible, shrouded in mystery by the animism of its traditional religions. Yet the fields appeared to be ripe for harvest in Asia, where

> **Methodism in China** began with the work of missionaries in the middle of the 1800s. By the time a century had passed, the Methodists were a thriving church. The rise of the communist party in 1949, however, pushed Methodism and other Christian denominations to Taiwan and parts of South Asia.

open doors, politically and economically, beckoned the churches to devote resources as never before. In such a context, successful evangelism and church planting seemed not only possible but profitable.

By the time of Edinburgh, Methodists had already served in China for more than half a century. British Methodists first gained access to China, which had a long history of opposition to foreign religions, through the Treaty of Nanking and the imperialist conflicts of the so-called Opium Wars (1839–1844 and 1856–1860). British sovereignty over Hong Kong from 1841 only strained missionary access to the mainland. First arriving in 1847 (MEC) and 1848 (MECS), American Methodists had comparably better success in China through medical and educational missions under pioneering men and women such as Moses and Jane White, their colleague Judson Dwight Collins, and Young John Allen (Lin Lezhi).[3]

Few Methodists will recognize his name, but Robert Samuel Maclay (1824–1907) did more to promote the growth of Methodism in Asia during the late nineteenth century than almost any other missionary in the region. In his *Life Among the Chinese* (1861), Maclay provided a detailed ethnography of Chinese culture, concluding with an impassioned appeal for American Methodists to enlist in God's kingdom work.[4] Maclay thought that political change brought unprecedented opportunities for Christian evangelism, allowing new access to a people almost wholly unaware of Jesus Christ. In a reversal of religious imagery, Maclay implored his readers to cast off their *own* darkness by gaining familiarity with a people in need of Christ: "The time has gone by when ignorance of China characterized alike all classes of society, and when Christians might innocently shut out from their sympathies and evangelism its myriads of people."[5] Instead, he claimed in language reminiscent of an ancient campaign, "Christians must at once gird themselves for this conquest, or the present golden opportunity may pass away forever."[6] He calculated the number of districts, the missionaries that would be required, and the cost for their support. Maclay proposed that if all Protestant denominations did their part (and Methodists surely could contribute their fair share), China might soon have missionaries working in every region of the nation.

One of the foremost Methodist missionaries to Asia, **Robert Samuel Maclay** (1824–1907), served in China, Japan, and Korea. Maclay received ordination from the Methodist Episcopal Church in Baltimore and, in 1847, was appointed to work in China. He served as superintendent of the China Mission from 1852 and subsequently led MEC missions in Japan and Korea.

Figure 11.2. Robert Samuel Maclay

Although Methodists devoted substantial resources in the coming years, nothing like the sort of broad network of missionaries to China that Maclay envisioned ever materialized. Institutional success would have required an unprecedented commitment to the task. To be sure, Christian denominations from different parts of the world sent thousands of missionaries to work in China, but church growth was ultimately thwarted by hostility toward foreign religion and political events beyond their control. As controversy between conservative and liberal Christians raged in the West (particularly in the so-called Fundamentalist-Modernist controversy in the United States), the number of missionaries to China gradually declined. Over time, the Methodist movement became as diverse as the land itself—established at different times and different places, by different bodies of believers with different theological dispositions—yet all belonged to a single Wesleyan heritage.

If, on the other hand, success is measured not by the growth of Methodism as an institution but by the multiplication of Christian disciples, then Methodism in China produced extraordinary fruit. The bold and uncompromising witness of a man widely known as the "John Wesley of China" had a far-reaching impact that extends to the present day.[7] John Sung (1901–1944), whose official name (Shangjie) combines characters for "honorable" and "integrity," was raised the son of poor converts to Christianity. His father was a Methodist Episcopal Church minister to a large church in Fujian province in southeastern China. As a child, Sung assisted his father, who was known for his dynamic preaching; Chinese Christians affectionately referred to the boy as "Little Preacher."

In 1920 John Sung began studies at Ohio Wesleyan in the United States. He preached in local churches, excelled academically, and earned several degrees, including a doctorate in chemistry at Ohio State University. But the course of Sung's life changed dramatically while studying at Union Theological Seminary in New York. Sung deliberated a career in chemistry but felt impressed to reexamine his prior call to Christian evangelism. Union seemed an ideal place for Sung, with leading theologians to learn from in the classroom, but the combative outlook on faith and science overwhelmed him. As in previous institutions, Sung also took on an intense academic workload, hoping to complete a three-year program in only one year. Under the influence of theological modernism, Sung gradually lost faith in the power of prayer and devoted himself to Buddhist meditation instead. Friends worried that mental illness, manifest in depression and increasing paranoia, had overwhelmed his ability to continue as a student. Amid all these pressures, Sung finally and unexpectedly found spiritual release in a powerful conversion experience:

> As days passed, my spirit was [so] weighed down that I felt no peace. On the night of 10 February [1927], I wept and prayed in desperation. Then my sinful

life was played out before me scene after scene, even those secret ones. I recalled a copy of the New Testament at the bottom of a chest. I dug it out and flipped open to Luke 23. I felt as though my spirit had floated out of my body and I was following Jesus, cross on back as He walked towards Golgotha. I could also feel the weight of my sins almost crushing me to death.[8]

Sung's vision of death alongside his savior at the crucifixion brought him to a place of new birth. He changed his name to "John" (after John the Baptist) and began telling everyone around him to repent. This, of course, did not sit well with many of his colleagues at the seminary. Accusingly, he told one liberal professor (the noted theologian Harry Emerson Fosdick), "You are of the devil. You made me lose my faith, and you are causing these other young men to lose their faith."[9] Fosdick and others worried that intense emotional strain had led to a complete mental breakdown and arranged for Sung to be treated at a psychiatric institute at the seminary's expense.

Sung received treatment for several months. Although he rejected their assessment of his mental health, he devoted himself to rest, prayer, and study

Figure 11.3. John Sung with Bethel Evangelistic Band, 1931 (Sung is at far left; Chinese evangelist Andrew Gih is second from right)

of the Bible.[10] Ironically, this period of calm served as the key to his subsequent ministry. Eventually, he sought assistance and release through intervention by the Chinese consul. On his return voyage home, Sung tossed all his academic awards into the ocean, save the PhD diploma he preserved for his parents. Years after his release, the consul related to a missionary, "Sung was no more crazy than you or I; he just had a good case of old-fashioned religion, and it was so unusual in New York City that they thought he was crazy."[11]

Upon return to China in 1927, Sung embarked on an unprecedented evangelistic campaign. He began by assisting in class leaders' training sessions for the Methodist Episcopal Mission and soon led evangelistic outreaches under the Hinghwa Conference of the Methodist Episcopal Church. Although Western clothing was growing increasingly popular in China, Sung wore only the gown of a Chinese laborer as a sign of his commitment to the commoner. His dramatic style drew crowds to hear the young preacher. One Methodist missionary recorded a typical scene:

> He would race back and forth on the platform or leap over the Communion rail and stand in the aisles. At times he would walk down the aisles and point his finger in the face of someone in the audience, then rush back to the front of the church and perhaps stand on the Communion rail to finish his sermon! People in considerable numbers came forward after every meeting to pray and to accept Christ.[12]

Sung's command of the Bible, animated preaching (though often unconventional, to be sure), and commitment to a message of repentance attracted listeners first by the hundreds and then by the thousands.[13]

By the mid-1930s, Sung had emerged as one of the most well-known evangelists in all of Asia, traveling widely throughout China, Singapore, Malaysia, Thailand, Indonesia, and beyond. His work among the Methodists remained constant (he was formally ordained an elder by his conference in 1938), but his conflict with liberal Methodist missionaries, association with indigenous churches, and tendency to reject the interference of Western denominations diminished his rep-

The renowned Chinese evangelist **John Sung** taught an uncompromising message of repentance that transformed Christianity in the region. In his *Diary*, Sung records a hymn he composed that captures the simplicity of his Spirit-filled witness:

> My all to Him I give
> A life off'ring filled with the Holy Spirit,
> A member of His body, I shall become
> Clear is my heart, my eyes no longer dim.
> Yes, the Lord's will be done, as I
> Walk along the heav'nly road with Him.[15]

utation among Methodists abroad.[14] Everywhere he went, Sung preached a striking message of repentance from sin and baptism in the Spirit. "Oratorical prowess does not convict the sinner," Sung noted in one diary. "It is the power of God that leaves sinners at a loss for words. Some sinners lack the strength to confess their sins, because of social status. But they cannot rest until they make a clean break from their sins through confession."[16] As he preached, the people responded with tearful confessions. Others claimed healing from longstanding ailments. By the time of his death from tuberculosis in 1944, some estimate that nearly 10 percent of all Christians in China had come to faith through his ministry.[17]

In a period when the social aspect of evangelism led missionaries to emphasize education, medicine, and matters of justice, John Sung's unrelenting denunciation of sin appeared out of touch to many of his contemporaries. Yet John Wesley's sermons persistently underscore the centrality of repentance both for unbelievers and believers alike. Wesley's sermon "The Way to the Kingdom" (1746), for example, provides a characteristic denunciation of sin. His text for the sermon, "The kingdom of God is at hand: repent, ye, and believe the gospel" (Mk 1:15), appears nearly two hundred times in personal records of sermons delivered between 1742 and 1790.[18] Against an optimistic account of humanity, Wesley proclaimed an unswerving gospel of repentance in the knowledge that sin has left all people depraved: "Know thyself to be a sinner, and what manner of sinner thou art. . . . Know that thou art totally corrupted in every power, in every faculty of thy soul. . . . The eyes of thine understanding are darkened, so that they cannot discern God or the things of God. The clouds of ignorance and error rest upon thee, and cover thee with the shadow of death."[19]

Wesley refused to limit repentance to those outside the church. In his sermon "The Repentance of Believers" (1767), Wesley explained that by repentance believers gain "a conviction of our utter sinfulness and guiltiness and helplessness."[20] Against the tendency to imagine that justification eliminates the power of sin, Wesley claimed that the children of God recognize that they are helpless sinners apart from the ongoing work of grace. Though its power no longer reigns as the guiding principle of the individual's life, sin remains. Pride, jealousy,

Dr. Mary Stone (Shi Meiyu) (1873–1954), the renowned Chinese physician, resigned from the MEC's Woman's Foreign Missionary Society in protest against modern liberalism before cofounding the Bethel Mission of Shanghai, a vast ministry that "consisted of a hospital, nursing school, seminary, high school, and a 1,500-seat tabernacle."

Figure 11.4. Dr. Mary Stone

anger, and self-will all endure, and only the Holy Spirit will bring about entire sanctification.

> By repentance we feel the sin remaining in our hearts, and cleaving to our words and actions. By faith we receive the power of God in Christ, purifying our hearts and cleansing our hands. By repentance we are still sensible that we deserve punishment for all our tempers and words and actions. By faith we are conscious that our advocate with the Father is continually pleading for us, and thereby continually turning aside all condemnation and punishment from us. By repentance we have an abiding conviction that there is no help in us. By faith we receive not only mercy, but "grace to help in *every* time of need."[21]

All are helpless without Christ. All depend on the power of the Holy Spirit to conquer the ever-present tendency to sin. The "John Wesley of China," though primarily working among an unreached people, simply extended the teachings of Wesley to Asia.

The influence of indigenous leaders such as John Sung proved especially important in the years that followed. In 1933 British Methodists in China, including the United Methodist Free Churches, the Bible Christians, and the Methodist New Connexion, united in a single body.[22] Similarly, several American Methodist denominations—including former missions of the MEC, MECS, and MPC—merged in 1940 to form the Methodist Church in China.[23] Despite these unions, the tides of political change were greater than the churches could withstand. Missionary activity in China ended with the culmination of the Chinese civil war (the conflict was particularly intense from 1945 until its conclusion in 1950). The rise of communism forced reorganization of the Christian churches under the supervision of the Chinese government, eliminating denominational distinctions among Prot-estants. China established a policy known as the "three-self church," which severed ties with Western ecclesial authorities in favor of churches that were self-governing, self-supporting, and self-propagating.[24] Ironically, these principles of autonomy mirrored those increasingly favored by many mis-sionaries and even reflected the goals established at the Edinburgh World Missionary Conference. However, China's policy of exclusion differed by threatening to dissolve not only the paternal oversight but even the fraternal relationships enjoyed by Christian denominations. Methodist missionaries were required to leave, but many joined the work in Southeast Asian nations such as Indonesia, Malaysia, and Singapore, where Methodists previously had established thriving churches in the latter half of the nineteenth century.[25] Chinese Methodists lost their denominational identity, but John Sung's legacy continues to be revered by Christians throughout the region.

Much more could be said of the establishment and growth of Methodism in Asia. After years serving in China, R. S. Maclay extended the reach of Methodism as a missionary in Japan between 1873 and 1885. Japan had been closed to missionary presence for more than two centuries, but the United States forced Japan to enter into trade in 1873. Within a year, numerous religious bodies flooded Japan, including the Methodists, who established stations in Tokyo, Nagasaki, and elsewhere. In a matter of years, the mission ordained its first Japanese pastor, Yoitsu Honda, and soon developed an annual conference with nearly twenty Japanese ministers. Honda eventually served as the first bishop of the united Japan Methodist Church (composed of MEC, MECS, and Canadian Methodists) in 1907. In later years, political tensions with the West increased exponentially, and in 1941 the Japanese government forced all Protestant churches, as well as the Greek Orthodox Church, to merge their property in the formation of a single ecclesial body: The United Church of Christ in Japan (known in Japanese as "Kyodan"). After the war, the Methodist Board of Missions assessed the state of the churches and determined that American bombs had destroyed nearly half the churches in the nation and almost every church in Tokyo. In Hiroshima and Nagasaki, cities devastated by the use of atomic bombs by the United States, hundreds of Methodists were killed along with the destruction of churches and schools in these communities.

> **Methodism in Southeast Asia** traces its roots to the pioneering work of missionaries such as the Indian-born William Fitzjames Oldham (1857–1937) in Singapore. Oldham helped establish Methodism through work in education, served as missionary bishop for the region, and directed the expansion of Methodism into Malaysia and the Philippines. Other evangelists from China and Sri Lanka furthered Methodist ministry. Today, in addition to many autonomous Methodist churches, other Wesleyan bodies such as the Church of the Nazarene have active church and educational ministries throughout the region.

Many credit Maclay with the introduction of Methodism in Korea, too, after he received permission from the government for limited medical and

Figure 11.5. Methodist Episcopal Church Sunday school, Korea

educational activity in 1884. When MEC and MECS missionaries arrived
the following year (in part by request of the Korean people), they engaged
in limited evangelism and only gradually introduced public worship as more
and more Koreans joined the church. Secret meetings were common.
Baptisms were unique and sacred occasions. Many burned their fetishes,
believed to ward off evil spirits, anxious of the consequences. One early
chronicler remarked, "Did it cost them anything? The cost was frightful. . . .
Ostracism from their friends and relatives, and persecution was sure to
follow."[26] Although the Protestant missionaries in Korea (including Methodists and Presbyterians) agreed in 1908 to form the United Church of
Christ in Korea, the sending churches from North America refused. Nonetheless, the churches agreed to a single Bible translation, a common hymnal,
and regional boundaries to their work. Under Japanese rule, Methodist
churches in Korea suffered persecution and strict political control. Some
churches were closed, others were repurposed, and the Korean Methodist
bishop was required to forbid the use of the Old Testament and the book of
Revelation for its condemnation of the powers of this world.[27] In the 1930s
Korean Methodists, along with other Christians, faced the challenge of the

Shinto shrine controversy, as the Japanese government required attendance at Shinto rites that many Christians deemed incompatible with their faith. Refusal often led to arrest, and some missionaries were deported. Finally, in 1937, the Korean Methodist Church agreed to comply with shrine attendance on patriotic (rather than religious) grounds.[28] Just months before Japan surrendered to the United States in 1945, the government forced the merger of all Korean churches. Methodists later returned to their previous ecclesial structures, but Korean Methodism ever since shares many features of Presbyterian church polity (such as a ministerial appointment system rather than itineracy).[29] Today, Korean Methodism is among the most robust bodies of Methodism in the world, with a devoted membership and a stout commitment to evangelism in Russia, Africa, and further abroad.[30]

At the Edinburgh World Missionary Conference of 1910, the Methodist layman John Mott articulated a plan for world evangelism in the clearest terms. Representatives from Britain, America, and Europe pledged their energy and financial resources to the work of world evangelism. Mott offered a final, inspirational prayer: "God grant that we all of us may in these next moments solemnly resolve henceforth so to plan and so to act, so to live and so to sacrifice, that our spirit of reality may become contagious among those to whom we go . . . and that before many of us taste death we shall see the Kingdom of God come with power."[31] None present could possibly have predicted what lay ahead when Mott stepped away from the lectern. Within the decade, the onset of the Great War set nations at odds in the deadliest conflict the world had ever seen, dashing hope in their spiritual commission in the process. Their focus on Asia proved fruitful in many respects, yet they could not have foreseen the cultural changes that would politicize atheism in communist-controlled nations such as China or the Soviet Union, nor had they anticipated the exponential growth of Christianity in Africa. Ironically, the two World Wars hastened the rise of autonomous churches, as meagre resources left Protestant denominations incapable of exerting the influence they had once maintained. Instead of world evangelism, the conference provided the groundwork for the twentieth-century ecumenical movement and the formation of the World Council of Churches (1948).[32] Yet the future of global Methodism arguably took its most surprising turn in the one region conference organizers had intentionally ignored: Latin America.

CHAPTER TWELVE

....

Inspired Voices

JOHN WESLEY READ SPANISH. He learned the language in 1736, hoping to communicate with Native Americans who had acquired it from Jesuit and Franciscan missionaries.[1] In the end, the plan came to nothing—Governor Oglethorpe in Georgia opposed the idea. Still, Wesley made use of his new proficiency in reading seventeenth-century mystics such as Miguel de Molinos. Perhaps more important, his knowledge of Spanish reveals a deeper lesson about the man: John Wesley was willing to learn more to reach many.

Expansion into Central and South America would seem a natural avenue for such a mission-minded people as the Methodists. Like their founder, Methodists were willing to sacrifice for the good of others. Dr. Thomas Coke, as noted previously, discovered to his surprise that Methodism had already reached the Caribbean when he unexpectedly landed on the island of Antigua in 1786. By the time Coke set sail on his fateful journey to India and Ceylon (today Sri Lanka), a mission halfway around the world, Methodists had already established a network of preaching circuits serving thousands of believers in islands throughout the Caribbean. Still, while Methodism quickly spread in some places, expansion into other unreached areas did not come so easily. In this chapter, I will explain how two trajectories of belief and practice shaped the growth of Methodism in Latin America and why tensions between these two visions of Methodism may portend the future the movement.

The prior establishment of Roman Catholicism distinguishes the work of Methodist missionaries in Latin America from their ministry in so many other parts of the world. Consider this: Protestantism dates from the early 1500s (Luther famously published his Ninety-Five Theses in 1517), but it took more than *three hundred years* for the first Protestant sermon to be preached in Latin America. By that time, Roman Catholicism already had deep roots, and Protestants often faced political roadblocks to their evangelistic plans.

The first sermon delivered in Spanish by a Methodist occurred in 1853. Benigno Cárdenas had been a Roman Catholic priest before the appointment of a French-born bishop incited him to protest. As with other Roman Catholics in New Mexico, Cárdenas felt that Rome neglected the churches in the region. The appointment of the new bishop poured salt in their wounds, particularly among priests who felt a strong sense of nationalism or served in far-flung dioceses.[2] Cárdenas traveled to Rome to make his voice heard, but the trip seemed destined to fail almost from the beginning. On his return voyage, Cárdenas stopped in London and met William Rule, a British Methodist who had previously served in Spain. Rule encouraged Cárdenas to join the Methodists. Soon, under the auspices of the Methodist Episcopal Church, Cárdenas was headed home to form a society. Local authorities denied Cárdenas access to a hall for services, so (in the spirit of early British Methodists) he decided to hold an open-air service in the main plaza in front of the governor's palace in Santa Fe. On November 20, 1853, Cárdenas surrendered his Roman Catholic ministerial credentials and delivered the first sermon in Spanish by any Methodist.

> The **first sermon delivered in Spanish** was given by a former Roman Catholic priest named Benigno Cárdenas. Cárdenas discovered Methodism in London while returning from a trip to Rome, where he protested against the decision to appoint a French bishop to oversee the Roman Catholics in New Mexico. In 1853 Cárdenas addressed a crowd in the plaza in Santa Fe, marking the commencement of Methodist ministry in Spanish.

More than three decades earlier, an anonymous layperson had formed a small class of English-speaking Methodists in Argentina and wrote to the Methodist Episcopal Missionary Society in New York requesting denominational support. There was no immediate response. Then, in 1835, Bishop James O. Andrew (whose slaveholding later brought the Methodist Episcopal Church to schism) sent Fountain E. Pitts to survey ministry opportunities in Argentina, Uruguay, and Brazil. The following year, American Methodist missionaries arrived in Rio de Janeiro and Buenos Aires. Their work, however, was short lived. Financial support from the US soon evaporated in the wake of schism, missionary families suffered dire health problems, and opposition from Roman Catholics continually hampered their work.[3] As a result, Methodism managed only tepid growth among English-speaking people until the Scottish-born Methodist James Francis Thomson began preaching the first Protestant sermons in Spanish in South America on May 25, 1867. Thomson, a trailblazing figure in Protestant missions, subsequently worked his way into the interior of Argentina and later preached extensively in both Uruguay (1868) and Paraguay (1881). Yet Thomson's message almost by necessity involved not only a call to faith in Christ but simultaneously a rejection of Roman Catholicism.

Anti-Catholicism contributed to the decision to appoint William Butler to the mission in Mexico in 1872. Butler and his wife Clementina had previously served in India, where they came to distrust the evangelistic appeal of Roman Catholicism. They now believed that the Catholic presence in Latin America was likely ineffective too. As secretary of the American and Foreign Christian Union from 1869, Butler traveled widely in Mexico. Yet Butler and others knew that the most fruitful ministry would be accomplished by those who had been born and raised in the area. The contributions of the Woman's Foreign Missionary Society once again proved crucial to

Figure 12.1. William Butler

the growth of Methodism. Hundreds of women served in education, nursing, and Bible teaching, slowly shaping the faith of nations. Some locals feared that Methodist missionaries were political agents working to annex more and more land to the US, but others felt empowered by the gospel and responded to the opportunity to engage in dialogue about the Bible and matters of faith.[4]

Latent distrust for Catholicism also figured in the appointment of Alejo Hernández (1842–1875) to ministry in Mexico City by the MECS in 1872. Hernández, the first Mexican Methodist minister, had studied for the priesthood at Aguascalientes, Mexico, when he joined Benito Juárez's

Resistance Army following the French invasion of Mexico in 1862. Already frustrated by the Roman Catholic Church's support for the invasion, Hernández read an anti-Catholic tract and traveled to Brownsville, Texas, where he hoped he might access a Spanish Bible. At Brownsville, Hernández visited an English church and unexpectedly underwent a profound conversion of faith. He later described the experience in words strikingly similar to John Wesley's at Aldersgate: "I felt that God's Spirit was there, although I could not understand a word that was being said. I felt my heart strangely warmed. . . . Never did I hear an organ play so sweetly, never did human voices sound so lovely to me, never did people look so beautiful as on that occasion. I went away weeping for joy."[5] Hernández returned to Mexico and in 1873 organized the first Methodist church in Mexico City.

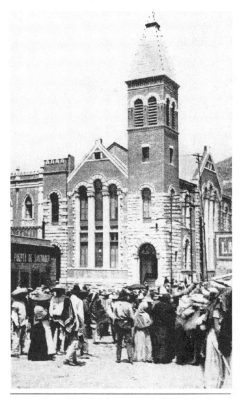

Figure 12.2. Methodist Episcopal Church, Pachuca, Mexico, c. 1918

Inspired by the influence of William Taylor (1821–1902), the Methodist missionary to Africa and Asia, a vision for self-supporting Methodist churches in Latin America became more and more prominent. Teachers and preachers worked assiduously along the west coast of South America and deeper inland, sharing Wesleyan beliefs with the people in Bolivia, Peru, Chile, Venezuela, Costa Rica, and Panama.[6] Methodists established annual conferences in these and other nations, yet the failure of American Methodists to elect resident episcopal bishops in places like Brazil and Mexico eventually stultified growth. Although petitions for resident leadership were sent to the General Conferences of 1922 and 1926,

Although many associate Latin American liberation theology with Roman Catholicism, the Methodist theologian **José Míguez Bonino** (1924–2012) is widely remembered as one of the most important figures of the movement. Bonino was born in Argentina and educated in Buenos Aires before studying at Emory University and Union Theological Seminary. After his ordination in 1948, Bonino served as a pastor and professor, an observer at the Second Vatican Council, and a member of the presidium of the World Council of Churches.

Figure 12.3. José Míguez Bonino, 1974

the church refused to act. In 1930, wearied by resistance and indecisiveness, local leaders formed both the Methodist Church of Brazil and the Methodist Church of Mexico. Decades later, other nations followed a similar path.[7]

Latin American Methodism steadily diversified across nations, cultures, and dialects. In some regions, Wesleyan beliefs and practices reflected these new contexts, while in others Wesleyan thought remain mediated by the forms of worship and customs of sending churches from abroad. This variation, as explained by the noted Argentinian Methodist theologian José Míguez Bonino, resulted in forms of Latin American Methodism initiated by (1) the missionary voices of the British and American Methodists who first established English churches, (2) the holiness heritage of Free Methodists, Nazarenes, Salvation Army, and other Wesleyan churches, or (3) a Pentecostal variety of Methodism that focused on the gifts of the Spirit, such as speaking in tongues.[8] The early history of Latin American Methodism reflects British and American missionary expansion, but that lineage may be less influential than that of the Methodist churches influenced by the broader Pentecostal renewal of the early 1900s.

Twentieth-century Methodists, along with other Latin American Protestants, confronted a perennial problem: what Bonino aptly called a "crisis of conscience." From the introduction of Roman Catholicism in the sixteenth century to the arrival of Protestantism in the nineteenth, Latin American churches contributed to the sharp divide between rich and poor through alliances with powerful political parties. One midcentury letter of caution to the pope at the Vatican illustrates the concern: "Beware, brother Paul. Religion and the Church have constantly been used in Latin America to justify and buttress injustice, oppression, repression, exploitation, persecution, the murder of the poor."[9] Protestants, including Methodists, often imagined that they enjoyed a position of autonomy that distinguished their churches from the collusion they detected among Roman Catholics—Bonino describes, for example, growing up in an "aggressive and even violent" confrontation with Catholicism.[10] Gradually, however, even Protestants began to recognize that their own churches had become complicit in the misuse of political power by sanctioning the benevolent colonialism of the churches that first shared the gospel with them.

As a result, Methodists in Latin America have needed to read *against* and *within* mediating traditions. In fact, a willingness to challenge mediating church authorities gave rise to one of the most vibrant Wesleyan bodies in Latin America today. The Methodist Pentecostal Church (MPC) of Chile finds its origin in a revival inspired by international connections among Methodists in India, Britain, and North America. In the early years of the twentieth century, the American Methodist missionary Willis Collins Hoover (1856–1936) was serving as district superintendent and pastor of a large congregation in Valparaíso, Chile, with his wife. Around 1908, Mary Anne Hoover, who had studied at the Methodist Chicago Training School for Home and Foreign Missions, received a publication from her former classmate and Methodist missioner Minnie Abrams (1859–1912). The pamphlet, *The Baptism of the Holy Ghost and Fire* (1906), explained Abrams's experiences in the so-called Mukti revivals in India, where Abrams worked among hundreds of widowed girls alongside the educator and social reformer Pandita Ramabai (1858–1922). The Mukti revivals began with a renewed emphasis on holiness (influenced, in part, by the Keswick movement in England), but soon some women reported Pentecostal experiences such as speaking in unknown languages (spiritual "tongues" akin to the earliest Christians in the book of Acts), prophetic utterances, and miraculous visions. Abrams and other leaders of the Mukti movement regarded this "baptism of the Spirit" as a third work of God available to every Christian after justification and entire sanctification.

Bolstered by these reports, the Hoovers encouraged their Methodist congregation in Chile to seek revival in their own church. They began with extended periods of prayer. People unexpectedly repented of secret sins. Debts were paid, relationships healed, and several notoriously immoral individuals were converted. Others experienced dramatic reactions to what they regarded as the work of the Spirit—tears, laughter, groaning, strange tongues, bold witness, and ecstatic visions became more and more common.[11] Hundreds of people began to attend church services, but with expansion came criticism too. Some pastors in the area deemed the revival a sham. Others complained to the bishop and sought out political avenues to suppress the spread of their alleged fanaticism.

When the Missionary Society of the Methodist Episcopal Church heard news of the revival, allegations of misconduct and discredit to the good reputation of Methodism in the region outweighed other reports of conversions, rising membership, and broad spiritual renewal. Remarkably, Methodist spirituality gave rise to accusations of enthusiasm once again. At the annual conference in Valparaíso (1910), the MEC bishop formed a disciplinary commission to prepare charges against Hoover. The commission determined that Hoover had taught and disseminated "false and anti-Methodist doctrines," including teachings on the manifestations of the Spirit, belief in the demonic, the practice of raising hands in worship, and sundry miraculous claims. The commission recommended the following resolution:

Figure 12.4. Willis Collins Hoover

> Inasmuch as certain false doctrines such as the teaching that the baptism in the Holy Spirit is accompanied by the gift of tongues, visions, miracles of healing and other manifestations, have been disseminated in various parts of this Conference and represented as the doctrines of the Methodist Episcopal Church, we, by this present declaration, state that those doctrines are anti-Methodist, contrary to the Scriptures and irrational, and our members are put on notice that they ought not to accept them as the teachings of our church.[12]

Removed from his role as district superintendent and unable to reconcile with the bishop, Hoover appealed to the early history of Methodism and attempted to publish translations of Wesley's journals for a local newspaper as evidence of his faithfulness to the long heritage of the movement. All to no avail. In 1910, with the encouragement of his wife and congregation, Hoover resigned from ministry as a missionary in the MEC.

I am breaking relations with the church organization I have served all my life. Nevertheless, I want my brothers to know I have not ceased being a Methodist. I follow Wesley faithfully. I have not separated myself from Wesley's doctrines, nor those of the church. If I withdraw and take another name it is only because they want to dismiss me without showing proof of error. I put myself in the hands of God to serve Chile with all my heart, as I have always done. My heart is here. The voice of God is here. . . . . This separation is not a war. It is a separation not from Methodism, but simply from the government of the Methodist Church, because of conscience.[13]

Hoover's church divided in the wake of his forced resignation, but hundreds of members joined with two affiliated groups of former Methodist Chileans caught up in the same revival and formed La Iglesia Metodista Pentecostal (The Methodist Pentecostal Church). The new church quickly spread throughout Chile and, despite another church split in 1932, became the largest Protestant denomination in the nation.[14]

The history of **Methodism in Chile** serves as an important reminder of competing forces within Latin American Christianity, including churches derived from British and American Methodist missionaries, the Holiness Movement, and Pentecostalism. After the Methodist Episcopal Church established a district in the South American annual conference in 1893, a revival led by the American missionaries Willis and Mary Anne Hoover led to the formation of the Methodist Pentecostal Church in 1909.

Members of the Methodist Pentecostal Church in Chile, with Hoover serving as superintendent, believed that they had remained faithful to Wesleyan teaching. How true was their claim? Although Wesley rarely used the phrase "baptism with the Holy Ghost," he certainly identified entire sanctification and the doctrine of perfection with the fullness of the Spirit promised to those who find new life in Christ.[15] Wesley seems to have been convinced, too, by the theological assertions made by his protégé John Fletcher, which linked Christian perfection to "baptism in the Spirit." To our knowledge, John Wesley never experienced any proto-Pentecostal gifts of the Spirit, but he questioned the condemnation of Montanists in the early church (who were known for their ecstatic prophecies) as a conflict of authority rather than a rejection of their spirituality. While MEC leaders rejected the claim that Spirit baptism denotes a necessary "step" in the Christian life (whether evidenced by speaking in tongues or not), Hoover and others were hardly innovating in any "anti-Methodist" or "irrational" manner, as charged by the commission.

The rise of the Methodist Pentecostal Church in Chile reflects not so much a battle over doctrine, then, as the promotion of ennobling experiences of the Spirit. In their acceptance of inward renewal by the baptism of the Holy Spirit, Chileans made Methodism their own as they began participating in worship using their own gifts and speaking in their own tongues (even giving voice to heavenly languages). Spiritual gifts democratized Chilean Methodism. The organization of the church (polity), adherence to class meetings, and the persistence in historic Methodist practices such as infant baptism remained fully intact, even while new methods of evangelism and new patterns in worship began to emerge.[16] The Methodist Pentecostal Church flourished as the people were liberated from the demands of conformity to North American cultural forms. From this perspective, the Methodist Pentecostal Church and the MEC were "simply two cultural variations of the same Methodist tradition."[17] Despite their condemnation, Chilean Methodists simultaneously recovered an early Methodist tradition (similar to the "enthusiasm" that left the Wesleys preaching in the open air outside many Church of England parishes) and challenged mediating traditions in favor of the needs of believers in their own context: "The difference between the Methodists and us does not lie in a different doctrine. It is just that they have merely the Methodist doctrines whilst we experience them."[18]

The Pentecostal revival of Methodism in Chile is a dramatic incident but certainly not an isolated one. In fact, many Protestants throughout Latin America, even if they do not explicitly identify as Pentecostal, worship in just such a fashion and believe that the Holy Spirit works miraculously in their lives. In Brazil, for example, many Methodists could easily be mistaken for Pentecostals, with "forms of worship, preaching, and prayer" that reflect a Pentecostal ethos. For this reason, Methodist churches are often effective

For centuries, Roman Catholicism and Christianity were practically synonymous in Latin America. During the nineteenth century, Protestants gradually made inroads into these countries through the work of laypeople and foreign missionaries. Since the middle of the twentieth century, most Methodist churches in Latin America have become **autonomous**, including the largest such body, the Methodist Church in Brazil. Theological and political antagonism between Protestants and Roman Catholics remain a longstanding source of conflict.

at attracting the poor and illiterate "who cannot read hymn-books or church bulletins" but recognize that they belong to the family of God.[19]

Still, Bonino and other Latin American Methodists have argued that more work remains to be done. Above all, they have suffered from a dearth of Methodist literature in the vernacular, leaving many unable to plumb the depths of their own Christian heritage.[20] While many missionaries to Latin America have emphasized Wesley's teachings on piety, holiness, and individual spiritual renewal, Wesley also wrote pointedly on matters of social and economic concern, such as the plight of the poor. In his *Thoughts on the Present Scarcity of Provisions* (1773), for example, Wesley provided a first-hand account of the suffering he encountered in his travels.

> Why are thousands of people starving, perishing for want, in every part of the nation? The fact I know; I have seen it with my eyes, in every corner of the land. I have known those who could only afford to eat a little coarse food once every day. I have known one in London (and one that a few years before had all the conveniences of life) picking up from a dunghill stinking sprats, and carrying them home for herself and her children. I have known another gathering the bones which the dogs had left in the streets, and making broth of them, to prolong a wretched life! I have heard a third artlessly declare, "Indeed I was very faint, and so weak I could hardly walk, until my dog, finding nothing at home, went out, and brought in a good sort of bone, which I took out of his mouth, and made a pure dinner!" Such is the case at this day of multitudes of people, in a land flowing, as it were, with milk and honey! abounding with all the necessaries, the inconveniencies, the superfluities of life![21]

The proper response to such poverty, according to Wesley, involved both individual sacrifice and government intervention to force down the price of food. Wesley avoided generalities. Businesses that once employed many people now only could afford to employ a few since demand for products had decreased with rising costs. The price of bread had inflated with the rise of the distilleries and the production of alcohol. The proliferation of horses and carriages from industrialization had inflated the price of oats and simultaneously decreased the number of farmers who bred cattle, sheep, and other livestock to feed the towns. Rents on properties had increased as landholders sought to maintain exorbitant lifestyles through increasing incomes, and inordinate taxes on land only heightened the crisis. Instead, Wesley proposed a series of acts that might counter the trend and help the neediest individuals. Prohibiting distilleries would sink the price of corn and end the scourge of drunkenness, and taxes on the export of horses and

John Wesley believed that Methodists had personal responsibility to **care for the poor** and found several ways to provide for them through the work of the societies. His threefold model of Christian financial stewardship—*gain* all you can, *save* all you can, *give* all you can—prioritizes helping others against the temptation to accumulate wealth. In South America, the wide reach of Methodist and Wesleyan denominations such as the Salvation Army have maintained this much-neglected aspect of Wesleyan theology.

Figure 12.5. Salvation Army cart requesting donations of used clothing, shoes, newspapers, and sundry items for minors, Brazil, 1930

the ownership of carriages would rebalance the livestock supply and reduce the national debt. Wesley's solution—the discouragement of luxuries through targeted taxation—may or may not be good economic policy, but Wesley was no capitalist. He thought that Christian social policy ought to reflect biblical teachings on concern for the poor, even in a nation such as his own, "where there is no fear of God, where there is such a deep, avowed, thorough contempt for all religion."[22]

Latin American Methodism has much to gain from the recovery of Wesleyan social ethics and much to lose from its neglect.[23] Still, the widely reported saying that "Roman Catholicism chose the poor, but the poor chose Pentecostalism" should also serve as a warning for Methodists. Reading against mediating traditions involves more than replacing the nineteenth-century Methodist teachings on personal holiness, for instance, with a revival of Wesleyan social concern. Latin American Methodism participated in a protest against power in part by embracing the work of the Spirit among the laity. When the Spirit descended upon the people, their bodies became the mouthpieces of God, and their dignity as image-bearers could be recognized.[24] In this, we may discover that the future of Methodism worldwide depends on those who reject the tendency to homogenize and embrace the diversity that has always existed in the movement.

EPILOGUE

....

Hope for the Future

SEARCH ONLINE FOR "METHODIST CHURCH," and you may discover the website of the World Methodist Council (WMC). With photos of churches and leaders from around the world, the WMC includes an overview of its vibrant, international church family. "The World Methodist Council is made up of 80 Methodist, Wesleyan and related Uniting and United churches representing over 80 million members in 138 countries."[1] Methodism began in Oxford, England, in the 1720s with just a few individuals. By the time of John Wesley's death in 1791, however, there were more than 57,000 Methodists in Britain and, perhaps surprisingly, an equal number across the Atlantic. In fact, it wasn't long before Methodism constituted the single largest denomination in the United States. By 1900, Methodist membership in the United States had grown to nearly 4.5 million members, and at the time of the formation of the United Methodist Church in 1968, there were more than 10.5 million Methodists in the United States alone.[2] Yet few American Methodists today appreciate the sizeable body of Methodists around the world. Indeed, right now, there are about three times more Methodists in Ghana than in Great Britain, and there are about as many Methodists in Africa as there are in the United States.

> The **World Methodist Council** (WMC) is an association of churches that find their roots in the Methodist or Wesleyan tradition, including a number of United or Uniting churches around the world. The WMC, which began at a conference at the Wesley Chapel in London, England, in 1881, works to support member churches through support for evangelism, educational programming, and ecumenical engagement.

Methodism is diverse. Although this large family traces its roots back to the teachings of John and Charles Wesley, the expansion of global Methodism emerged amid a rather complex network of theological, geographical, and cultural influences that mediated the spread of one of the most influential forms of Christianity in the world today. In this book, I've traced some of the many strands of growth in Wesleyan and Methodist churches across time and place to reveal the inherent adaptability of this global movement. Wherever Methodists sent missionaries and evangelists, they soon discovered that— almost inevitably—classes had already formed, lay leaders had already established patterns of Bible study and accountability, and the teachings of the Wesleys had been promoted to encourage holy living and the transformation of local communities.

Methodism flourished most when Wesleyans adapted their founders' influence to the needs of the people. The earliest Methodists in Britain preached not to establish a new church but to renew the Church of England.

Figure E.1. John Wesley, 1788

Heart religion proved attractive to broad swaths of the population that longed for a deeper piety and spiritual expression than they typically encountered in the established church. Revivalism and field preaching offered a dynamic of faith—often described, in Wesley's terms, as the "witness of the Spirit"—that met a deeply felt need among Christians who continued to identify with the Anglican Prayer Book.

In North America, though John Wesley's writings were always valued, Asbury and others recognized that "Daddy" Wesley couldn't rule them from afar. Wesley had little knowledge of the beliefs and practices of a truly *American* Methodism. Wesley couldn't fully appreciate what it meant that Methodists had been imbued with the spirit of democracy or the experience of striking out into frontier spaces. Asbury's influence, along with that of so many other men and women, appealed to early Americans because

American Methodism met people in the particularity of their context. Methodists knew what it was to be outsiders—scorned by the established church, even as the colonists felt silenced by the crown—but they adapted to American life in the formation of a new, more democratic connection.

As Methodism spread around the world, the uplifting message of a God who pours out the Holy Spirit on all people ennobled and dignified those who felt the crushing weight of colonial powers. In Sri Lanka and India, Methodism flourished most when the links to the old world died—whether in the literal passing of Dr. Thomas Coke, the embrace of "round tables," or a realization of Christ along the Indian road. And in remote areas of Africa, where traditional religions seemed an insuperable obstacle to evangelism, Methodism succeeded by becoming truly African—whether in witness in the inland districts of Ghana's Ashanti region or in martyrdom in the harsh climate of East Africa. In Asia, Methodists preached good news to those who longed for reconciliation with God and provided a language of repentance, renewal, and discipleship. In Latin America, Methodism often outpaced the theological boundaries of the missionary church as Spirit-inspired utterances brought renewal that contravened established norms. In very different ways, wherever they went, Methodists fulfilled John Wesley's prescient claim, "I look upon all the world as my parish."

In the world of art, experts can sometimes confirm the legitimacy of an artwork by looking for a *pentimento*—the trace evidence of a painting underneath the visible exterior. As layers of paint fade over time, or through the assistance of X-ray or infrared technology, experts can detect signs of an earlier image that preceded the composition a viewer sees on the surface. The subject who sat for a portrait, for instance, may have remained the same, but small adjustments in perspective or positioning may become visible beneath the image.

Methodists often debate the marks of ecclesial authenticity. "Hasn't contemporary Methodism departed from its roots in Wesley?" one friend recently asked me. The question reveals a deep yearning to find the "true" Methodism in a past now lost from sight but remaining underneath the brushstrokes of subsequent generations. In Italian, *pentimento* means "repentance," much like the English word *penitent*. The search for "true"

Methodism suggests as much: in order to return to the original, repentance is required. In many ways, this book shows how complicated such a task may be, since Methodism never developed in the linear process so often assumed in controversies over authenticity.

What is Methodism? The question may be answered from a number of different angles. *Historically*, the movement originated in England during the early eighteenth century, as a small group of young men at Oxford shared their belief that the love of God in Christ might be known everywhere. *Theologically*, the movement centers on biblical teachings about God's gracious work of love extended freely to all people by the power of the Holy Spirit. *Ecclesially*, the movement encompasses a range of different church polities (governments) that share in common a commitment to connectional ministry among people in need of God's love. In short, Methodists are a diverse body of Protestants who found inspiration in the teachings of John and Charles Wesley, discovered the love of God in an experience of grace, and formed connections in life and ministry through networks that span the world.

Several features of the movement stand out for ongoing deliberation. Rather than imagining Wesleyan or Methodist beliefs and practices in isolation, however, I believe that major Methodist themes must be considered in mutually informing pairs held in tension.

Grace and responsibility. Methodists combine two pivotal ideas: God's gracious work of love restores people to lives of responsibility. On our own, we are incapable of following the ways of God. Sin abounds. Yet through the gracious work of God in Christ, sinners are redeemed, reconciled, and renewed by the power of the Spirit. This change leads not to inaction but action; instead of waiting in silence, Methodists seek God through the means of grace and pursue holiness with their entire lives. John Wesley wasn't shy about telling Methodists how to live. He gave guidance on how to use their time, what activities they should and shouldn't participate in, and how they ought to spend their money. God's grace remains at the center. Opinions may have changed about cultural practices, but the Wesleyan belief that Christian responsibility differs from cultural norms remains strong.

Biblical and sacramental. Wesley was a man of one book: the Bible. Methodists follow a similar pattern of faith rooted in Anglican and Pietist influences that make Scripture the center of faith and life. While the Wesleyan Quadrilateral, theorized by the American theologian Albert Outler, has often been taught as something closer to an equilateral, in Wesley's thought the Bible remained the most significant vehicle of God's revelatory work in the world. The rule of Scripture testifies to Christ, yet Christians encounter Christ through not only the Word but also the mediation of the sacraments. Early Methodists attended the Lord's Supper regularly and practiced baptism as a means of grace; this is the very reason why the power of ordination (and the consequent authority to administer the sacraments) proved necessary (if controversial) in the earliest years of the movement.

Societies and classes. Early Methodism spread far and wide because of its commitment to interpersonal relationships. Wherever Methodists went, they gathered with others in community. Societies of larger meetings for hearing the Word and receiving the sacraments brought cohesion to the group. Hymn singing, for example, not only taught the people what to believe but also gave them a sense of fellowship. Large gatherings alone weren't sufficient. The Methodists also depended on smaller groups—classes or bands—that generated accountability, required active sharing of personal goods for the needy, and encouraged a life of faith. Love feasts, which didn't depend on the authority of an ordained minister, brought the community together for times of personal witness and intimate sharing. In time, Sunday schools displaced the classes, reducing mutual accountability and leaving spiritual formation to the influence of the

The **Wesleyan Quadrilateral**, first theorized by Albert Outler, depicts the relationship between four interrelated means of knowing God: Scripture (that is, the Bible) (S), *church traditions* (T), and *reason* (R) all reflect Wesley's Church of England heritage, while Wesley's reliance on religious *experience* (E) indicates a valuable (if sometimes unreliable) source of witness. Some present the Wesleyan Quadrilateral as four interchangeable and equally authoritative options for doctrine and practice, but Wesley's insistence on the primacy of Scripture may be discerned in the repeated claim that he was "a man of one book."

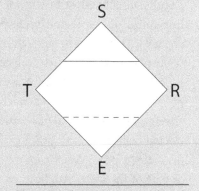

Figure E.2. The Wesleyan Quadrilateral

minister. The shift gradually lessened cohesion. For many decades of the twentieth century, attendance at both worship and Sunday school was a matter of deep importance (and American Methodists regularly kept records and offered tokens of reward for those who maintained their commitments), but as American culture changed, the emphasis on personal accountability diminished along with the influence of the movement numerically.

Laity and clergy. The empowerment of laity to do the work of ministry remains an ideal that pervades Methodism. In one UMC congregation I belonged to many years ago, the top of the weekly bulletin opened with the name of the pastor, followed by a striking reminder: "All members ministers." A commitment to lay ministry complements an itinerant clergy. Itineracy, a distinctive initiated by John Wesley, has fundamentally shaped the life of the church: remain in most Methodist congregations long enough, and the clergy will eventually move on to service elsewhere. In this way, the identity of each congregation rests with its members far more than pastors who provide leadership for a time.

The episcopacy, in such a light, is peripheral to contemporary Methodist identity—a remnant of Methodism's Church of England roots. This is not a political statement or a sign of disrespect—Methodists often have received decisive, life-giving leadership from their bishops—but the episcopacy remains secondary in a measured view of world Methodism. Wesley's reaction to Coke and Asbury proves the point. After Wesley's death, the British Methodists established a polity that relied on a rotating presidency of the conference. Methodists formed a *connection*, a communion of likeminded clergy and laity. Most British Methodists were members of the Church of England, so it may seem strange at first that they didn't form a parallel episcopacy with bishops to guide the church. The reason was simple: they didn't really plan to separate from the church so much as renew it from within.

In North America, by contrast, Methodists chafed under the authority of political and ecclesial powers across the ocean. Ironically, even with their strong preference for democratic structures, early American Methodists elected bishops to lead the church—despite threats of schism and fears of despotic leaders.[3] American Methodists continued to imagine themselves as part of the wider Anglican communion, even as so much of American society resisted such a model of church leadership, but their bishops have had relatively little societal influence by comparison. Even Francis Asbury, the greatest American Methodist, yielded to the authority of the conference in his elevation to the episcopacy.

British and American Methodist missionaries replicated these disparate forms of church government around the world. Yet, broadly speaking, British Methodists have tended over time to relinquish churches to indigenous leadership (a move that followed practices of decolonialization), while American Methodists have tended to exert paternal authority from afar, especially in Africa and parts of Asia. Still, there is no one defining polity beyond the connectional conference. While it may be tempting for some Methodists to regard the episcopacy as a central feature of Methodism, a more decisive mark may be discovered in the mutuality of active ministry and deliberative conferencing by laity and clergy together.[4]

Social concern and personal piety. The God who saves by grace empowers people for responsible action. Methodists believe that works of service manifest a heart strangely warmed. From their earliest days, Methodists have worked in the prisons, established orphanages, and built centers for education. The vast Methodist publishing industry springs from a heart to share the good news through the printed word. Classes took donations (and leaders made up the difference for the poorest members) in order to support those in need. Wesley expected Methodists to attend to the needs of the community but also spoke unceasingly of the requirements of the holy life. He continually called for repentance and could be impatient with the "almost" Christian who compromised in an inordinate love for pleasures of the world. Wesley expected that life in Christ came with a new awareness of the Spirit's work, and he thought such a love for God would extend effortlessly in a love of neighbor.

These beliefs and practices, features of Methodism that characterize the movement from its earliest days, remain relevant today. Not all Wesleyans feel equal commitment to these characteristics, to be sure. Still, these ideals belong at the heart of any people called Methodist.

In this book, I've included not only cherished stories of Methodism's past but also lesser-known events that complicate a uniform account of Methodist belief and practice. Recent historians have worked to demonstrate how some of the most beloved stories—Wesley's "heart strangely warmed" experience at Aldersgate, for instance—may not be the ones that Wesley himself saw as most important. There is good reason to ask difficult questions about cherished traditions. Indeed, even Charles Wesley looked back to his "Day of Pentecost" and wondered if too much attention to a day long past might distract him from the more important matter of faith *in the present*: "My dearest Sally," he wrote to his wife, "This I once called the anniversary of my conversion. Just twenty-two years ago I thought I received the first grain of faith. But what does that avail me, if I have not the Spirit now?"[5] While Methodists might demand too much from such fabled moments as the Epworth rectory fire or the Aldersgate conversion, we might also consider how these stories have not only obscured the past in favor of partisan theological positions but also proved "instrumental in opening a future."[6]

Two vital beliefs are often set in opposition in accounts of what constitutes "authentic" Methodism. On one hand, some maintain that Methodism has flourished around the world through the promotion of historic Christian beliefs about the transformative power of God in an individual's life. In such a view, true Methodism is known in an articulation of beliefs about repentance, conversion, assurance, and growth in holiness through a process of sanctification. While tending to encourage a formulaic account of the Christian life, these patterns (and the stories Methodists have repeated along with them) have inspired an abiding belief that God's providential hand continues to work through personal encounters that transform people from sin to salvation and increasing holiness in every aspect of life. On the other hand, some Methodists assert that true Methodism may be found wherever members minister in solidarity with the needy, oppressed, and outcast. For these individuals, Methodism is a powerful movement of justice and liberation that restores people to positions of dignity in this worldly experience.

Those who wish to follow Christ in the manner of the Wesleys would be wise to recover the full range of these convictions. Sharp divisions across denominations in the early twentieth century set those who emphasized individual piety against those who advocated for social concerns. For some, the spiritual life is the source of transformation, so the heart should be prioritized above any other need, no matter how basic. Other Methodists, by contrast, have so stressed social interests that any talk of God's transformative work in the lives of sinful humans is regarded as secondary at best. Whenever Methodists have separated these two aspects of the movement, they have failed to live out the legacy of John and Charles Wesley and risked dividing the movement once again.

Unity is not uniformity. The Ghanaian theologian Mercy Amba Oduyoye rightly challenges the temptation to build the church on a weak foundation: "All 'towers of Babel' aimed at structuring a monolith for a Church came to nothing. It seems to me that even today all such efforts are doomed to crumble."[7] Rather, Methodists must respect the diversity of the churches by finding their unity in Jesus Christ. Even the term *centrist*, admirably advocated by some, can appear to signal a weak and lukewarm homogeneity that unwittingly departs from essentials of the gospel. I propose, instead, the term *Broad Church Methodism* to identify a historical reality, namely, the unmistakable breadth of the church, and to indicate the need for generosity if Methodists hope to remain united within a global connection.

Schism, as Wesley counsels in his sermon on the topic, marks a church that has divided into parties, resulting from anger, resentment, and a loss of mutual affection. Separation, for Wesley, involves a "grievous breach of the law of love" and presents a stumbling block to those outside the church.[8] Division diminishes the effectiveness of ministry—vast resources are lost in the act and efforts abroad are inevitably redoubled, even where agreements to work together are promised. As with conflict in families, it's the children who suffer most. In much the same way, conflict disrupts the growth of those who look to the church for stability in the early stages of faith. The younger Methodist churches inevitably endure the loss of wisdom gained from years of experience in any rending of the connection. Older Methodist churches, for their part, risk repeating the paternalism of previous generations in their failure to listen to growing churches built on a dynamism akin to that of the earliest years of the movement. Onlookers see division, and their hearts harden to the good news. Of course, parties that separate almost always hold their own judgments sacrosanct, and the decision to separate is almost always deemed unavoidable. To compromise, in such a light, appears to equivocate in matters of profound significance, either condoning injustice or corrupting truth. But that which is intolerable in times of excess may be endured in times of want. Methodists should wisely weigh the consequences of schism and, in the words of Wesley, "consider it calmly."

There is good reason to believe that Methodism will press forward in ministry well into the future, nevertheless. Methodist churches around the

world continue to work across diverse cultures with inspired and often courageous labor. The reality of effective ministry gives good reason to hope.
While membership declines in many of the older Methodist bodies,
churches inspired by a Wesleyan vision of Pentecost continue to thrive in
nations around the world. These churches, too, are diverse—they ought not
be idealized or sentimentalized, as if they contain the singular remedy to
Western secularity or unbelief—yet their perspectives on faith and life may
yet help bring a new vitality into churches now struggling to make disciples,
especially in communities where religious devotion is but one among many
options for living a rightly ordered life. If British, American, and other
Methodists around the world hope to participate in such a renewal together,
then they must attend more diligently to their own history, discern the legitimacy of new developments, and embrace the gracious work of the Spirit
in the days ahead.

Notes

PROLOGUE: METHODISM IN CRISIS

[1]A closer look at data on Christian denominations around the world may be found in *World Christian Encyclopedia: A Comparative Survey of Churches and Religions in the Modern World*, 2nd ed., ed. David B. Barrett, George T. Kurian, and Todd M. Johnson (Oxford: Oxford University Press, 2001), 3–18.

[2]Michael Lipka, "Mainline Protestants Make up Shrinking Number of U.S. Adults," Pew Research Center: Fact Tank, May 18, 2015.

[3]Scott J. Jones, *The Once and Future Wesleyan Movement* (Nashville: Abingdon, 2016), 10.

[4]David Hempton, *Methodism: Empire of the Spirit* (New Haven: Yale University Press, 2005), 211–16.

[5]Among the most helpful and widely referenced sources, see Richard P. Heitzenrater, *Wesley and the People Called Methodists*, 2nd ed. (Nashville: Abingdon, 2013); Randy L. Maddox, *Responsible Grace: John Wesley's Practical Theology* (Nashville: Kingswood, 1994); and Kenneth Cracknell and Susan J. White, *An Introduction to World Methodism* (Cambridge: Cambridge University Press, 2005); Charles Yrigoyen Jr. and Susan E. Warrick, eds., *Historical Dictionary of Methodism* (Lanham, MD: Scarecrow, 2013).

1: WARM HEARTS

[1]Susanna Wesley, *Susanna Wesley: The Complete Writings*, ed. Charles Wallace Jr. (New York: Oxford University Press, 1997), 67.

[2]Susanna Wesley, *Susanna Wesley*, 79.

[3]On John Wesley's relationship with Anglicanism, see Frank Baker, *John Wesley and the Church of England* (London: Epworth, 2000), and Ryan Nicholas Danker, *Wesley and the Anglicans: Political Division in Early Evangelicalism* (Downers Grove, IL: IVP Academic, 2016); for more on John Wesley's life, ministry, and writings, see Heitzenrater, *Wesley and the People Called Methodists*, and Henry D. Rack, *Reasonable Enthusiast: John Wesley and the Rise of Methodism* (London: Epworth, 1992).

[4]Susanna Wesley, *Susanna Wesley*, 82–83.

[5]Those who first used the obscure term *Methodists* of the Wesley circle seem to have objected especially to their asceticism: "Many began noticing with some alarm the seemingly fanatical practices of fasting on Wednesdays and Fridays, the annoying habit of getting up at four and five o'clock in the morning, and the radical extent to which Wesley and his friends carried their frugality and their various methods of self-denial" (Heitzenrater, *Wesley and the People Called Methodists*, 47).

[6]John Wesley, January 17–February 1, 1736, *Journal and Diaries (1735-38)*, ed. W. Reginald Ward and Richard P. Heitzenrater, vol. 18, *The Bicentennial Edition of the Works of John Wesley* (Nashville: Abingdon, 1988), 141–45.

[7]John Wesley, January 24, 1738, *Journal and Diaries*, 18:211.

[8]John Wesley, May 24, 1738, *Journals and Diaries*, 18:249–50.

[9]John Wesley, Sermon 2, "The Almost Christian," in *Works* §1.13, 136–37.

[10]David J. Hart and David J. Jeremy, eds., *Brands Plucked from the Burning: Essays on Methodist Memorialisation and Remembering* (Evesham: Wesley Historical Society, 2013), 84.

[11]John Wesley, "Thoughts upon Methodism," §2, in *The Methodist Societies: History, Nature, and Design*, ed. Rupert E. Davies, vol. 9, *The Bicentennial Edition of the Works of John Wesley* (Nashville: Abingdon, 1989), 527.

[12]John Wesley, "Thoughts upon Methodism," §1, 527.

2: DIVINE POWER

[1]Barry Schwartz, "Collective Forgetting and the Symbolic Power of Oneness: The Strange Apotheosis of Rosa Parks," *Social Psychology Quarterly* 72, no. 2 (2009): 123.

[2]Schwartz, "Collective Forgetting," 127.

[3]Charles Wesley, *Manuscript Journal of the Reverend Charles Wesley, MA*, ed. S. T. Kimbrough Jr. and Kenneth G. C. Newport, 2 vols. (Nashville: Kingswood, 2008), 1:101.

[4]Charles Wesley, *Manuscript Journal*, 1:102.

[5]Charles Wesley, *Manuscript Journal*, 1:103.

[6]Charles Wesley, *Manuscript Journal*, 1:104. Though remarkably similar, Charles's account predates John Wesley's famous record at Aldersgate: "I spent some hours this evening in private with Martin Luther, who was greatly blessed to me, especially his conclusion of the second chapter. I laboured, waited, and prayed to see 'who loved *me*, and gave himself for *me*'" (104).

[7]Charles Wesley, *Manuscript Journal*, 1:104.

[8]Charles Wesley, *Manuscript Journal*, 1:105.

[9]John Wesley, ed., *Collection of Psalms and Hymns* (Charlestown: Lewis Timothy, 1737), 22–23. Kimbrough and Newport attribute the likely hymn to George Hickes's *Devotions in the Ancient Way of Offices* (1700).

[10]Charles Wesley, *Manuscript Journal*, 1:106.

[11]Charles Wesley, *Manuscript Journal*, 1:107.

[12] Augustine, *Confessions* 8.12.

[13]Charles Wesley, *Manuscript Journal*, 1:108 (Ps 39:8, from the Book of Common Prayer).

[14]Outler notes that the Wesleys advanced a view of the Spirit's work in salvation "that has no exact equivalent in 'Western Spirituality' up to their time" (quoted in John R. Tyson, ed., *Charles Wesley: A Reader* [Oxford: Oxford University Press, 1989], 43).

[15]Tyson, *Charles Wesley*, 43–44.

[16]Charles explains, "The sound of her voice was entirely changed into that of Mrs. Musgrave (if I can be sure of anything sensible)" (*Manuscript Journal*, 1:108).

[17]Charles Wesley, *Manuscript Journal*, 1:107.

[18]Charles Wesley, *Manuscript Journal*, 1:109.

[19]Charles Wesley, *Manuscript Journal*, 1:111. In fact, both John's Aldersgate and Charles's Pentecost experience were equally trinitarian events, but their unique interpretations of these experiences exemplify the subtle fissures that divided later Methodists.

[20]Susanna Wesley, *Susanna Wesley: The Complete Writings*, ed. Charles Wallace Jr. (New York: Oxford University Press, 1997), 176.

[21]Tyson, *Charles Wesley*, 21; see also *A Collection of Hymns for the Use of the People Called Methodists*, ed. Franz Hildebrandt and Oliver Beckerlegge, vol. 7, *The Bicentennial Edition of the Works of John Wesley* (Oxford: Clarendon, 1983).

[22]Tyson, *Charles Wesley*, 198–200.

[23]Richard P. Heitzenrater, *Wesley and the People Called Methodists* (Nashville: Abingdon, 1995), 100. For an insightful look at the economics of the growing movement, see Clive Murray Norris, *The Financing of John Wesley's Methodism, c. 1740–1800* (Oxford: Oxford University Press, 2017).

3: PERFECT LOVE

[1]George Whitefield, "The Good Shepherd: A Farewell Sermon," in *Eighteen Sermons, Preached by the Late Rev. George Whitefield*, ed. Joseph Gurney and Andrew Gifford (London: Joseph Gurney, 1771), 434–39; cf. Jeffrey W. Barbeau, *Religion in Romantic England: An Anthology of Primary Sources* (Waco: Baylor University Press, 2018), 46–50.

[2]Whitefield, "Good Shepherd," 434; Barbeau, *Religion in Romantic England*, 48.

[3]George Whitefield, *Short Account*, quoted in Mark K. Olson, "Whitefield's Conversion and Early Theological Formation," in *George Whitefield: Life, Context, and Legacy*, ed. Geordan Hammond and David Ceri Jones (Oxford: Oxford University Press, 2016), 30.

[4]Quoted in Olson, "Whitefield's Conversion," 33.

[5]For more on Whitefield's life and times, see Harry S. Stout, The Divine Dramatist: *George Whitefield and the Rise of Modern Evangelicalism* (Grand Rapids: Eerdmans, 1991).

[6]John Wesley, Sermon 37, "The Nature of Enthusiasm," §12, in *Works*, 2:50.

[7]John Wesley, Sermon 37, "The Nature of Enthusiasm," §19–20, in *Works*, 2:53–54.

[8]John Wesley, Sermon 37, "The Nature of Enthusiasm," §39, in *Works*, 2:60.

[9]John Wesley, Sermon 4, "Scriptural Christianity," §3, in *Works*, 1:160 (emphasis added).

[10]John Wesley, Sermon 4, "Scriptural Christianity," §3, in *Works*, 1:161.

[11]The Toleration Act of 1689 had allowed nonconforming (that is, non-Anglican) Protestants to meet freely upon taking oaths of allegiance to the King (thereby minimizing concerns that political insurrection would occur through such gatherings). Against John Wesley's insistence that Methodists were not dissenters, a trustee of the New Room registered the building as such during remodeling (Richard P. Heitzenrater, *Wesley and the People Called Methodists* [Nashville: Abingdon, 1995], 170), and similar registrations were made for chapels established by other Methodists, such as the Selina Hastings, Countess of Huntingdon.

[12]Albert C. Outler, ed., *John Wesley* (New York: Oxford University Press, 1964), 178.

[13]John Wesley, "The Nature, Design, and General Rules, of the United Societies," in *The Methodist Societies: History, Nature, and Design*, ed. Rupert E. Davies, vol. 9, *The Bicentennial Edition of the Works of John Wesley* (Nashville: Abingdon, 1989), 70–73.

[14]John Wesley, "The Rules of the Band Societies," in *Methodist Societies*, 78.

[15]On the relationship between Wesley and the doctrine of *theosis*, see Jeffrey W. Barbeau, "John Wesley and the Early Church: History, Antiquity, and the Spirit of God," in *Evangelicals and the Early Church: Recovery, Reform, Renewal*, ed. George Kalantzis and Andrew Tooley (Eugene, OR: Cascade, 2012), 52–76.

[16]John R. Tyson, ed., *Charles Wesley: A Reader* (Oxford: Oxford University Press, 1989), 39–40, and John R. Tyson, *Charles Wesley on Sanctification: A Biographical and Theological Study* (Salem, OH: Schmul, 1992), chaps. 6–7.

[17]Tyson, *Charles Wesley*, 199.

[18]Heitzenrater, *Wesley and the People Called Methodists*, 138.

[19]The 1766 examination included such questions as, "Do you know the Rules of the Society? Of the Bands? Do you keep them? Do you take no snuff? Tobacco? Drams [alcohol]? Do you constantly attend the church and sacrament? . . . Are you determined to employ all your time in the work of God? Will you preach every morning and evening? Endeavouring not to speak too loud or too long? . . . Will you diligently and earnestly instruct the children, and visit from house to house?" (Heitzenrater, *Wesley and the People Called Methodists*, 235).

[20]John Wesley, *A Plain Account of Christian Perfection*, §20, in *Doctrinal and Controversial Treatises II*, ed. Paul Wesley Chilcote and Kenneth J. Collins, vol. 13, *The Bicentennial Edition of the Works of John Wesley* (Nashville: Abingdon, 2012), 179.

[21]Henry D. Rack, *Reasonable Enthusiast: John Wesley and the Rise of Methodism* (London: Epworth, 1992), 338–39.

[22]Rack, *Reasonable Enthusiast*, 339; John Wesley, *Plain Account of Christian Perfection*, §22.

[23]John Wesley, *Plain Account of Christian Perfection*, §22.

[24]William Warburton, *The Doctrine of Grace or, The Office and Operations of the Holy Spirit Vindicated from the Insults of Infidelity and the Abuses of Fanaticism*, 3rd ed. (London: A. Millar and J. and R. Tonson, 1763), 82–83; cf. Barbeau, *Religion in Romantic England*, 182–86.

[25]Heitzenrater, *Wesley and the People Called Methodists*, 167.

[26]On Calvinistic Methodism, see David Ceri Jones, Boyd Stanley Schlenther, and Eryn Mant White, *The Elect Methodists: Calvinistic Methodism in England and Wales, 1735–1811* (Cardiff: University of Wales Press, 2012).

[27]John Wesley, Sermon 53, "On the Death of George Whitefield," §2.4, in *Works*, 2.338.

[28]Heitzenrater, *Wesley and the People Called Methodists*, 290.

4: Costly Obedience

[1]*John Wesley*, screenplay by Lawrence Barrett (Radio and Film Commission of the Methodist Church, 1954).

[2]On the Deed of Declaration, see Richard P. Heitzenrater, *Wesley and the People Called Methodists* (Nashville: Abingdon, 1995), 282–85.

[3]Coke already had been ordained an Anglican presbyter, like Wesley.

[4]Rupert Davies, *Methodism* (London: Epworth, 1976), 108–9.

[5]Charles Wesley, "MS. Ordination Hymns: V, Epigram," in *Charles Wesley: A Reader*, ed. John R. Tyson (Oxford: Oxford University Press, 1989), 429.

[6]Charles Wesley, "MS. Brothers: Hymn IX," in Tyson, *Charles Wesley*, 430.

[7]Charles Wesley, Letter to John Wesley, August 14, 1785, in Tyson, *Charles Wesley*, 434.

[8]John Wesley, Letter to Charles Wesley, August 19, 1785, in Tyson, *Charles Wesley*, 435.

[9]John Wesley, Sermon 75, "On Schism," §2.17, in *Works*, 3:67.

[10]In his funeral sermon, Wesley lamented the loss in most elevated language: "Many exemplary men have I known, holy in heart and life, within fourscore years. But one equal to him I have not known—one so inwardly and outwardly devoted to God. So unblameable a character in every respect I have not found either in Europe or America. Nor do I expect to find another such on this side of eternity" (John Wesley, Sermon 114, "On the Death of John Fletcher," §3.12, in *Works*, 3:628).

[11]Davies, *Methodism*, 111.

[12]Davies, *Methodism*, 111.

[13]Jean Miller Schmidt, *Grace Sufficient: A History of Women in American Methodism, 1760–1939* (Nashville: Abingdon, 1999); Paul Wesley Chilcote, ed., *Her Own Story: Autobiographical Portraits of Early Methodist Women* (Nashville: Kingswood, 2001).

[14]Other branches and related groups include the Bible Christians (1815), the Wesleyan Reformers (1849), and, under the leadership of William and Catherine Booth, the Salvation Army (1865).

[15]For more on Methodist double allegiance during the period, see Frances Knight, *The Nineteenth-Century Church and English Society* (Cambridge: Cambridge University Press, 1995), 24–36.

[16]On Bunting, see Davies, *Methodism*, 121–22; Kenneth Cracknell and Susan J. White, *An Introduction to World Methodism* (Cambridge: Cambridge University Press, 2005), 33–34.

[17]Leigh Hunt, "An Attempt to Shew the Folly and Danger of Methodism. In a Series of Essays," *The Examiner*, nos. 19–22, 24, 28–29, 33, 35 (May–August 1808): 301–2, 334, 381–82, 445, 524–25, 555–56; see Jeffrey W. Barbeau, *Religion in Romantic England: An Anthology of Primary Sources* (Waco: Baylor University Press, 2018), 199–205.

[18]Cracknell and White, *Introduction to World Methodism*, 34.

[19]John Wesley, Sermon 139, "On the Sabbath," §1.1–2, in *Works*, 4:270.

[20]John Wesley, Sermon 143, "Public Diversions Denounced," in *Works*, 4:318–28; cf. Sermon 79, "On Dissipation," in *Works*, 3:115–25.

[21]Quoted in Timothy Larsen, *Friends of Religious Equality: Nonconformist Politics in Mid-Victorian England* (Rochester, NY: Boydell, 1999), 195–96.

[22]William Arthur, *"The People's Day": An Appeal to the Right Hon. Lord Stanley, M.P., Against His Advocacy of a French Sunday* (London: Hamilton, Adams, 1855), 16.

[23]Davies, *Methodism*, 153–54. In several ways, Lidgett's life and work parallels the evolution of the American social gospel movement.

[24]John Scott Lidgett, *The Spiritual Principle of the Atonement, as a Satisfaction Made to God for the Sins of the World*, 2nd ed. (London: Charles H. Kelly, 1898), 14; cf. J. Scott Lidgett, *The Fatherhood of God, in Christian Truth and Life* (Edinburgh: T&T Clark, 1902), 101–2.

[25]"Wesley relied upon immediate contact with the Living Spirit of Christ, whose Authority alone is final and satisfying, and who remoulds and vitalizes the past by His continuous influence and action upon prophetic individuals" (J. Scott Lidgett, *God, Christ and the Church* [London: Hodder and Stoughton, 1927], 318).

[26]Lidgett, *God, Christ and the Church*, 319.

[27]Thomas A. Langford, *Practical Divinity: Theology in the Wesleyan Tradition*, 2 vols. (Nashville: Abingdon, 1998–1999), 1:51, 57.

5: REVIVAL FIRE

[1]Frances Asbury, *The Journals and Letters of Francis Asbury*, 3 vols., ed. Elmer T. Clark, J. Manning Potts, Jacob S. Payton (London: Epworth; Nashville, Abingdon, 1958), 1:4–5 (hereafter *JLFA*).

[2]John Wigger, *American Saint: Francis Asbury and the Methodists* (Oxford: Oxford University Press, 2009), 44.

[3]*JLFA*, 1:195.

[4]In December 1776, Asbury confided in his journal, "My present practice is, to set apart about three hours out of every twenty-four for private prayer; but Satan labours much to interrupt me; nevertheless, my soul enjoys a sweet and peaceful nearness to God, for the most part, in these duties" (*JLFA*, 1:206).

[5]Wigger, *American Saint*, 77.

[6]Rebecca Ridgely, "Reminiscences," in *Early Methodist Life and Spirituality: A Reader*, ed. Lester Ruth (Nashville: Kingswood, 2005), 73–74.

[7]*JLFA*, 1:211.

[8]See Russell E. Richey, *Early American Methodism* (Bloomington: Indiana University Press, 1991), 88–91.

[9]*JLFA*, 1:346–47, 381n115; Wigger, *American Saint*, 111–25.

[10]*JLFA*, 1:471.

[11]Coke makes no mention of Asbury's cautionary response, but his journal mentions plans for the journey: "Mr. *Asbury* has also drawn up for me a route of about eight hundred or a thousand miles in the mean time. He has given me his black (*Harry* by name,) [that is, Harry Hosier] and borrowed an excellent horse for me. I exceedingly reverence Mr. *Asbury*; he has so much simplicity, like a little child, so much wisdom and consideration, so much meekness and love; and under all this, though hardly to be perceived, so much command and authority" (Thomas Coke, *The Journals of Thomas Coke*, ed. John A. Vickers [Nashville: Kingswood, 2005], 35).

[12]Coke, *Journals of Thomas Coke*, 38–39.

[13]Early American republicanism came to the foreground in a dispute over episcopal authority when James O'Kelly (1735–1826) unsuccessfully called for clergy to have the right to accept or reject itineracy appointments. For more on how early American political thought shaped the O'Kelly affair, see Richey, *Early American Methodism*, 88–91.

[14]*JLFA*, 3:31 (October 3, 1783).

[15]*JLFA*, 1:450.

[16]Wigger, *American Saint*, 72.

[17]Although he was far less active than in other years of ministry, Asbury nonetheless traveled widely and preached at least ninety-five times during this period of relative seclusion (Wigger, *American Saint*, 103).

[18]*JLFA*, 1:425. Coke praised Asbury's fidelity to the cause: "he has the highest esteem for our dear father Mr. *Wesley*. Indeed he has entered into the deep things of God" (Coke, *Journals of Thomas Coke*, 38).

[19]Richard P. Heitzenrater, *Wesley and the People Called Methodists* (Nashville: Abingdon, 1995), 289.

[20]*The Methodist Experience in America, Vol. 2: Sourcebook*, ed. Russell E. Richey, Kenneth E. Rowe, and Jean Miller Schmidt (Nashville: Abingdon, 2000), 62.

[21]Symptomatic of Anglican prejudice against Methodist lay preachers, the representatives almost entirely neglected Asbury while pandering to Coke (Wigger, *American Saint*, 145–46).

[22]A regrettable lapse in judgment that was later amended (Wigger, *American Saint*, 140).

[23]*JLFA*, 3:62–63.

[24]*JLFA*, 3:75.

[25]*JLFA*, 3:65.

[26]*JLFA*, 1:673.

[27]Wigger, *American Saint*, 382.

[28]*JLFA*, 2:797.

6: Everlasting Freedom

[1]John Wigger, *American Saint: Francis Asbury and the Methodists* (Oxford: Oxford University Press, 2009), 149.

[2]Frances Asbury, *The Journals and Letters of Francis Asbury*, 3 vols., ed. Elmer T. Clark, J. Manning Potts, Jacob S. Payton (London: Epworth; Nashville, Abingdon, 1958), 1:362 (hereafter *JLFA*). Freeborn Garrettson made similar plans for Nova Scotia, writing to Asbury that Hosier "would be very useful" in reaching several thousand people in the region (Nathan Bangs, *The Life of the Rev. Freeborn Garrettson* [New York: G. Land & C. B. Tibbett, 1845], 161).

[3]*JLFA*, 1:403.

[4]On Hosier and other early leaders, see J. Gordon Melton, *A Will to Choose: The Origins of African American Methodism* (Lanham: Rowman & Littlefield, 2007).

[5]Thomas Coke, *The Journals of Thomas Coke*, ed. John A. Vickers (Nashville: Kingswood, 2005), 35 (November 29, 1784).

[6]Coke, *Journals of Thomas Coke*, 37. These comments preceded Hosier saving Coke from drowning on an ill-timed trip crossing the Cambridge Ferry (*Journals of Thomas Coke*, 39; cf. John Vickers, *Thomas Coke: Apostle of Methodism* [Nashville: Abingdon, 1969], 84).

[7]Ezekiel Cooper in Wigger, *American Saint*, 285–86. Notably, in 1786, Hosier was the first of any Methodist to garner the interest of New York newspapers (*JLFA*, 1:494).

[8]*JLFA*, 1:413.

[9]Bangs, *Life of the Rev. Freeborn Garrettson*, 195 (cf. 187–89, 191–92, 194).

[10]Late in his life, Hosier allegedly struggled with alcoholism, which may be interpreted either as the hindrance to his advancement in the MEC or a part of the aftermath of racial discrimination against him (see Warren Thomas Smith, *Harry Hosier: Circuit Rider* [Nashville: Upper Room, 1981], 57–58).

[11]*JLFA*, 1:274.

[12]Asbury complains in one letter that some Methodists were too forceful in their methods, since preaching on the evils of slavery wasn't always possible (*JLFA*, 3:258).

[13]*JLFA*, 3:160.

[14]William Knox, *Three Tracts Respecting the Conversion and Instruction of the Free Indians and Negroe [sic] Slaves in the Colonies*, new ed. (London: J. Debrett, 1789), 24–25.

[15]Knox, *Three Tracts*, 27.

[16]Wesley alludes to Is 26:21; see John Wesley, *Journals and Diaries 1 (1735–1738)*, ed. W. Reginald Ward and Richard P. Heitzenrater, vol. 18, *Bicentennial Edition of the Works of John Wesley* (Nashville: Abingdon, 1988), 180–81 (April 1737); on Wesley's early encounters with the slave system, see Geordan Hammond, *John Wesley in America: Restoring Primitive Christianity* (Oxford: Oxford University Press, 2014), 150–51.

[17]John Wesley, *Thoughts upon Slavery* (Philadelphia: Joseph Crukshank, 1774), 55.

[18]John H. Wigger, *Taking Heaven by Storm: Methodism and the Rise of Popular Christianity in America* (New York: Oxford University Press, 1998), 140.

[19]Wigger, *Taking Heaven by Storm*, 140.

[20]Wigger, *American Saint*, 467n33.

[21]Russell E. Richey, *Early American Methodism* (Bloomington: Indiana University Press, 1991), 59.

[22]Richard Allen, *Life, Experience, and Gospel Labors of the Rt. Rev. Richard Allen* (Nashville: Abingdon, 1960), 15.

[23]A comparable incident is found in the life of John J. Jacob, a slaveholder from West Virginia who was converted and freed his slaves in 1788. He then began itinerating, "being desirous to glorify God, in my conduct, by doing to others as I would have them do unto Me" (*JLFA*, 3:260).

[24]Allen, *Life, Experience, and Gospel Labors*, 26.

[25]Wigger refutes the commonplace assertion that the withdrawal from St. George's took place in 1787 since both the construction of the balcony and the assignment of McClaskey as presiding elder both occurred in 1792 (*American Saint*, 490n12). Allen himself mentions building the gallery in his *Life, Experience, and Gospel Labors* (26).

[26]Allen, *Life, Experience, and Gospel Labors*, 25.

[27]Allen, *Life, Experience, and Gospel Labors*, 29. This is consistent with his criticism of a growing Methodist desire for respectability that began at the Christmas

Conference (see *Life, Experience, and Gospel Labors*, 22). Absalom Jones and others who favored the Episcopal Church founded the African Episcopal Church of St. Thomas the same year. Jones was ordained deacon in the Episcopal Church in 1795 and the first African American priest in 1804. On Allen and Jones, see also Carol V. R. George, *Segregated Sabbaths: Richard Allen and the Emergence of Independent Black Churches, 1760-1840* (Oxford: Oxford University Press, 1973).

[28]For Allen's account of the Philadelphia epidemic of 1793, which killed more than 10 percent of the city's population, see *Life, Experience, and Gospel Labors*, 48-65.

[29]*JLFA*, 2:18; Wigger, *American Saint*, 250-52.

[30]On Richard Allen and Bethel church, see also *JLFA*, 2:64, 235; 3:366-67.

[31]Daniel Coker (1780-1846) was among Allen's collaborators and one of the most significant black leaders of the time; see also Will B. Gravely, "African Methodisms and the Rise of Black Denominationalism," and Doris Andrews, "The African Methodists of Philadelphia, 1794-1802," in *Perspectives on American Methodism: Interpretive Essays*, ed. Russell E. Richey, Kenneth E. Rowe, and Jean Miller Schmidt, 108-26, 145-58 (Nashville: Kingswood, 1993).

[32]Numerous examples may be found in Cynthia Lynn Lyerly's *Methodism and the Southern Mind, 1770-1810* (New York: Oxford University Press, 1998), 119-45; cf. Wigger, *Taking Heaven by Storm*, 125-50.

[33]The vote, 117 to 56, fell largely along geographical lines. However, some delegates from Illinois and Philadelphia also supported his reinstatement (*Journal of the General Conference of the Methodist Episcopal Church, Held in the City of New York, 1844* [New York: G. Lane and C. B. Tippett, 1844], 33-34).

[34]*Journal of the General Conference of the Methodist Episcopal Church, 1844*, 58.

[35]*Journal of the General Conference of the Methodist Episcopal Church, 1844*, 63-64.

[36]*Journal of the General Conference of the Methodist Episcopal Church, 1844*, 63-64; the number of slaves inherited by his former wife appears in the "Reply to the Protest," 201. For Bishop Andrew's self-defense, "I am a slaveholder for conscience' sake," see "General Conference Delegates Debate Slavery and Episcopacy," in *The Methodist Experience in America, Vol. 2: Sourcebook*, ed. Russell E. Richey, Kenneth E. Rowe, and Jean Miller Schmidt (Nashville: Abingdon, 2000), 270-78. Norwood explains that legislation in southern states allowed for emancipation "in almost every case" if either the slave was removed from the state or the former owner guaranteed financial support (Frederick A. Norwood, *The Story of American Methodism: A History of the United Methodists and Their Relations* [Nashville: Abingdon, 1974], 204).

[37]*Journal of the General Conference of the Methodist Episcopal Church, 1844*, 76.

[38]*Journal of the General Conference of the Methodist Episcopal Church, 1844*, 83-84.

[39]*Journal of the General Conference of the Methodist Episcopal Church, 1844*, 186-98; the committee reply to the protest may be found on 199-210.

7: HOLY PEOPLE

[1]Luke T. Harrington, "How Methodists Invented Your Kid's Grape Juice Sugar High: The Weird Story Behind the Church's Go-To Communion Wine Substitute," *Christianity Today*, September 16, 2016.

[2]The discussion of the Methodist temperance movement in this chapter owes much to the best book on the subject, Jennifer L. Woodruff Tait, *The Poisoned Chalice: Eucharistic Grape Juice and Common-Sense Realism in Victorian Methodism* (Tuscaloosa: University of Alabama Press, 2011). See also Woodruff Tait's accessible correction to Harrington, "Raise a Juice Box to the Temperance Movement: The Teetotaling History Behind America's Favorite Communion Wine Substitute," *Christianity Today*, April 28, 2017.

[3]For example, the Congregationalist Moses Stuart's "What Is the Duty of the Churches, in Regard to the Use of Fermented (Alcoholic) Wine, in Celebrating the Lord's Supper?," *The Methodist Magazine and Quarterly Review* (October 1835): 411–39.

[4]Woodruff Tait, *Poisoned Chalice*, 9. Woodruff Tait elsewhere offers this startling fact: "The bar tab for George Washington's farewell party by his troops in 1787—a party attended by 55 people—ran to 60 bottles of claret, 54 bottles of Madeira, 22 bottles of porter, 12 bottles of beer, 8 bottles of hard cider, 8 bottles of whiskey, and 7 bowls of spiked punch" ("Raise a Juice Box to the Temperance Movement," para. 11).

[5]Woodruff Tait, *Poisoned Chalice*, 9. Consumption never rose above three gallons of absolute alcohol again and remains at less than a gallon to this day.

[6]John Wesley, Sermon 13, "On Sin in Believers," §4.12–13, in *Works*, 1:331–32.

[7]Adam Clarke, *A Dissertation on the Use and Abuse of Tobacco*, in *A Discourse on the Nature, Design, and Institution of the Holy Eucharist* (New York: E. Sargeant and Griffin and Rudd, 1812), 237; cf. Jeffrey W. Barbeau, *Religion in Romantic England: An Anthology of Primary Sources* (Waco: Baylor University Press, 2018), 325–30.

[8]John Wesley, Sermon 16, "The Means of Grace," in *Works*, 1:376–97.

[9]John Wesley, "A Word to a Drunkard," in *The Works of the Rev. John Wesley* (London: Wesleyan Conference Office, 1872), 11:169.

[10]Moses M. Henkle, *Primary Platform of Methodism, or, Exposition of the General Rules* (Louisville: Morton & Griswold, 1851).

[11]Matthew Simpson, "Our Martyr President," in *Our Martyr President, Abraham Lincoln* (New York: Tibbals & Whiting, 1865), 408.

[12]*Address to Christians Throughout the World* (Richmond, 1863), 7–8.

[13]Frederick A. Norwood, *The Story of American Methodism: A History of the United Methodists and Their Relations* (Nashville: Abingdon, 1974), 274–76.

[14]William Apess, *A Son of the Forest* (New York, 1829), 38.

[15]Apess, *Son of the Forest*, 39–40.

[16]Apess, *Son of the Forest*, 41. Apess claims that the Methodists did more to help Native Americans than any other denomination (73); cf. Philip F. Gura, *The Life of William Apess, Pequot* (Chapel Hill: University of North Carolina Press, 2015).

[17]Consider, too, the case of Peter Jones (1802–1856), a member of the Ojibwa people who served as a Methodist minister in Canada and wrote numerous books including biblical translations, hymnals, and a history of the Ojibwa people.

[18]Homer Noley, *First White Frost: Native Americans and United Methodism* (Nashville: Abingdon, 1991), 128–29.

[19]Quoted in Noley, *First White Frost*, 129.

[20]Gary L. Roberts, *Massacre at Sand Creek: How Methodists Were Involved in an American Tragedy* (Nashville: Abingdon, 2016).

[21]Wesley, Sermon 43, "The Scripture Way of Salvation," §3:18, in *Works* 2:169.

[22]One of the earliest descriptions of this doctrine appears in *The Altar Covenant* (1837), though Palmer expanded on the process in many other works in subsequent years (*Phoebe Palmer: Selected Writings*, ed. Thomas C. Oden [New York: Paulist, 1988], 107–30, esp. 121); cf. Elaine A. Heath, *Naked Faith: The Mystical Theology of Phoebe Palmer* (Cambridge: James Clarke, 2009), 23–28.

[23]Phoebe Palmer, *Entire Devotion to God* (1845), in *Phoebe Palmer: Selected Writings*, 187.

[24]Oden, introduction to *Phoebe Palmer: Selected Writings*, 12.

[25]Norwood, *Story of American Methodism*, 294.

[26]Douglas M. Strong, "Free Methodist Church," in *Historical Dictionary of Methodism*, ed. Charles Yrigoyen Jr. and Susan E. Warrick, 158–59 (Lanham, MD: Scarecrow, 2013).

[27]Holiness churches founded colleges, too, such as Asbury (Kentucky) and Taylor (Indiana). By the turn of the twentieth century, the Holiness Movement experienced its own renewal, as many of the earliest leaders of Pentecostalism came from the ranks of Methodist and Holiness churches. Charles Parham, one of the most influential voices in early American Pentecostalism, began as an MEC supply preacher before leaving in opposition to denominationalism. On the relationship between Methodist, Holiness, and Pentecostal churches, see Vinson Synan, *The Holiness-Pentecostal Tradition: Charismatic Movements in the Twentieth Century* (Grand Rapids: Eerdmans, 1997).

[28]*Journal of the General Conference of the M.E.C.S., 1894* (quoted in Synan, *Holiness-Pentecostal Tradition*, 40).

[29]Carl Bangs, *Phineas F. Bresee: His Life in Methodism, the Holiness Movement, and the Church of the Nazarene* (Kansas City: Beacon Hill, 1995), 196.

[30]The original name, The Pentecostal Church of the Nazarene, was formed in the 1907 merger of Bresee's Church of the Nazarene (1895) and the Association of

Pentecostal Churches of America (1896) headed by H. F. Reynolds in New York. The following year, Holiness churches originating in Texas and Tennessee joined the work in the formation of the new denomination.

[31]The Church of the Nazarene also established several colleges and universities such as Point Loma (California) and Olivet Nazarene (Illinois). For more on the Church of the Nazarene, see Bangs, *Phineas F. Bresee: Our Watchword and Song: The Centennial History of the Church of the Nazarene*, ed. Floyd T. Cunningham et al. (Kansas City: Beacon Hill, 2013); J. Fred Parker, *Mission to the World: A History of Missions in the Church of the Nazarene Through 1985* (Kansas City: Nazarene Publishing House, 1988).

[32]Willard heard Phoebe Palmer speak near her home outside Chicago and read many of her works (Ruth Bordin, *Frances Willard: A Biography* [Chapel Hill: University of North Carolina Press, 1986], 156).

[33]Frances E. Willard, *Woman in the Pulpit* (Boston: D. Lothrop, 1888), 46–47.

[34]Bordin, *Frances Willard*, 160–68.

[35]Courtney Aldrich, "Many U.S. Presidents Have Methodist Ties," UMC.org (accessed April 23, 2018).

8: United Ministry

[1]Harold Frederic, *The Damnation of Theron Ware* (1896; New York: Penguin, 1986), 204.

[2]Dickinson perceives signs of factionalism in the novel: "At the time Frederic was writing, American Methodism was being torn apart by conflict between liberals, who held an optimistic belief in the inevitability of progress, and conservatives, who balked at the modernising trends of liberals, and Frederic places this conflict at the heart of his novel" (David Dickinson, *Yet Alive? Methodists in British Fiction Since 1890* [Newcastle upon Tyne: Cambridge Scholars, 2016], 36).

[3]On Wesley and history, see Jeffrey W. Barbeau, "John Wesley and the Early Church: History, Antiquity, and the Spirit of God," in *Evangelicals and the Early Church: Recovery, Reform, Renewal*, ed. George Kalantzis and Andrew Tooley (Eugene, OR: Cascade, 2012), 52–76.

[4]Frederick A. Norwood, *The Story of American Methodism: A History of the United Methodists and Their Relations* (Nashville: Abingdon, 1974), 217–20; Stan Ingersol, "Education," in *The Cambridge Companion to American Methodism*, ed. Jason E. Vickers (New York: Cambridge University Press, 2013), 261–78.

[5]Methodist-affiliated institutions in the early twentieth century included schools of higher education such as Boston University (Massachusetts), Syracuse University (New York), Northwestern University (Illinois), and the University of Southern California (California), as well as seminaries such as Garrett Biblical Institute (Illinois), Iliff School of Theology (Colorado), Perkins School of Theology (Texas), and Duke Divinity School (North Carolina).

[6]Ingersol, "Education," 272.

[7]Consider the different beliefs of noted American Methodists John B. Cobb Jr. (who takes up Wesley's thought in *Grace and Responsibility: A Wesleyan Theology for Today* [Nashville: Abingdon, 1995]) and Stanley Hauerwas (who reflects on his Methodist heritage in *Hannah's Child: A Theologian's Memoir* [Grand Rapids: Eerdmans, 2010]); on the latter, see Jeffrey W. Barbeau, "The Conversion of Stanley Hauerwas," *Transpositions: Theology, Imagination, and the Arts*, March 27, 2017, www.transpositions.co.uk/the-conversion-of-stanley-hauerwas/.

[8]On Boston Personalism, see Douglas M. Strong, "The Nineteenth Century: Expansion and Fragmentation," in *Cambridge Companion to American Methodism*, 83; "Border Parker Bowne and Henry Clay Morrison," in *From Aldersgate to Azusa Street: Wesleyan, Holiness, and Pentecostal Visions of the New Creation*, ed. Henry H. Knight (Eugene, OR: Pickwick, 2010); Paul Deats and Carol Robb, *The Boston Personalist Tradition in Philosophy, Social Ethics, and Theology* (Louvain: Peeters, 1986).

[9]For example, Vanderbilt Divinity School separated from the MECS in 1914 after a decade-long legal attempt to wrest control of the institution from the authority of the church (the US Supreme Court eventually decided the case in favor of Vanderbilt; see Norwood, *Story of American Methodism*, 303–4; Ingersol, "Education," 274–75).

[10]Mott earned a Nobel Peace Prize for his efforts on behalf of POWs during World War I. For more on Mott's life and work, see Charles Howard Hopkins, *John R. Mott, 1865–1955: A Biography* (Grand Rapids: Eerdmans, 1980).

[11]John R. Mott, *The Future Leadership of the Church* (New York: Student Volunteer Movement for Foreign Missions, 1908), 4.

[12]Hopkins, *John R. Mott*, 325.

[13]Edith L. Blumhofer, *Her Heart Can See: The Life and Hymns of Fanny J. Crosby* (Grand Rapids: Eerdmans, 2005).

[14]Philip William Otterbein (1726–1813) and Jacob Albright (1759–1808), the founders of the United Brethren in Christ (1814) and Evangelical Church (1816), promoted teachings and practices associated with Methodism among German-speaking Americans during the late eighteenth and early nineteenth centuries.

[15]Wendy J. Deichmann, "The Twentieth Century: Reform, Redefinition, Renewal," in *Cambridge Companion to American Methodism*, 111.

[16]In 1956, capitalizing on these vast resources, the MC required that all candidates for ministry obtain a graduate (seminary) education to receive ordination.

[17]The Fundamentalist Methodist Conference continues today in southern Missouri, emphasizing local church authority and believer's baptism.

[18]More than forty women preachers have been identified from the earliest years of the movement. For more on women's unique contributions to Methodism, see Jean Miller Schmidt, *Grace Sufficient: A History of Women in American Methodism*,

1760-1939 (Nashville: Abingdon, 1999), esp. 13–32; Paul Wesley Chilcote, ed., *Her Own Story: Autobiographical Portraits of Early Methodist Women* (Nashville: Kingswood, 2001).

[19]Schmidt, *Grace Sufficient*, 63.

[20]In addition to other sources on Methodist women in this chapter, see Rosemary Skinner Keller, *Georgia Harkness: For Such a Time as This* (Nashville: Abingdon, 1992).

[21]Georgia Harkness, "The Ministry as a Vocation for Women," *The Christian Advocate* (April 10, 1924): 454–55, quoted in Schmidt, *Grace Sufficient*, 274; Laceye C. Warner, "American Methodist Women: Roles and Contributions," in *Cambridge Companion to American Methodism*, 328; on Harkness as a "theologian of the people" and other key leaders during this time, see Rosemary Skinner Keller, ed., *Spirituality and Social Responsibility: Vocational Vision of Women in the United Methodist Tradition* (Nashville: Abingdon, 1993).

[22]The AMEZ eliminated gender specifications for ordination in 1868, ordaining the first female deacon in 1896 and first female elder in 1898 (Norwood, *Story of American Methodism*, 352).

[23]Schmidt, *Grace Sufficient*, 281.

[24]The first woman to receive ordination in the MC was Maud Keister Jenson (1904–1998), who had previously served with her husband as a missionary to Korea (see Warner, "American Methodist Women," 328–29). Women similarly lost ground in the merger that formed the EUB, since the United Brethren Church had affirmed the ordination of women for more than fifty years before the union put an end to the practice (see Deichmann, "Twentieth Century," 108).

[25]Georgia Harkness, *The Church and Its Laity* (New York: Abingdon, 1962), 16.

[26]Harkness, *Church and Its Laity*, 202.

[27]Details of the merger may be found in Paul Washburn, *An Unfinished Church: A Brief History of the Union of the Evangelical United Brethren Church and the Methodist Church* (Nashville: Abingdon, 1984).

[28]Albert C. Outler, "Visions and Dreams: A Sermon for the Uniting Conference of the United Methodist Church (Dallas, Texas; April 23, 1968)," *Perkins Journal* (Spring 1974): 36–41 (37).

[29]Four years later, the general conference formally designated the Oklahoma Indian Missionary Conference to represent United Methodist churches (mostly in Oklahoma) in the denomination. Unlike the African American Central Jurisdiction, which avoided integration between black and white churches, the Oklahoma Indian Missionary Conference created space for Native American UMC churches to preserve identity and memory.

[30]Roy Nichols (1918–2002) served as the first African American bishop after the dissolution of the Central Jurisdiction. Abel Tendekayi Muzorewa (1925–2010) became the first indigenous pastor serving as a bishop (he later served as the prime

minister of Zimbabwe). Marjorie Swank Matthews (1916–1986) was elected the first female bishop in 1980. Warner's cautionary remark about the twenty-first century UMC should also be noted: "With women consisting of 40–60 percent of seminary students, only 10–15 percent of clergy in UM annual conferences are women" ("American Methodist Women," 329).

[31]For a thorough review of American Methodist stances on sexuality, with attention to contentious issues such as birth control, sexual education, and abortion, see Ashley Boggan Dreff, *Entangled: A History of American Methodism, Politics, and Sexuality* (Nashville: New Room, 2018).

[32]I am indebted to Robert W. Sledge's article for a detailed description of these events ("The Saddest Day: Gene Leggett and the Origins of the Incompatible Clause," *Methodist History* 55 [2017]: 145–79); cf. Boggan Dreff, *Entangled*, 228–35.

[33]Leggett's statement to the Board of the Ministry, Southwest Texas Conference (May 31, 1971), quoted in Sledge, "Saddest Day," 157.

[34]Don Hand, who had been elected as a lay delegate to general conference at the same gathering that voted on Gene Leggett's ordination, introduced the final emendation. An attorney by profession, Hand thought the proposed language came to him in a moment of inspiration: "At the time I spoke, I experienced the strange sensation that the words were not mine" (Sledge, "Saddest Day," 172).

9: Round Tables

[1]A compelling account of Coke's final days may be found in John A. Vickers, *Thomas Coke: Apostle of Methodism* (Nashville: Abingdon, 1969), 355–66.

[2]The term *majority world* will be used throughout this book to indicate non-Western nations and churches (replacing the problematic label "third world").

[3]William Carey, *An Enquiry into the Obligations of Christians, to Use Means for the Conversion of the Heathens* (Leicester: Ann Ireland, 1792); cf. Jeffrey W. Barbeau, *Religion in Romantic England: An Anthology of Primary Sources* (Waco: Baylor University Press, 2018), 436–42.

[4]Coke published a three-volume *History of the West Indies* between 1808 and 1811. On developments in the Caribbean islands, see Kenneth Cracknell and Susan J. White, *An Introduction to World Methodism* (Cambridge: Cambridge University Press, 2005), 70; Methodist Church [Great Britain], *Kindling of the Flame* (British Guiana District: Methodist Bicentenary Celebrations in the Western Area, 1960); Noel F. Titus, *The Development of Methodism in Barbados, 1823–1883* (Bern: Peter Lang, 1994). Today, Methodist churches in the Caribbean islands, along with Central American nations such as Belize, Panama, and Costa Rica, continue to thrive as members of the Methodist Church of the Caribbean and Americas (MCCA).

[5]Letter to John Wesley Suter, November 30, 1813, in *The Letters of Dr. Thomas Coke*, ed. John A. Vickers (Nashville: Kingswood, 2013), 705.

[6]Vickers, *Thomas Coke*, 366.

[7]William Butler (who had been an assistant to James Lynch in Ireland before moving to the United States) and his wife, Clementina Rowe Butler, arrived as MEC missionaries in September 1856. The MEC formed the North India Conference in 1869, with schools, chapels, orphanages, and a printing press for the distribution of Christian literature around the region (for more on the Butlers and their work in Asia, New England, and Mexico, see Charles Yrigoyen Jr. and Susan E. Warrick, eds., *Historical Dictionary of Methodism* [Lanham, MD: Scarecrow, 2013], 78–79).

[8]E. Stanley Jones, *A Song of Ascents: A Spiritual Autobiography* (Nashville: Abingdon, 1968), 75.

[9]E. Stanley Jones, *The Christ of the Indian Road* (Nashville: Abingdon, 1925), 38.

[10]Jones, *Christ of the Indian Road*, 211.

[11]Jones, *Christ of the Indian Road*, 215.

[12]Jones, *Christ of the Indian Road*, 215.

[13]In 1930 Jones first established a Christian ashram at the foot of the Himalayas at Sat Tal. After Gandhi's death, Jones wrote, "I bow to Mahatma Gandhi, but I kneel at the feet of Christ and give him my full and final allegiance . . . a little man, who fought a system in the framework of which I stand, has taught me more of the spirit of Christ than perhaps any other man in East or West . . . [by his death] he marched into the soul of humanity in the most triumphal march that any man ever made since the death and resurrection of the Son of God" (*Gandhi: Portrayal of a Friend* [Nashville: Abingdon, 1948], 8). Martin Luther King Jr. later claimed that Jones's book influenced his decision to embrace Gandhi's principles of nonviolent resistance.

[14]Jones suggested that Methodist class meetings were "the germ of an idea" for Christian ashrams (*Song of Ascents*, 42). However, he rejected any identification of ashrams with denominational divisions.

[15]"E. Stanley Jones on the Ashram Ideal," in *History of Christianity in India: Source Materials*, ed. M. K. Kuriakose (Delhi: ISPCK, 1999), 347–48.

[16]John Wesley, Sermon 39, "Catholic Spirit," §1.6, in *Works* 2:84–85.

[17]Wesley's sermon "On the Trinity" illustrates this same tension. He says, on one hand, "I dare not insist upon anyone's using the word 'Trinity' or 'Person,'" but, on the other, "I do not see how it is possible for any to have vital religion who denies that these three are one" (Sermon 55, §4, 18, in *Works* 2:377–78, 386). On Wesley's Christology, see David A. Graham, "The Chalcedonian Logic of John Wesley's Christology," *International Journal of Systematic Theology* 20 (2018): 84–103.

[18]John Wesley, Sermon 39, "Catholic Spirit," §1.6, in *Works* 2:93.

[19]E. Stanley Jones, *The Christ of Every Road* (Nashville: Abingdon, 1930), 186; on Pentecost, see Jones, *Song of Ascents*, 57–60, 70.

[20]Jones, *Christ of the Indian Road*, 221. Notably, Jones's family opposed the election. Upon hearing the news, Jones's daughter Eunice promptly wrote "fourteen reasons why her father should not be a bishop" (Martha Gunsalus Chamberlain, *A Love Affair with India: The Story of the Wife and Daughter of E. Stanley Jones* [Madison, NJ: General Commission on Archives and History, 2009], 58).

[21]The most thorough examination of Niles's life and influence is Christopher L. Furtado, *The Contribution of Dr. D. T. Niles to the Church Universal and Local* (Madras: Christian Literature Society, 1978); see also, Jeffrey W. Barbeau, "D. T. Niles, the Church, and the Fellowship of the Spirit," *Methodist Review: A Journal of Wesleyan and Methodist Studies* 8 (2016): 43–75, and W. J. T. Small, ed., *A History of the Methodist Church in Ceylon, 1814–1964* (Ceylon: Wesley Press, 1972), 463–64, 632.

[22]D. T. Niles, *The Preacher's Calling to Be Servant* (New York: Harper, 1959), 129.

[23]D. T. Niles, *Sir, We Would See Jesus* (London: Student Christian Movement, 1938), 96.

[24]D. T. Niles, *Who Is This Jesus?* (Nashville; Abingdon, 1968), 89.

[25]When the Swiss Reformed theologian Karl Barth suggested that other religions are "just unbelief," Niles responded in a memorable snippet of dialogue: "'How many Hindus, Dr. Barth, have you met?' He answered, 'No one.' I said, 'How then do you know that Hinduism is unbelief?' He said, 'A priori.' I simply shook my head and smiled" (D. T. Niles, "Karl Barth—A Personal Memory," *South East Asia Journal of Theology* 11 [1969]: 10–11).

[26]Niles, *Preacher's Calling to Be Servant*, 54; D. T. Niles, "The Church's Call to Mission and Unity," *The Ecumenical Review* 5 (1953): 245.

[27]Both of these churches maintain membership in the World Methodist Council.

[28]Niles, *Who Is This Jesus?*, 106.

10: OUTSTRETCHED HANDS

[1]Mercy Amba Oduyoye, *Hearing and Knowing: Theological Reflections on Christianity in Africa* (Maryknoll, NY: Orbis, 1986), 38.

[2]Quoted in Casely B. Essamuah, *Genuinely Ghanaian: A History of the Methodist Church Ghana, 1961–2000* (Trenton, NJ: Africa World Press, 2010), 7.

[3]Quoted in Bengt Sundkler and Christopher Steed, *A History of the Church in Africa* (Cambridge: Cambridge University Press, 2000), 203.

[4]See Essamuah, *Genuinely Ghanaian*, 10.

[5]Wilkinson and other settlers soon came into conflict with the directors of the Sierra Leone Company, who failed to follow through on promises of land (twenty acres for men, ten acres for women, and five acres for any additional children in a family) and impartial governance of the region. In 1800, rising tensions led to a rebellion that left two Methodists dead and scores more exiled to other areas along the coast. Wilkinson, for his part, never regained the following he once enjoyed. For more

on Methodism in the region, see Charles Marke, *Origin of Wesleyan Methodism in Sierra Leone and History of Its Missions* (London: Charles H. Kelly, 1913).

[6]Boston King, *The Life of Boston King*, ed. Ruth Holmes Whitehead and Carmelita A. M. Robertson (Halifax: The Nova Scotia Museum and Numbus Publishing, 2003), 22. King wrote his memoir while attending Kingswood School and first published his story in *The Methodist Magazine* in March and April 1798.

[7]King, *Life of Boston King*, 23.

[8]King, *Life of Boston King*, 24.

[9]On Freeman, see F. Deaville Walker, *Thomas Birch Freeman: The Son of an African* (London: Student Christian Movement, 1929); Seth Aryeetey Aryee, "The Bible and the Crown: Thomas Birch Freeman's Synthesis of Christianity and Social Reform in Ghana (1838–1890)" (PhD diss., Drew University, 1993).

[10]Quoted in M. M. Familusi, *Methodism in Nigeria (1842–1992)* (Ibadan: NPS Educational Publishers, 1992), 8.

[11]Essamuah, *Genuinely Ghanaian*, 13; see also F. L. Bartels, *The Roots of Ghana Methodism* (Cambridge: Cambridge University Press, 1965).

[12]Freeman not only returned to Kumasi in 1843 but also traveled widely in Nigeria, where he established churches and encouraged agricultural trade. Today, United Methodism in Nigeria owes a considerable debt to the devoted labors of EUB missionaries and indigenous leaders; see Peter Marubitoba Dong et al., *The History of the United Methodist Church in Nigeria* (Nashville: Abingdon, 2000).

[13]Paraphrasing Ps 68:31; Thomas B. Freeman, *Journal of Two Visits to the Kingdom of Ashanti, in Western Africa* (London: John Mason, 1843), 85.

[14]John Wesley, Sermon 63, "The General Spread of the Gospel," §1, in *Works*, 2:485.

[15]John Wesley, Sermon 63, "The General Spread of the Gospel," §12.

[16]John Wesley, Sermon 63, "The General Spread of the Gospel," §17.

[17]Shaw received ordination in London in November 1819. Richard Watson, the noted teacher and minister, delivered the charge to ministry (William Shaw, *The Story of My Mission in South-Eastern Africa* [London: Hamilton, Adams, 1860], 7); see also Leslie A. Hewson, *They Seek a City: Methodism in Grahamstown* (Grahamstown, South Africa: Institute of Social and Economic Research, 1981).

[18]Shaw, *Story of My Mission in South-Eastern Africa*, 187. Methodists in other regions of Africa attribute the growth of the movement to the Spirit's power; see, for example, John Wesley Z. Kurewa, *The Church in Mission: A Short History of the United Methodist Church in Zimbabwe, 1897–1997* (Nashville: Abingdon, 1997), 67–79.

[19]Shaw, *Story of My Mission in South-Eastern Africa*, 124.

[20]Joan A. Millard, "Are They Not Methodist Too? Case Studies of Some African Independent Churches That Call Themselves Methodist," in *The Global Impact of the Wesleyan Traditions and Their Related Movements*, ed. Charles Yrigoyen Jr., Pietist and Wesleyan Studies 14, 105–17 (Lanham, MD: Scarecrow, 2002), 111.

[21]Millard, "Are They Not Methodist Too?," 110–12.

[22]Stephen Ward Angell, *Bishop Henry McNeal Turner and African-American Religion in the South* (Knoxville: University of Tennessee Press, 1992), 230.

[23]Methodism in South Africa continued to struggle with race, segregation, and apartheid during the twentieth century. Prominent leadership roles in the church went to white ministers, and the nation's political divide was realized in the local church. Nevertheless, in later years, the church provided support for Nelson Mandela (1918–2013), who was educated in Methodist schools throughout his youth and cared for during his imprisonment (see Kenneth Cracknell and Susan J. White, *An Introduction to World Methodism* [Cambridge: Cambridge University Press, 2005], 77; Dion Forster, "Mandela and the Methodists: Faith, Fallacy, and Fact," *Studia Historiae Ecclesiasticae* 40 [2014]: 87–115).

[24]The formation of the Harris churches of West Africa are a similar case: William Wadé Harris (1860–1929) had been a Liberian Methodist but later developed a large network of churches out of his evangelistic activity throughout West Africa. Millard gives several excellent examples of independent churches in Africa that formed in response to Methodist practices of segregation ("Are They Not Methodist Too?," 105–17).

[25]Zablon John Nthamburi, *A History of the Methodist Church in Kenya* (Nairobi: Uzima, 1982).

[26]On early East African pioneers, see Nthamburi, *History of the Methodist Church in Kenya*, 34–38.

[27]Mercy Amba Oduyoye, *Leadership Development in the Methodist Church Nigeria: 1842–1962* (Ibadan: Sefer, 1992), 88; on Methodist women in Africa, see 63–88.

[28]From a letter by Rev. Charles New, December 28, 1874, quoted in *Church Missionary Intelligencer* 11 (April 1875): 110.

[29]In 1890, through contributions made by the Anglican Church Mission Society, Methodists, and the British government, East African slaves were released, and the slave trade was abolished in the region. Domestic slavery, to the disappointment of missionaries, remained.

[30]Nthamburi, *History of the Methodist Church in Kenya*, 50–54.

[31]Mercy Amba Oduyoye, *The Wesleyan Presence in Nigeria, 1842–1962: An Exploration of Power, Control and Partnership in Mission* (Ibadan: Sefer, 1992), vii.

[32]Nthamburi, *History of the Methodist Church in Kenya*, 70–88. On Zimbabwean Methodist efforts to address faith and culture in matters of marriage, polygamy, and the like, see Kurewa, *Church in Mission*, 81–92.

[33]Michael Kasongo, *History of the Methodist Church in the Central Congo* (Lanham, MD: University Press of America, 1998), 47.

[34]Oduyoye, *Hearing and Knowing*, 35.

[35]Oduyoye, *Wesleyan Presence in Nigeria*, 85; on the challenges of collaboration between Methodist missionaries and Africans in Nigeria, including the significance

of local language, training centers, and women in ministry, see Oduyoye, *Leadership Development in the Methodist Church Nigeria.*

[36]Bishop Abel Muzorewa (1925–2010) of Zimbabwe, for example, recognized the debt African leaders owe to Christian missionaries for education and training, while calling into question the mistakes made along the way, such as banning respected customs and the tendency to make converts "in their own image" (Abel Muzorewa, "Bishop Muzorewa Cites Missionary 'Mistakes' Made in Africa by West," in *The Methodist Experience in America, Vol. 2: Sourcebook,* ed. Russell E. Richey, Kenneth E. Rowe, and Jean Miller Schmidt [Nashville: Abingdon, 2000], 641–42).

[37]Paul Chilcote, with Katheru Gichaara and Patrick Matsikenyiri, "A Singing and Dancing Church: Methodist Worship in Kenya and Zimbabwe," in *The Sunday Service of the Methodists: Twentieth-Century Worship in Worldwide Methodism, Studies in Honor of James F. White,* ed. Karen B. Westerfield Tucker, 227–47 (Nashville: Kingswood, 1996), 243.

[38]John Wesley, "The General Spread of the Gospel," §27, in *Works,* 2:499 (cf. Rev 19:6).

11: Spiritual Conquest

[1]Churches in the central conferences of the UMC and other Wesleyan denominations continue to be active throughout Europe, including France, Italy, Germany, Poland, Hungary, and Croatia (see statistical information online at the World Methodist Council; cf. Kenneth Cracknell and Susan J. White, *An Introduction to World Methodism* [Cambridge: Cambridge University Press, 2005], 88–89; Charles Yrigoyen Jr. and Susan E. Warrick, eds., *Historical Dictionary of Methodism* [Lanham, MD: Scarecrow, 2013], 137–44).

[2]John R. Mott, "Closing Address," in *Addresses and Papers of John R. Mott,* 6 vols. (New York: Association Press, 1947), 5:19–20.

[3]Missionary commitment to medicine and education is a hallmark of Christian missions, and played an important role in the establishment of Methodist churches in Asia, including in Malaysia, Indonesia, the Philippines, and Myanmar (see "Asia," in *Historical Dictionary of Methodism,* 37–46).

[4]R. S. Maclay, *Life Among the Chinese* (New York: Carlton & Porter, 1861).

[5]Maclay, *Life Among the Chinese,* 369.

[6]Maclay, *Life Among the Chinese,* 380.

[7]Sung's name is conspicuously absent in some literature on Methodism in China, I think due to his combative attitude toward liberalism and the extent of his influence beyond the Methodist churches. On Sung's life and thought, see Lim Ka-Tong, *The Life and Ministry of John Sung* (Singapore: Genesis, 2012); Leslie T. Lyall, *John Sung* (London: China Inland Mission, 1954); and Timothy Tow, *John Sung My Teacher* (Singapore: Christian Life Publishers, 1985).

[8]John Sung, *The Diary of John Sung: Extracts from His Journals and Notes*, trans. Thng Pheng Soon (Singapore: Genesis, 2012), 31.

[9]Sung, *Diary of John Sung*, 32.

[10]Lyall provocatively declares, "The mental hospital thus became John Sung's real theological college! It was there that he began to appreciate the deep truths of God's Word and it was there that he was taught the difficult lesson of quiet submission to the will of God" (*John Sung*, 38).

[11]Lim, *Life and Ministry of John Sung*, 72.

[12]Quoted in Lim, *Life and Ministry of John Sung*, 90.

[13]Lyall explains that Sung's "untenable" exegesis "would have horrified the great Bible teachers of our time." He was known for preaching from vast sections of the Bible, chapter by chapter, in order to develop spiritual connections throughout the entire canon (Lyall, *John Sung*, 145).

[14] Lim, *Life and Ministry of John Sung*, 119; cf. Mark A. Noll and Carolyn Nystrom, *Clouds of Witnesses: Christian Voices from Africa and Asia* (Downers Grove, IL: InterVarsity, 2011), 201–13.

[15]Sung, *Diary of John Sung*, 73.

[16]Sung, *Diary of John Sung*, 109.

[17]Lim, *Life and Ministry of John Sung*, xiii.

[18]Albert C. Outler and Richard P. Heitzenrater, eds., *John Wesley's Sermons: An Anthology* (Nashville: Abingdon, 1991), 123; cf. John Wesley, Sermon 7, "The Way to the Kingdom," in *Works* 1:217–32.

[19]John Wesley, Sermon 7, "The Way to the Kingdom," §2.1, in *Works* 1:225–26.

[20]John Wesley, Sermon 14, "The Repentance of Believers," §2, in *Works* 1:335.

[21]John Wesley, Sermon 14, "The Repentance of Believers," §2.6, in *Works* 1:349–50.

[22]Walter N. Lacy, *A Hundred Years of China Methodism* (New York: Abingdon-Cokesbury, 1948). For a helpful look at the state of British Methodism in China just prior to the establishment of communism, see Harold B. Rattenbury, *The Seven Churches of China, Being a Picture of the Seven China Districts of the Methodist Church* (London: Cargate, 1934).

[23]Notably, missionaries from the United Brethren, Evangelical Association, Free Methodists, and Church of the Nazarene all served in China during this time (see "Asia," in *Historical Dictionary of Methodism*, 40–41).

[24]For more on the "three-self church," see Daniel H. Bays, *A New History of Christianity in China* (Malden, MA: Wiley-Blackwell, 2012).

[25]For the rise of Methodism in the region, see Theodore R. Doraisamy, *The March of Methodism in Singapore and Malaysia, 1885–1980* (Singapore: Methodist Book Room, 1982).

[26]Mattie Wilcox Noble, "Reminiscences of Early Christians in Korea," in *Within the Gate*, ed. Charles A. Sauer (Seoul: Korean Methodist News Service, 1934), 67–68. Numerous essays in this volume are helpful for understanding early Korean Methodism.

[27]James Huntley Grayson, *Korea: A Religious History*, rev. ed. (London: Routledge-Curzon, 1989), 162.

[28]Paul Yong Pyo Hong, "Spreading the Holiness Fire: A History of the OMS Korea Holiness Church, 1904–1957" (PhD diss., Fuller Theological Seminary, 1996), 221.

[29]The similarity between the churches also reflects their shared hymnal and Bible translations. Presbyterians, for their part, took up the practice of Methodist class meetings (Grayson, *Korea*, 166). The Church of the Nazarene actively evangelized in Korea, forming one of the strongest bodies of Nazarenes outside the United States in the twentieth century ("Asia," in *Historical Dictionary of Methodism*, 42). For an account of Korean Methodist worship, see Edward W. Poitras (Pak Tae In), "Ten Thousand Tongues Sing: Worship among Methodists in Korea," in *The Sunday Service of the Methodists: Twentieth Century Worship in Worldwide Methodism*, ed. Karen B. Westerfield Tucker (Nashville: Kingswood, 1996), 195–208.

[30]The division of Korea in 1945 practically eliminated Methodism in the North. For more on Methodism in Korea, see Mi-Soon Im, "The Role of Single Women Missionaries of the Methodist Episcopal Church, South, in Korea, 1897–1940" (PhD diss., Boston University School of Theology, 2008). On Methodism in the former Soviet Union, see S. T. Kimbrough, Jr., ed., *Methodism in Russia and the Baltic States: History and Renewal* (Nashville: Abingdon, 1995), esp. 198–99 (on Korean missionaries to Russia).

[31]Mott, "Closing Address," 5:22.

[32]John Mott, whose efforts in wartime relief work had already earned him a Nobel Peace Prize in 1946, was named the honorary president of the inaugural meeting of the World Council of Churches.

12: INSPIRED VOICES

[1]Justo L. González, "Overview," in *Each in Our Own Tongue: A History of Hispanic United Methodism*, ed. Justo L. González (Nashville: Abingdon, 1991), 20–21. Elsewhere, Wesley indicates that he learned Spanish to speak to Jewish parishioners, "some of whom seem nearer the mind of Christ than many of those who call him Lord" (quoted in Justo L. González, "Can Wesley Be Read in Spanish?," in *Rethinking Wesley's Theology for Contemporary Methodism*, ed. Randy L. Maddox [Nashville: Kingswood, 1998], 162).

[2]Joel N. Martínez, "The South Central Jurisdiction," in *Each in Our Own Tongue*, 40.

[3]The first Protestant church building was built in Buenos Aires in 1843. On the state of Methodist missions in the region, see Paulo Ayres Mattos, "Methodism in Latin America and the Caribbean," in *T&T Clark Companion to Methodism*, ed. Charles Yrigoyen Jr. (London: Bloomsbury, 2010), 206; cf. "Latin America and the Caribbean," in *Historical Dictionary of Methodism*, ed. Charles Yrigoyen Jr. and Susan E. Warrick (Lanham, MD: Scarecrow, 2013), 219–26.

[4]John Wesley Butler, *History of the Methodist Episcopal Church in Mexico* (New York: Methodist Book Concern, 1918), 51–52, 54. Mary Hastings, for example, worked twenty-five years developing a school of five hundred in Pachuca; she was the first Methodist missionary buried in Mexico (Butler, *History of the Methodist Episcopal Church in Mexico*, 60).

[5]Quoted in Martínez, "South Central Jurisdiction," 42.

[6]The collaborative spirit of the Edinburgh Missionary Conference led to the formation of the Committee on Cooperation for Latin America (CCLA) in 1913. Three years later, in a meeting in Panama, Protestant mission boards established a comity agreement that decreased competition among the denominations. The Church of the Nazarene, for example, has a sizeable presence in Guatemala, Haiti, Peru, and Bolivia (Mattos, "Methodism in Latin America and the Caribbean," 211). For an overview of Methodist missions in Latin America, see Pablo R. Andiñach, "Methodism in Latin America," in *The Oxford Handbook of Methodist Studies*, ed. William J. Abraham and James E. Kirby (Oxford: Oxford University Press, 2009), 139–54.

[7]The United Methodist General Conference Commission on Structure of Methodism Overseas (COSMOS) successfully petitioned General Conference to allow churches to choose autonomy if they wished. Although they still send nonvoting delegates to General Conference, Methodists in Cuba, Chile, Argentina, Uruguay, Peru, Bolivia, Costa Rica, and Panama each elected to function as autonomous bodies in subsequent years.

[8]Bonino received his education at Facultad Evangélica Teologiá in Buenos Aires before attending Emory and Union Theological Seminary in the United States. He was the only Latin American Protestant observer at the Second Vatican Council. Bonino identified the diverse streams of Wesleyan and Methodist churches in several works, including "Wesley in Latin America: A Theological and Historical Reflection," in *Rethinking Wesley's Theology for Contemporary Methodism*, ed. Randy L. Maddox (Nashville: Kingswood, 1998), 169–82; and *Faces of Latin American Protestantism: 1993 Carnahan Lectures*, trans. Eugene L. Stockwell (Grand Rapids: Eerdmans, 1995).

[9]José Míguez Bonino, *Doing Theology in a Revolutionary Situation* (Philadelphia: Fortress, 1975), 17.

[10]José Míguez Bonino, "Catholic and Protestant, but Missionary: John Wesley's Explicit and Implicit Ecclesiology and the Methodist Mission in Latin America," in *The Global Impact of the Wesleyan Traditions and Their Related Movements*, ed. Charles Yrigoyen Jr., 69–73 (Lanham, MD: Scarecrow, 2002), 69.

[11]Willis Collins Hoover, *History of the Pentecostal Revival in Chile*, trans. Mario G. Hoover (Santiago: Eben-Ezer, 2000); cf. Walter J. Hollenweger, "Methodism's Past in Pentecostalism's Present: A Case Study of a Cultural Clash in Chile," *Methodist History* 20 (1982): 169–82.

[12]Hoover, *History of the Pentecostal Revival in Chile*, 72–73.

[13]Hoover, *History of the Pentecostal Revival in Chile*, 87–88.

[14]Approximately 75 percent of Chilean Protestants belong to La Iglesia Metodista Pentecostal (Kenneth Cracknell and Susan J. White, *An Introduction to World Methodism* [Cambridge: Cambridge University Press, 2005], 87). Hoover's memoir contrasts with other accounts that emphasize the significance of the two churches he joined in 1910 and the subsequent split of 1932 (see Frans H. Kamsteeg, *Prophetic Pentecostalism in Chile: A Case Study on Religion and Development Policy* [Lanham, MD: Scarecrow, 1998], 68–75).

[15]The most extensive study of these questions may be found in Laurence W. Wood, *The Meaning of Pentecost in Early Methodism: Rediscovering John Fletcher as John Wesley's Vindicator and Designated Successor* (Lanham, MD: Scarecrow, 2002), 176.

[16]Mattos, "Methodism in Latin America and the Caribbean," 212. Unlike some other Pentecostal churches, such as the Assemblies of God, the Methodist Pentecostal Church rejects an emphasis on tongues as a definite mark of Spirit baptism.

[17]Hollenweger, "Methodism's Past in Pentecostalism's Present," 181.

[18]Quoted in Hollenweger, "Methodism's Past in Pentecostalism's Present," 176.

[19]Cracknell and White, *Introduction to World Methodism*, 87–88.

[20]Bonino lamented that at the end of the twentieth century, Wesley's actual writings remained largely untranslated in Spanish, except for the standard fifty-two sermons and a few other texts ("Wesley in Latin America," 173). Latin American Methodists subsequently took up the task in a fourteen-volume collection of Wesley's works in Spanish (see L. Elbert Wethington, "The Impact of *Obras de Wesley* in the Hispanic World," in *The Global Impact of the Wesleyan Traditions and Their Related Movements*, ed. Charles Yrigoyen Jr., 275–84 [Lanham, MD: Scarecrow, 2002]); cf. Jason E. Vickers, "The Wesleys' Role in World Methodism," in *The Ashgate Research Companion to World Methodism*, ed. William Gibson, Peter Forsaith, and Martin Wellings (Burlington, VT: Ashgate, 2013), 115.

[21]John Wesley, "Thoughts on the Present Scarcity of Provisions," in *The Works of John Wesley*, 3rd ed., 14 vols. (1872; Grand Rapids: Baker, 1984), 11:54.

[22]Wesley, "Thoughts on the Present Scarcity of Provisions," 59. For more on Wesley's social concerns, see Theodore W. Jennings Jr., *Good News to the Poor: John Wesley's Evangelical Economics* (Nashville: Abingdon, 1990).

[23]Methodist theologian Elsa Tamez, for instance, draws attention to the liberation of women in works such as "Cultural Violence against Women in Latin America," in *Women Resisting Violence: Spirituality for Life*, ed. Mary John Mananzan et al., 11–19 (Maryknoll, NY: Orbis, 1996); *Struggles for Power in Early Christianity: A Study of the First Letter to Timothy*, trans. Gloria Kinsler (Maryknoll, NY: Orbis, 2007).

[24]On the relationship between human dignity and the Christian doctrine of justification, see Elsa Tamez, *The Amnesty of Grace: Justification by Faith from a Latin American Perspective*, trans. Sharon H. Ringe (Nashville: Abingdon, 1993), 24–26.

Epilogue: Hope for the Future

[1]From "Our Worldwide Church Family," World Methodist Council, www.world-methodistcouncil.org/about/member-churches/. Data reported as of June 2018.

[2]David Hempton, *Methodism: Empire of the Spirit* (New Haven: Yale University Press, 2005), 211–16.

[3]On the constitutional basis of American Methodism, see William B. Lawrence and Sally Curtis Askew, "Constitutional Methodism in Crisis: Historical and Operational Perspectives on Divisions Threatening United Methodism," *Methodist Review* 10 (2018): 23–72.

[4]Bonino's comment on Wesley's attitude to church polity is helpful: "He accepted the ministerial structure of the Church of England as the most convenient, scriptural, and reasonable, but not the only possible or essential structure. However, when strict obedience to church order threatened mission he believed he had received from God, he did not hesitate to break with order" (José Míguez Bonino, "Catholic and Protestant, but Missionary: John Wesley's Explicit and Implicit Ecclesiology and the Methodist Mission in Latin America," in *The Global Impact of the Wesleyan Traditions and Their Related Movements*, ed. Charles Yrigoyen Jr., 69–73 [Lanham, MD: Scarecrow, 2002], 73).

[5]*Charles Wesley: A Reader*, ed. John R. Tyson (Oxford: Oxford University Press, 1989), 110 (Journal, Whitsunday, 1760). Charles continues in a touching remark identifying his marriage to Sally as a means of grace: "Eleven years ago He gave me another token of His love, in my beloved friend; and surely He never meant us to part on the other side of time. His design in uniting us here was, that we should continue one to all eternity." Elsewhere, I refer to this as "among the most romantic statements ever penned to a lover" ("All Loves Excelling: How Romance Inspired Charles Wesley's View of God," *Christianity Today* (February 13, 2019) [online]). By contrast, John Wesley's marriage to Mary ("Molly") Vazeille seemed destined to fail almost from the start.

[6]Jason E. Vickers, "The Wesleys' Role in World Methodism," in *The Ashgate Research Companion to World Methodism*, ed. William Gibson, Peter Forsaith, and Martin Wellings (Burlington, VT: Ashgate, 2013), 116.

[7]Mercy Amba Oduyoye, *The Wesleyan Presence in Nigeria 1842–1962: An Exploration of Power, Control and Partnership in Mission* (Ibadan: Sefer, 1992), 95.

[8]John Wesley, Sermon 75, "On Schism," in *Works*, 3:59–69.

Image Credits

Figure 1.1. *The rescue of the young John Wesley from the burning parsonage at Epworth, Lincolnshire.* Mezzotint by S. W. Reynolds after H. P. Parker / Wellcome Library, London, Wikimedia Commons

Figure 1.2. *Susanna Wesley, mother of John Wesley, the founder of Methodism.* Engraving. W. B. Daniels, *The Illustrated History of Methodism in Great Britain, America, and Australia* (1884) / Wikimedia Commons

Figure 1.3. *John Wesley M. H.* John Faber / Library of Congress Prints and Photographs Division

Figure 1.4. *The rescue of the young John Wesley from the burning parsonage at Epworth, Lincolnshire.* Mezzotint by S. W. Reynolds after H. P. Parker / Wellcome Library, London, Wikimedia Commons

Figure 2.1. *Charles Wesley.* Sarah Tytler, *The Countess of Huntingdon and Her Circle* (London: Sir Isaac Pitman and Sons, Ltd, 1907) / Wikimedia Commons

Figure 2.2. *John Wesley "field preaching" outside a church.* Engraving / Wellcome Library, London, Wikimedia Commons

Figure 3.1. *George Whitefield.* Sarah Tytler, *The Countess of Huntingdon and Her Circle* (London: Sir Isaac Pitman and Sons, Ltd, 1907): photo by Emery Walker / Wikimedia Commons

Figure 3.2. *Credulity, Superstition, and Fanaticism.* William Hogarth, April 1762. The image is a re-imagining of his earlier work, *Enthusiasm Delineated. The Genius of William Hogarth*, Stuart Barton and Tony Curtis, eds. (Lyle Publications, 1972) / Wikimedia Commons

Figure 3.3. *Portrait of The Right Honourable Selina Countess of Huntingdon.* Welsh Portrait Collection at the National Library of Wales / R. Page, Wikimedia Commons

Figure 4.1. *Reverend John Fletcher, 1729–1785.* Thomas Blood, engraver / Wikimedia Commons

Figure 4.2. *Mary Bosanquet Fletcher.* David Atkinson Archive / Wikimedia Commons

Figure 4.3. *Salvation Army World War I poster.* Frederick Duncan / Wikimedia Commons

Figure 4.4. *Jabez Bunting.* Thomas Percival Bunting, *The Life of Jabez Bunting, D. D.* (London: Longman, Green, Longman, and Roberts, 1859)

Figure 4.5. *Reverend John Scott Lidgett – 1941*: PA Images / Alamy Stock Photo

Figure 5.1. *The Reverend Francis Asbury, Bishop of the Methodist Episcopal Church in the United States* / Library of Congress Prints and Photographs Division

Figure 5.2. *Captain Thos. Webb of the British Army One of the first Methodist Preachers in America, 1801-ca. 1886.* New York Public Library's Digital Library / Wikimedia Commons

Figure 5.3. *O'Kelly Chapel. The Life of Rev. James O'Kelly and the Early History of the Christian Church in the South (1910).* Internet Archive Book Images / Wikimedia Commons

Figure 5.4. *Christmas Conference Ordination of Asbury. The Ordination of Bishop Francis Asbury.* Thomas Coke Ruckle, painter; A. Gilchrist Campbell, engraver / Wikimedia Commons

Figure 6.1. *"Black Harry," Harry Hosier.* I. Garland Penn, *The Afro-American Press, and its Editors* (Springfield, MA: Wiley & Co. Publishing, 1891), 87.

Figure 6.2. *Reverend Freeborn Garrettson.* New York Public Library's Digital Library / Wikimedia Commons

Figure 6.3. *Richard Allen. Distinguished colored men,* Popular Graphic Arts / Library of Congress, Wikimedia Commons

Figure 6.4. *Bethel African Methodist Episcopal Church.* 419 South Sixth Street, Philadelphia, Philadelphia County, PA / Library of Congress Prints and Photographs Division

Figure 7.1. *Advertisement for Welch's grape juice.* Christian Herald Association, Tisch Library, Tufts University, Internet Archive Book Images / Wikimedia Commons

Figure 7.2. *William Apess. William Apess, A Son of the Forest* (New York: the author, 1831) / Wikimedia Commons

Figure 7.3. *John Wesley preaching to Native American Indians.* Engraving / Wellcome Library, London, Wikimedia Commons

Figure 7.4. *Phoebe Worrall Palmer.* Rev. Richard Wheatley, *The Life and Letters of Mrs. Phoebe Palmer* (1881) / public domain

Figure 7.5. *Frances Willard.* Photo taken before 1898, author unknown / Wikimedia Commons

Figure 8.1. *John R. Mott.* Materialscientist / Wikimedia Commons

Figure 8.2. *Lucy Rider Meyer.* J. F. Hurst, *The History of Methodism,* 1902 / Wikimedia Commons

Figure 8.3. *Dr. Georgia E. Harkness. Pulpit Digest,* November 1953 / Wikimedia Commons

Figure 9.1. *Thomas Coke.* Holland Nimmons McTyeire, *A History of Methodism,* Internet Archive Book Images / Wikimedia Commons

Figure 9.2. *E. Stanley Jones* / Courtesy of E. Stanley Jones Foundation Archives

Figure 9.3. *Rev. D. T. Niles* / World Council of Churches Archives

Figure 10.1. Josiah Wedgwood, "Am I Not a Man and a Brother?" 1787 medallion for the British anti-slavery campaign, / Kzirkel, Wikimedia Commons

Figure 10.2. *Thomas Birch Freeman.* Kandymotownie / Wikimedia Commons

Figure 10.3. *Bishop Henry McNeal Turner.* H. B. Parks, Charles Simpson Butcher, John Anderson Lankford, *Africa: The Problem of the New Century* / Wikimedia Commons

Figure 11.1. *The 1910 World Missionary Conference, Edinburgh* / Wikimedia Commons

Figure 11.2. *Robert Samuel Maclay.* Historic Images / Alamy Stock Photo

Figure 11.3. *John Sung and the Bethel Evangelistic Band.* Zanhe / Wikimedia Commons

Figure 11.4. *Mary Stone.* Margaret Ernestine Burton, *Women Workers of the Orient* (Central Committee on the United Study of Foreign Missions, 1918) / Wikimedia Commons

Figure 11.5. *Sunday school class in Korea.* Methodist Episcopal Church, Korean Digital Archive, University of Southern California Libraries / Wikimedia Commons

Figure 12.1. *William Butler.* Internet Archive Book Images / Wikimedia Commons

Figure 12.2. *Methodist Episcopal Church in Mexico.* John Wesley Butler, *History of the Methodist Episcopal Church in Mexico,* Pitts Theology Library, Emory University, Internet Archive Book Images / Wikimedia Commons

Figure 12.3. *José Míguez Bonino.* National Archives of The Netherlands / Wikimedia Commons

Figure 12.4. *Willis Collins Hoover* / Chilean Methodist Library

Figure 12.5. *Salvation Army cart. Charrete Doacoes.* Tgomame / Wikimedia Commons

Figure E.1. *John Wesley.* William Hamilton, *Portrait of John Wesley,* National Portrait Gallery, London / Wikimedia Commons

Figure E.2. *Wesleyan Quadrilateral.* Courtesy of Rebekah A. Barbeau

Index

Finding the Textbook You Need

The IVP Academic Textbook Selector
is an online tool for instantly finding the IVP books
suitable for over 250 courses across 24 disciplines.

ivpacademic.com